BOTTICELLI

☞ Books in the RENAISSANCE LIVES series explore and illustrate the life histories and achievements of significant artists, rulers, intellectuals and scientists in the early modern world. They delve into literature, philosophy, the history of art, science and natural history and cover narratives of exploration, statecraft and technology.

Series Editor: François Quiviger

Already published

Albrecht Dürer: Art and Autobiography *David Ekserdjian*
Aldus Manutius: The Invention of the Publisher *Oren Margolis*
Artemisia Gentileschi and Feminism in Early Modern Europe *Mary D. Garrard*
Blaise Pascal: Miracles and Reason *Mary Ann Caws*
Botticelli: Artist and Designer *Ana Debenedetti*
Caravaggio and the Creation of Modernity *Troy Thomas*
Descartes: The Renewal of Philosophy *Steven Nadler*
Donatello and the Dawn of Renaissance Art *A. Victor Coonin*
Erasmus of Rotterdam: The Spirit of a Scholar *William Barker*
Filippino Lippi: An Abundance of Invention *Jonathan K. Nelson*
Giorgione's Ambiguity *Tom Nichols*
Hans Holbein: The Artist in a Changing World *Jeanne Nuechterlein*
Hieronymus Bosch: Visions and Nightmares *Nils Büttner*
Isaac Newton and Natural Philosophy *Niccolò Guicciardini*
Jan van Eyck within His Art *Alfred Acres*
John Donne: In the Shadow of Religion *Andrew Hadfield*
John Evelyn: A Life of Domesticity *John Dixon Hunt*
Leonardo da Vinci: Self, Art and Nature *François Quiviger*
Leon Battista Alberti: The Chameleon's Eye *Caspar Pearson*
Lucas Cranach: From German Myth to Reformation *Jennifer Nelson*
Machiavelli: From Radical to Reactionary *Robert Black*
Michelangelo and the Viewer in His Time *Bernadine Barnes*
Paracelsus: An Alchemical Life *Bruce T. Moran*
Petrarch: Everywhere a Wanderer *Christopher S. Celenza*
Piero della Francesca and the Invention of the Artist *Machtelt Brüggen Israëls*
Piero di Cosimo: Eccentricity and Delight *Sarah Blake McHam*
Pieter Bruegel and the Idea of Human Nature *Elizabeth Alice Honig*
Raphael and the Antique *Claudia La Malfa*
Rembrandt's Holland *Larry Silver*
Robert Hooke's Experimental Philosophy *Felicity Henderson*
Rubens's Spirit: From Ingenuity to Genius *Alexander Marr*
Salvator Rosa: Paint and Performance *Helen Langdon*
Thomas Nashe and Late Elizabethan Writing *Andrew Hadfield*
Titian's Touch: Art, Magic and Philosophy *Maria H. Loh*
Tycho Brahe and the Measure of the Heavens *John Robert Christianson*
Ulisse Aldrovandi: Naturalist and Collector *Peter Mason*

BOTTICELLI

Artist and Designer

ANA DEBENEDETTI

REAKTION BOOKS

To my husband, Matteo Andreoletti

Published by Reaktion Books Ltd
Unit 32, Waterside
44–48 Wharf Road
London N1 7UX, UK
www.reaktionbooks.co.uk

First published 2021
First published in paperback 2024

Printed and bound in India by Replika Press Pvt. Ltd

A catalogue record for this book is available from the British Library

ISBN 978 1 78914 928 9

COVER: Detail of Botticelli, *Madonna of the Magnificat*, c. 1483, tempera on wood. Photo Heritage Images/Fine Art Images/akg-images.

CONTENTS

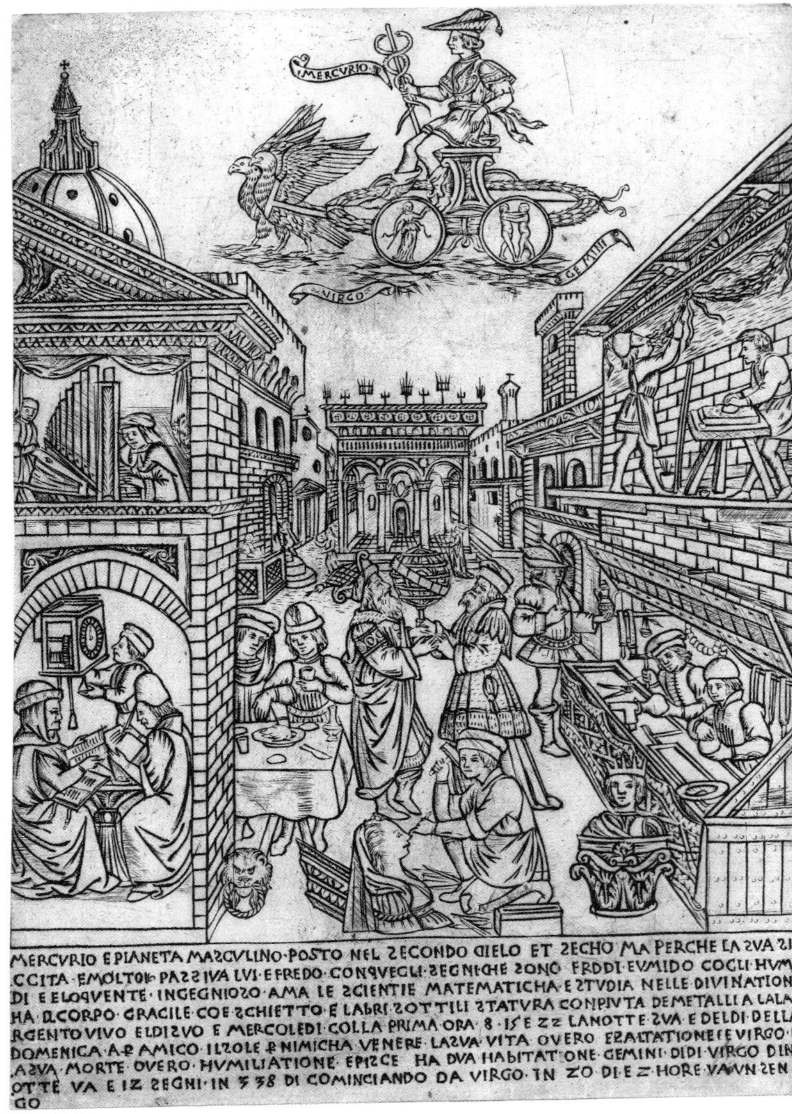
MERCVRIO
VIRGO
GEMINI
MERCVRIO E PIANETA MASCVLINO · POSTO NEL SECONDO CIELO ET SECHO MA PERCHE LA SVA SI
CCITA · EMOLTO PASSIVA LVI · E FREDO · CONQVEGLI · SEGNI CHE SONO FRDDI · EVMIDO COGLI · HVMI
DI E ELOQVENTE · INGEGNIOSO · AMA LE SCIENTIE MATEMATICHA · E STVDIA NELLE · DIVINATIONE
HA IL CORPO · GRACILE · COE SCHIETTO · E LABRI · SOTTILI STATVRA CONPIVTA DE METALLI A LALA
RGENTO VIVO ELDI SVO E MERCOLEDI · COLLA PRIMA · ORA · 8 · 15 E 22 LA NOTTE · SVA · E DELDI · DELLA
DOMENICA · A PAMICO · IL SOLE NIMICHA · VENERE · LA SVA · VITA · OVERO · EXALTATIONE E VIRGO · L
A SVA · MORTE · OVERO · HVMILIATIONE · E PISCE HA DVA · HABITATIONE · GEMINI · DIDI · VIRGO DIN
OTTE VA E I 12 SEGNI · IN 338 DI COMINCIANDO DA VIRGO · IN 20 DI · E 2 · HORE · VA VN SEN
GO

ONE

Becoming Botticelli

When considering the artistic personality of such a famous figure as Botticelli, it is necessary to step back in time and try to understand his milieu and what his birthplace might have looked like.

Wandering through the city of Florence in the 1460s must have felt not too dissimilar to what people may experience today, especially in the historic centre of the city. Along the busy banks of the Lungarno river, one would have encountered hordes of people of every class, from the common populace, *popolo minuto*, to the *ottimati*, the highest stratum of Florence's cultural and wealthy elite. While penetrating the dense network of streets and *chiassi* of the city, one would have mixed with craftsmen and merchants of all sorts, such as tanners (*galigaio*), poultry farmers or sellers (*galigai* and *pollaioli*), stockbreeders, brokers and shopkeepers, as well as many other characters who maintained the city in an intense state of animation. These included maids, nuns, elegant ladies and patricians, priests and monks. Closely connected professions gathered in specific zones, giving rise to street names that are still in use today: via dei Cacioli (cheesemongers), via de' Banderai (clothworkers), via dei Pellicciai (tanners and furriers), via dei Brigliai (rein-makers) and via dei Calzaiuoli

1 Baccio Baldini (attrib.), *Mercury*, from the series 'Planets', *c.* 1465, engraving.

(shoemakers). These streets were filled with open-topped shops, for the curiosity and the admiration of all, as represented in a famous engraving attributed to Baccio Baldini, a close collaborator of Botticelli (illus. 1).

Alessandro di Mariano di Vanni Filipepi (1445–1510), more famously known as Sandro Botticelli, was the son of a Florentine tanner, Mariano di Vanni di Amideo Filipepi (d. 1482), and his wife, Mona Smeralda. The last born of a family of eight children, Alessandro owes his nickname 'Botticelli' (little barrel) to his elder brother Giovanni, who was a successful broker. The reason for this nickname remains unknown: was Giovanni dealing in barrels at some point, was it a reference to his physical appearance, or was he just a jovial character? The latter may have been more likely if the 'Botticello' to whom Lorenzo de' Medici refers in his poem titled *I Beoni* (The Drinkers) is Sandro's brother.[1]

No documents so far have unveiled this mystery, but that Sandro was known as related to Giovanni specifically (*di Botticelli*, 'from the family of Botticelli') shows the extent of Giovanni's popularity in Florence. Sandro had three brothers who were all to influence his destiny somehow (another brother, Cosimo, died at a young age, and we hardly know anything about the fate of his three sisters, Lisa, Beatrice and Maddalena).[2] His extended family lived in nearby houses in via Nuova d'Ognissanti, now via del Porcellana, in the quarter of Santa Maria Novella near the church of Ognissanti.[3] His father Mariano ran a small shop with his two brothers, Francesco and Jacopo, a stone's throw away from his house, then on via della Gora, today called via Montebello. As was sometimes the case in fifteenth-century Florence, Sandro would later open his workshop at his father's house. When his eldest brother Giovanni inherited the house upon their father's death in 1482, Sandro carried on living and working there, but not always on good terms with his brother and sister-in-law Nera, and their five children, Maddalena, Benincasa, Fiammetta, Amideo and Jacopo. Sandro would even file a case against his nephew Benincasa in order to regain some peace and quiet.[4] The painter himself would eventually inherit the house together with his other brother Simone after Giovanni's death in 1494. An early account reports that he died there, in misery, on 17 May 1510, but he might have been admitted to a nearby hospital (Spedale de' Vespucci) whose founders, the Vespucci family, had long been his close neighbours and occasional patrons.[5] The family tomb is still visible today in a small chapel on the right-hand side of the nave of the church of Ognissanti.[6]

We know very little about Botticelli's life. Apart from a few archival documents, the main source of information is the biography written by Giorgio Vasari (1511–1574), the father of modern art history. In the two editions of his monumental *Lives of the Most Eminent Painters, Sculptors and Architects* – the first published in 1550, and a revised and augmented edition in 1568 – Vasari gives a short biography of Botticelli some forty years after his death. He was probably relying on the recent oral tradition and documents that unfortunately have not survived. This account was to prove a model for later biographers, until the new archive-based art history was born as a discipline in the late nineteenth century. As valued as Vasari's testimony may be, it is distanced by almost two generations from Botticelli's time and is therefore not entirely reliable. As we shall see, his account is nonetheless one of the primary important sources for the study of his oeuvre and those of his fellow artists.[7] Another important account of Botticelli's life is an anonymous codex kept in the Florence central library (Biblioteca nazionale centrale di Firenze) described as the Anonimo Magliabechiano, which includes a short biography dated, by consensus, to the late 1530s and early 1540s. For centuries these two texts have been the main sources available. Complementing them are accounts and stories that appear almost randomly in a series of texts written during Botticelli's lifetime but not directly focused on him. In addition, towards the end of the nineteenth century, art historians started to explore the surviving contracts, inventories and tax returns in the archives. Today these have still not been fully accounted for and analysed. This relatively recent campaign of research within the Florentine archives has revealed many important details of Botticelli's life and cultural milieu.

Botticelli was not born into a family of artists, but he relied on his family's skills and network to reach this professional category, as often happened in Florence. From the turn of the fifteenth century the Florentine republic had fostered a truly meritocratic system that, together with regular falls in population following recurrent episodes of plague and wars, promoted a great fluidity between professions.[8] We find artistic dynasties such as the Della Robbia, who maintained a family workshop over three generations for nearly a century, and others with no previous artistic connection, such as the brothers Antonio (1429–1498) and Piero (1443–1496) Benci, called Pollaiolo, who were the sons of a poultry seller (hence their name 'pollaiolo', which derives from *pollo*, meaning 'chicken'). They ran one of the most successful workshops in Florence in the second half of the fifteenth century (Quattrocento) and were, on a few occasions, direct rivals to Botticelli. Leonardo da Vinci (1452–1519) was the son of a solicitor, while Michelangelo's (1475–1564) father would occasionally act as the chief magistrate (*podestà*) of a small town outside Florence. As for many of his contemporaries, Botticelli's success results from a combination of factors. His brother Giovanni, who was 24 years older than him, occupied a successful position in the mercantile city of Florence, which positioned him at the heart of a dense network of clientage,[9] and most likely enabled him to protect and recommend his younger brother early on in his career. Giovanni was a marriage-broker (*sensale e faccendiere*) at the Monte delle doti, founded by the government of the Republic of Florence in 1425 to provide suitable dowries (*doti*) to Florentine brides.[10] Artistic commissions were mainly made on the occasion of weddings and births; their rhythm was generally determined by the cycle of social and domestic events of the Florentine people.

Vasari presents Botticelli's artistic vocation as the result of intellectual dissatisfaction: Sandro 'was ever restless and could not settled down at school to reading, writing and arithmetic. Accordingly, his father, in despair at his waywardness, put him with a goldsmith, who was known to him as Botticello, a very reputable master of the craft.'[11] According to the biographer, the discovery of drawing and painting was the revelation that the young boy was looking for. Under the guidance of this master that Vasari identified as one 'called Botticello', seemingly ignoring that Sandro in fact owed his nickname to his elder brother Giovanni 'Botticello', 'he devoted himself to drawing, became attracted to painting, and resolved to take it up'.[12] As attractive as these beginnings may sound, such a story is commonplace throughout Vasari's *Lives*. We find similar tales about the great masters of his time. For instance, Vasari narrates that Michelangelo was born under an 'artistic' lucky star and always found himself distracted as a young boy, until he discovered the art of drawing, to which he then dedicated all his free time.[13] Similarly, Vasari's Leonardo is as restless as Botticelli, drawing (and sculpting) being the only occupation that he never gave up despite paternal complaints and occasional caning.[14]

In those years, the idea of the artist being inspired by an inner force had just emerged: Marsilio Ficino (1433–1499), a key figure in the Medicean cultural world as shall be seen, used a Neoplatonic concept – 'furor divinus', a passion inspired by the divine – to explain this artistic predisposition.[15] By Vasari's time, almost a century later, this concept was widely accepted and almost a prerequisite when it came to explain the vocation of any important artist. Although these assertions served Vasari's greater purpose, positing the art of drawing as an intellectual activity at the heart of all the arts, they more importantly reveal that Botticelli was still seen two generations later as an important member of the artistic cultural elite that included such towering figures as Michelangelo and Leonardo, whose art never went out of fashion, unlike Botticelli's. Vasari made a point of stating that he himself had collected some of Botticelli's drawings, which came to form part of his collection gathered in a large album known as *Libro di disegni*; some surviving fragments are still recognizable today thanks to the beautiful mounts the historian, who was also an accomplished artist, designed himself.

Botticelli's important status is corroborated in other testimonies, for instance in Benedetto Dei's book of memory (*Ricordanze*), written circa 1470, which mentions Botticelli's workshop (*bottega*) as well established at such an early date. A decade later, before Botticelli was sent to Rome to decorate the Sistine Chapel, he was praised as a new Apelles of Cos in Ugolino Verino's *Carliade*, an epic poem on Charlemagne inspired by Virgil's Trojan legend of the *Aeneid*: 'Tuscus Alexander, Choi successor Apellis', which translates 'Tuscan Alexander, successor of Apelles of Cos', Botticelli's first name, Alessandro, into Latin. Apelles was the greatest painter of ancient Greece and was recorded as a model to follow by Leon Battista Alberti (1404–1472) in the *De pictura* (1435), the first treatise on painting written in humanist terms.[16] Botticelli, who was in many ways influenced by Alberti's writings, was to emulate the great painter in the 1480s and '90s with the execution of the famous paintings *Birth of Venus* and the *Calumny of Apelles*. Apelles' original was known to Renaissance men through a detailed description by the Greek poet Lucian, whom Alberti quoted in his own treatise.[17]

According to Vasari, Botticelli was placed with an acquaintance of his father in the workshop of a goldsmith 'called Botticello'.[18] This 'Botticello' goldsmith mentioned by Vasari is now generally identified as his brother Antonio, who like the painter himself was known as *di Botticelli*. Antonio, who was sixteen years older than Sandro, registered on 20 May 1462 with the Silk Guild of Florence (Arte della Seta, also called Por Santa Maria) to which silk merchants and related professionals working with similar luxury materials (silk, gold and silver threads, for example), such as goldsmiths, embroiderers and weavers, reported. However, it is important to note that Antonio is actually recorded as *battiloro* (from *battere l'oro*: 'manipulating, transforming gold').[19] *Battilori* were not, strictly speaking, goldsmiths, which better translates in English to the Italian *orafo* and the Latin *aurifex*, but their professions overlapped a great deal. *Battilori* hammered precious metals (mainly gold and silver, sometimes copper) into thin layers used to highlight important or ornamental details in textiles and finished paintings. Although gold has mostly survived in paintings where it has been used to bring out precious features, such as halos of the saints, rays of divine light and any lavish details in garments and architecture, it was also employed in textiles (tapestries, embroideries and brocades), as well as other goods such as small pieces of furniture, reliquaries and candelabra.[20] These foils were also used to gild the elaborate carved frames that typically adorned paintings and low reliefs and any details that the customers wanted to see highlighted with gold.[21]

More importantly, *battilori* (goldbeaters), did not draw, unlike *orafi* (goldsmiths). It is therefore unlikely that Antonio, who was exercising such a mechanical task, was directly involved in Botticelli's primary training. However, he must have provided his younger brother with direct access to a proper goldsmith's or painter's shop, where Botticelli probably received his first training. Antonio is also documented as a medal caster and gilder, and Botticelli might have paid homage to his brother's profession and assistance in his formative years, if we allow ourselves to see in his early *Portrait of a Man with a Medal of Cosimo the Elder* (illus. 2) a representation of

Antonio holding between his hands an example of his work.[22] The medal is indeed made of real raised stucco and gilded, while the simplicity of the sitter's garments hints towards the identification of a craftsman or a middle-class man, rather than a member of the Medici family or their immediate circle.

Antonio had a shop in via Porta Rossa (still extant today) in the Parte Guelfa of the city, in the quarters stretching between the Ponte Vecchio and the church of Orsanmichele, in the heart of the commercial centre, where those from closely related professions, including painters, gathered.[23] This well-known phenomenon of zoning had considerably developed in Florence in the first half of the Quattrocento, fostering associations and exchanges of expertise between shops.[24] In via Porta Rossa Neri di Bicci (1419–1492), one of the most prolific and successful painters in Florence, if not very innovative, ran a busy workshop. We find mention in Neri's account books of a payment to 'Antonio di Mariano battiloro', Botticelli's brother, but also other references attesting to repeated contacts with Fra Filippo Lippi (1406–1469), Botticelli's future master.[25] A stone's throw from Antonio's shop, in via Vacchereccia, was the shop of the goldsmith Maso Finiguerra (1426–1464), who likely played a key role in Botticelli's formative years. Sandro's father, Mariano, declared in his tax return of 1458 that the young Sandro '*sta allegare ed è malsano*'. This expression was often interpreted as 'is learning to read' – considering that *allegare* could in fact stand for *leggere* – and 'is of poor health'.[26] The other reading – to which I subscribe – refers on the contrary directly to goldsmithing work, whereby the contracted expression '*allegare*' alludes to the manipulation and fusion of metals. It would have been surprising that Botticelli

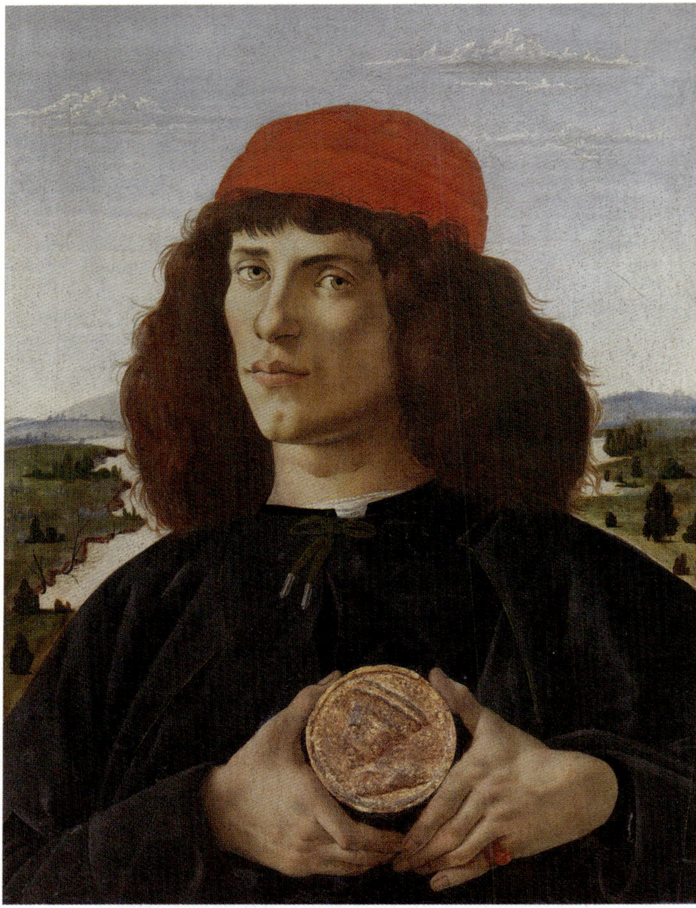

was still at school at the advanced age of thirteen while young boys before the age of ten were usually placed at the *scuola d'abbaco*, where they were taught basic mathematics and writing skills before joining a shop as an apprentice (*garzone*).[27] The Finiguerra family had their house in Borgognissanti, in the same neighbourhood as the Filipepis, who also appear as

2 Botticelli, *Portrait of a Man with a Medal of Cosimo the Elder*, c. 1474–5, tempera on wood and gilded stucco.

Maso's creditors on at least one occasion.[28] The two families were related by marriage as Maso's cousin Nera had married Giovanni 'Botticello' Filipepi and was thus sister-in-law to Antonio and Sandro. Antonio himself is recorded as training with an unidentified goldsmith in 1457, possibly Maso himself, before registering as *battiloro* at the Arte della Seta.[29]

The close connection between the two families led to the likely hypothesis that Sandro trained for some time with Maso Finiguerra. Botticelli's competence in drawing and his distinctive graphic style appear particularly close to that of Finiguerra. This resemblance is evident in the surviving set of 92 large drawings for Dante's poem the *Divine Comedy*, in which Botticelli was able to develop all his power of invention. Executed utilizing the complex technique of metalpoint, and subsequently highlighted with pen and brown ink, the drawings reveal hardly any changes of mind. The outline shows self-confidence with striking ease and grace while the compositions convey a sense of harmony, balance and movement. These qualities are also found in Maso's work. The similarity between their graphic style and compositional formulas, despite some inevitable differences inherent to their artistic personalities, suggests that Maso may have passed his singular manner on to Botticelli (see illus. 3 and 4).

Botticelli's beginnings were therefore facilitated by the dense network of alliances and trades fostered by his family, a characteristic trend of Florence's economic and social organization. Maso's shop in via Vacchereccia would soon be taken over by the goldsmith and sculptor Antonio del Pollaiolo (*c.* 1426–1498) in 1464, working with his younger brother Piero (1443–1496), who was primarily a painter. Nearby, in via dell'Agnolo, Andrea del Verrocchio (1435–1488) had also opened a multidisciplinary workshop.[30] Andrea del Verrocchio had begun his career as a goldsmith, but after 1457 requalified as a sculptor (because of a sudden drop in commissions in his former field) while also working as a painter. The influence of these artists on the young Botticelli remains a subject of debate today. They certainly provided a great model for Botticelli but it is unlikely, given the chronology of his formative years, that they contributed to his training. In fact, by the time Botticelli could have had access to their shops in the late 1460s, he was already fully trained and about to embark on the execution of his first documented masterpiece, in direct competition with the Pollaiolo brothers. This commission also prevented Botticelli from participating in the execution of Verrocchio's painting *The Baptism of Christ*, in which some scholars have perceived Botticelli's hand in the figure of the angel on the left hand-side.[31] Their geographical proximity, however, as well as relatively easy access to their works often displayed in public spaces, made it possible for a receptive and observing mind like Botticelli's to assimilate and emulate Verrocchio's and Pollaiolo's manner, without having trained directly under their supervision. Furthermore, the Pollaiolo brothers were probably close acquaintances of Botticelli's master, Filippo Lippi; they made the journey to see him in Spoleto when he fell ill in 1469. It is important to understand that the success of Florence as the greatest city of arts and crafts during the early Renaissance, and its increasing specialization in luxury goods, results from the close proximity and high level of exchange between the various professions active in that field.

In recent years, considerable progress has been made in researching the broader context of Renaissance art practice and its trade, the organization of the historic centre of the city and the place artists and craftsmen occupied both geographically and sociologically.[32] The permeability between artistic professions and the exchange of expertise between workshops is one of the great characteristics of Quattrocento Florence, and is key to understanding the workings of a successful workshop (*bottega*) such as Botticelli's. The Renaissance workshop had a strict internal hierarchy. At its head was the master (*capobottega*), who was required to register with the guild, and below him, in descending order, a number of collaborators (fully trained artists who decided not to open their own shops: Lorenzo di Credi (1459–1537), for instance, remained Verrocchio's life-long collaborator until he inherited the shop in 1488), together with more or less advanced apprentices (*garzoni* and younger *fanciulli di bottega*, whose training and salaries were regulated by the guild) as well as other mere handymen. The number of people employed depended on the size and level of the success of the *bottega*, which functioned typically as a great polyvalent hub, as exemplified by Verrocchio's shop. His workshop encompassed a wide variety of media, from painted panels to sculpture and other goods. It was not rare to see different types of craft in the same workshop. This great diversity, which helped them to respond quickly to any changes in demand on the market, was further strengthened by frequent partnership between artists who joined forces in order to endure the harsh competitiveness of the artistic business and stay afloat in difficult times. Throughout the fifteenth century, we find examples of such associations,

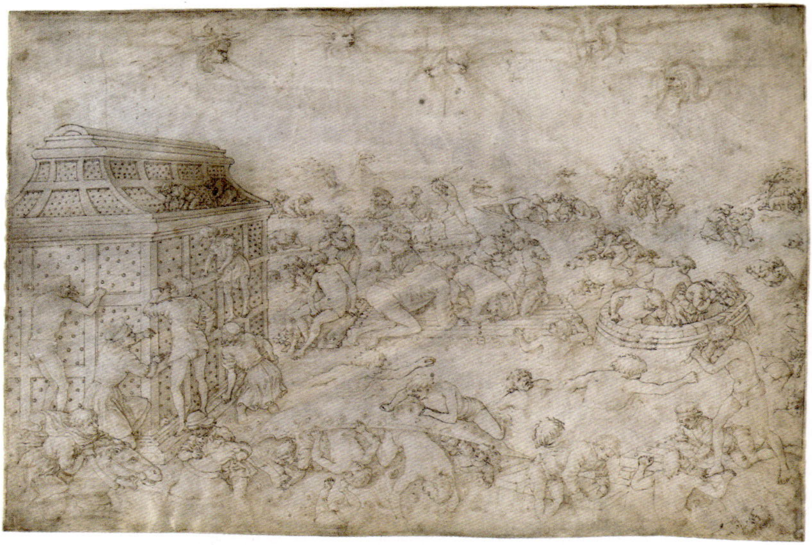

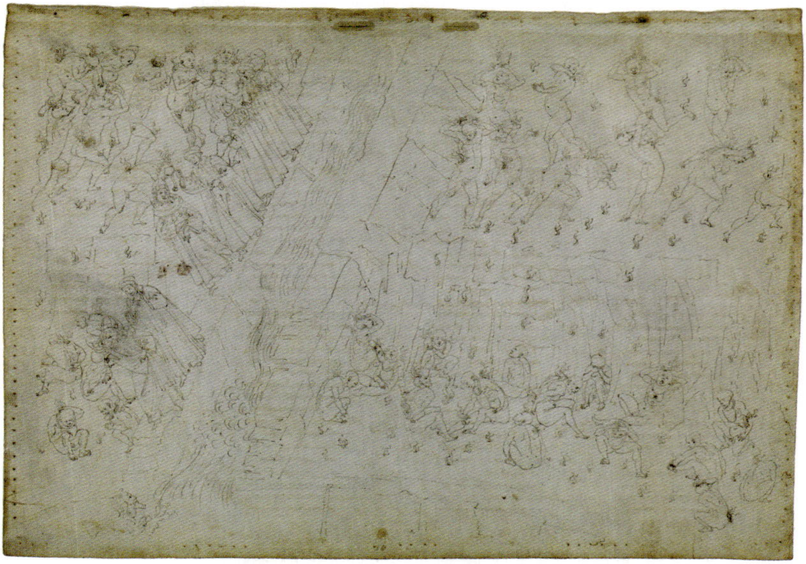

3 Maso Finiguerra, *The Flood*, *c.* 1460–64, pen and ink and wash on vellum.
4 Botticelli, 'Sodomites, Usurers in Hell', drawing for Dante's *Divine Comedy* (*Inferno*, XII), *c.* 1485–95.

which typically lasted for a period of three years. This is the case for the *compagnia* set up by Pesello and two other associates, Antonio di Jacopo and Cipriano di Cione, at the beginning of the century, for instance, for the career-long association between Marco del Buono (1402–1489) and Apollonio di Giovanni (*c.* 1416–1465), who specialized in paintings for pieces of furniture in the second half of the century.[33] Some *capobottega* extended their reach by setting up several workshops in the same city – like Neri di Bicci, who, in addition to his shop in via Porta Rossa, maintained his father's former shop in via San Salvadore in Oltrarno – or in different places, like Fra Filippo Lippi, who was a resident in the nearby city of Prato since May 1455 but kept a *bottega* in Florence, possibly in the same house, located in the quarter of San Pietro Maggiore, that his son, Filippino Lippi, would inherit in 1469.[34] At an uncertain date, most likely around 1459/60, Botticelli joined the Florentine workshop of the Carmelite friar Filippo Lippi. In 1459 Filippo had just completed one of his masterpieces, the altarpiece representing the *Adoration in the Wilderness* (now in the Gemäldegalerie, Berlin) for the Medici chapel in the Palazzo Medici in via Larga (today renamed via Cavour), which complemented the frescoes of Benozzo Gozzoli (1420–1497) depicting scenes of the journey of the Magi.

Manual work had been fundamental to the Carmelite rule since the thirteenth century and the artistic career entailed no conflict with the religious vocation. The order therefore counted such key figures for the development of Western art as the painter Lorenzo Monaco (1370–1425) and his disciple Fra Angelico (1400–1455).[35] Fra Filippo was heir to this tradition, and was in his turn considered as the leading painter in Florence, as several contemporary testimonies affirm. Cristoforo Landino (1424–1498), a professor at the University of Florence (then called the Studio) and one of the most important humanists of the century, gave Fra Filippo the highest praise in the introduction to his commentary on Dante's *Divine Comedy*, published in 1481. In this text, Landino describes the different qualities of the artists of his time (excluding those who were still alive, hence no mention of Botticelli): Fra Filippo is elegant (*gratioso*), rich (*ornato*) and exceedingly skilful (*artificioso sopra ogni modo*), very good at compositions and variety, at colours and relief, and at ornaments of every kind, whether imitations of the real or inventions.[36] Michael Baxandall gave a thorough analysis of this text encompassing a series of philological plays on words, such as Landino's peers would have enjoyed.[37] The Latin roots of these words provided contemporary readers with a much larger spectrum of meaning pertaining to literary and philosophical concepts in vogue at the time and with which a lay reader might have struggled. The same philological wordplays also had a part in devising the mythological compositions which Botticelli excelled at translating into paintings.

Almost three generations after Fra Filippo's death, Vasari was still paying homage to his talent by asserting that even Michelangelo 'has not only always praised him but imitated him in many things'.[38] A question then arose: how did Botticelli manage to approach such a master, who, in addition to his significant workload, commuted between Prato and Florence? No evidence has yet been found to document how Sandro entered Fra Filippo's workshop, apart from Vasari's late testimony, but part of the explanation may lie once again in the dense network of relationship and association which craftsmen and artists maintained. As already mentioned, Fra Filippo's name recurs frequently in Neri di Bicci's notebook, attesting to several reciprocal favours between the two men.[39] Neri was also acquainted with Antonio, Sandro's brother, and with Maso Finiguerra, whose kinship with the Filipepi was pointed out earlier. It is therefore very likely that this array of direct and indirect acquaintances and relationships had helped Botticelli on his way in Fra Filippo's shop in Florence. When Vasari stresses the close connection between goldsmiths and painters,[40] he does not only account for the fact that both disciplines were based on the art of drawing, thus sharing a great deal of expertise, but for a wider system of networks for mentoring and collaboration.

Very little is known about Fra Filippo's formative years. Together with his brother Giovanni, he entered the Carmelite convent of Santa Maria del Carmine in Florence, presumably following the death of their father, around 1411. He became a friar in 1421 at the age of fifteen.[41] His mother and sister lived in a house on the nearby piazza del Carmine. At that time (1425–7), Masaccio (*c.* 1401–1428), one of the greatest painters of his generation, was working in collaboration with the older Masolino da Panicale (1383–1447) on the frescoes of the Brancacci Chapel in that same church. Masaccio's frescoes were to provide an extraordinary visual repertory and an invaluable teaching aid to the young Filippo, whose style would in turn contribute in a distinctive way to Botticelli's own manner. A few decades later, between 1481 and 1485, Fra Filippo's son, Filippino Lippi (1457/8–1504), born out of wedlock to the nun Lucrezia Buti, would complete Masaccio's frescoes, which had been left unfinished after the latter's sudden and mysterious death at the young age of 28. Doubtless as a tribute to his family's story, Filippino represented himself among the crowd witnessing the *Dispute with Simon Magus*, and again in the *Crucifixion of St Peter* (illus. 5) together with a portrait of Botticelli, who became his master following Fra Filippo's death in 1469. Filippino was about thirteen when he entered Botticelli's workshop to become his disciple, thus closing the chapter of an extraordinary story of artistic transmission, collaboration and friendship.

In Florence, each trade corporation had its own training requirements. The statutes of the painters' guild (Arte dei Medici e Speziali) specified that the apprenticeship should last for a period of nine years, three to be paid for by the pupil, and six by the master.[42] The fact that a pupil received a salary after three years indicates that he was by then sufficiently trained to carry out small jobs within the *bottega*. In the first three years, however, the family paid for the master's time spent teaching his art's rudiments, and for bed and board. From Neri di Bicci's books, which record 22 years of artistic practice and are the most complete surviving accounts of the complex workings of a *bottega* in fifteenth-century Florence, we learn that the apprenticeship entailed not only working with the master but living with him; the young boy could be summoned at any time of the day and night at his master's whim. The apprenticeship therefore required a real commitment from both the master and the trainee, which was recognized by the many amendments and further contracts drafted between the two parties each time a change within the original agreement occurred. For example, Botticelli's

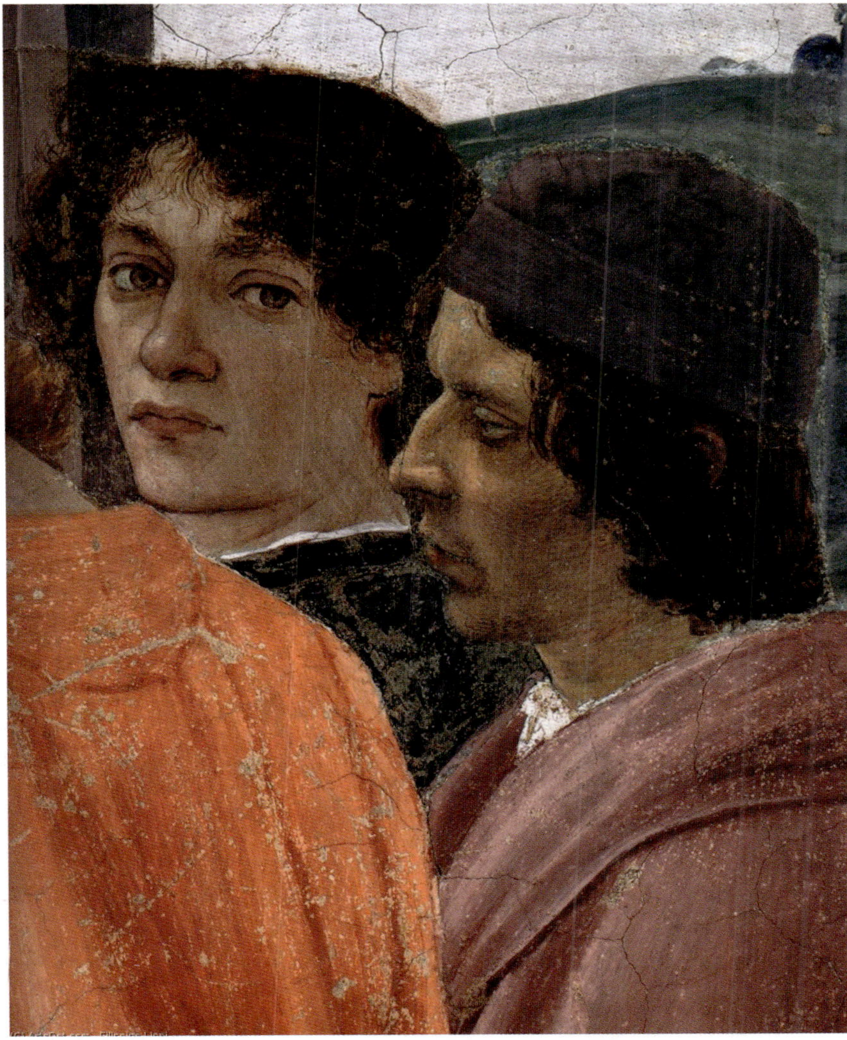

5 Filippino Lippi, *Crucifixion of St Peter*, fresco, 1482–5, detail of his self-portrait in the company of Botticelli.

collaborator-to-be Benedetto di Domenico, called Betto Pialla, entered Neri's *bottega* on 21 August 1463. A contract was then drafted between the two parties, which stated that Betto was to complete his apprenticeship by 30 December 1470. In the meantime, further contracts were drafted to record Betto's leaves, special tasks and changes in the end date of the initial contract.[43] Occasionally checked by the guild's solicitors, these contracts were extremely important; they guaranteed that the complex Florentine trade system was in good working order. Any irregularities were severely punished. Filippo Brunelleschi (1377–1446), for instance, was fined and imprisoned in 1434 after he refused to pay his guild dues.[44] When, in 1455, a conflict arose between Fra Filippo Lippi and Giovanni di Francesco (1412–1459), a former pupil who became Lippi's assistant, over a contract signed some fifteen years earlier, they were both imprisoned and tortured.[45]

In contrast, regulations over the total years under contract during the period of training were seldom applied and seemed to have indicated a broad timeframe rather than a fixed term of study. In practice, the apprenticeship hardly ever lasted that long, with some exceptions. For instance, Cennino Cennini (*c.* 1370–*c.* 1440) states in his treatise on painting, the *Craftsman's Handbook* (*Libro dell'arte*), written in about 1400, that his own apprenticeship with his master, the painter Agnolo Gaddi (fl. 1369–1396), lasted over twelve years.[46] However, from Neri di Bicci's memoirs, written a good half-century later, we learn that apprenticeship typically covered a period of about six years. It is most likely therefore that Botticelli remained Fra Filippo's apprentice for five to six years, coinciding with the period during which Fra Filippo was immersed in decorating the apse of Prato Cathedral (1452–65) with scenes of the lives of Stephen, the city's patron saint, and of John the Baptist, the patron saint of Florence.

We know nothing about the conditions of Botticelli's apprenticeship, as Fra Filippo's account books have not survived, but we can infer what he learned from his master in comparison with similar workshop practices and from what early artistic treatises recommended. Although it is difficult to distinguish how long different phases of learning lasted in each workshop, as it likely depended on the individual dexterity of the various candidates, Cennini identifies two main stages: first, the young boy started with direct handling of raw materials; then he would be allowed to move to the next stage, whereby he could be more closely involved in the production of artworks.[47] In other words, an education in technique preceded stylistic study. The first phase typically consisted of mechanical tasks, such as grinding the pigments or flattening and smoothing the surface of the panel, which was then covered with a thin layer of gesso in preparation for the composition to be drawn by senior assistants. The *garzone*'s role was therefore limited to observing the master and his more fully trained fellows, so as to familiarize himself with the specific style of the *capobottega*. The imitation of the master's style was fundamental to the success of the workshop, the production of which was by nature collaborative, in order to maintain a recognizable, reliable and consistent output. This is how many collaborators, more or less talented, have survived only as names in documents. Each work, whether produced by the *capobottega*, his assistants or in collaboration, was considered the master's work and purchased as such. Unevenness in the production was therefore inevitable, a trend which important patrons attempted to avoid by stipulating in contracts that specific aspects were to be executed exclusively by the master. But even so, these requests were not always respected. The second phase of the training was to learn how to draw. Paper was still rare at the time so this was done first on a small panel which could be recycled by applying a new layer of gesso. And only 'after a year or so', says Cennini, 'you may sometimes just draw on paper with a pen'.[48] Some of these drawings have survived and show that the apprentices served as models for each other in order to study different positions and perfect their knowledge of the anatomy of the body, which sometimes required them to pose naked or half-naked. Finally, the young apprentice came to learn to paint, which involved binding the pigments and applying the colours after the composition had been drawn on the support. The future painter would also learn how to mix the colours together in order to convey the sense of volume through light and shade, which, as Alberti puts it, brings the greatest beauty.[49]

When Botticelli joined Fra Filippo in Prato, he must have had good rudiments of draughtsmanship since he had already spent some time in a goldsmith's shop. As mentioned above, goldsmiths were particularly talented in the art of drawing, and were often called 'master draughtsmen' (*maestri di disegno*).[50] Draughtsmanship was the principal means by which to embellish precious silverware. Incising and embossing the hard surface of the metal required great manual dexterity and clear legibility in the design. Unfortunately, only a few drawings by Botticelli have survived out of the plethora he must have produced during his career (illus. 6). As already mentioned,

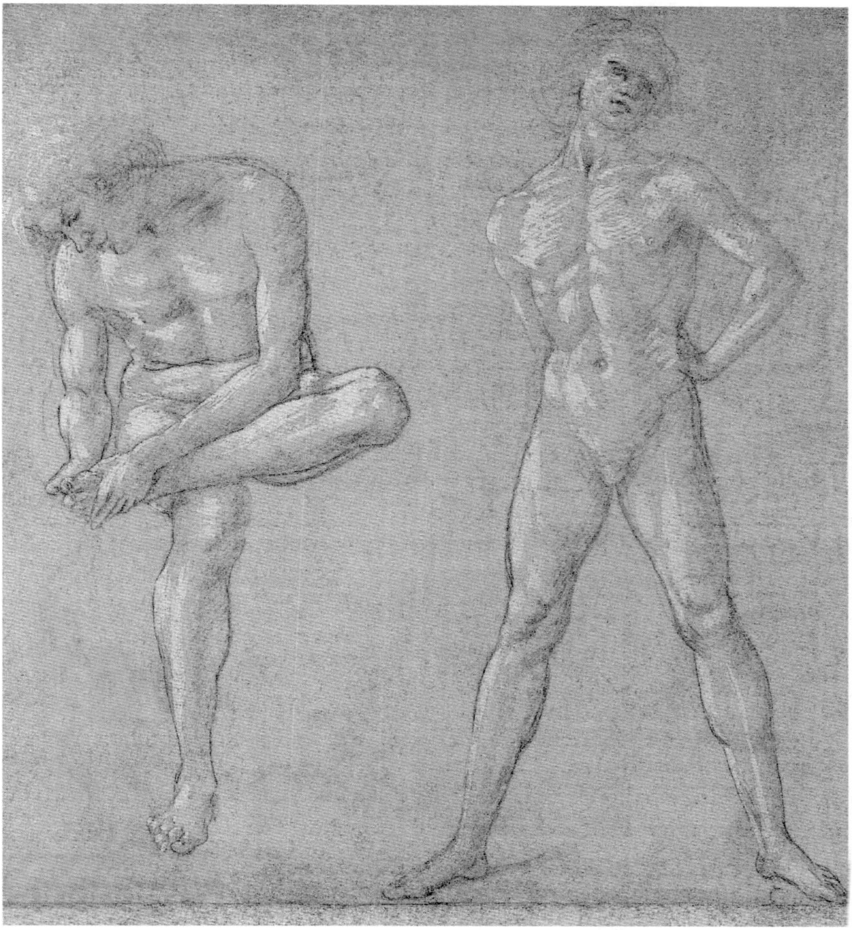

the drawings for Dante's poem the *Divine Comedy* bear witness to his dexterity and power of invention. Working with Fra Filippo in Prato gave Sandro his first experience of fresco painting on a monumental scale, providing him with useful skills for the future papal request to decorate the walls of the

6 Botticelli, *Study of Two Nudes*, c. 1470–75, metalpoint and lead white on white paper with pinkish yellow preparation.

Sistine Chapel in Rome two decades later (1481–2). By the time Botticelli arrived in Prato around 1459/60 an important part of the decoration was already completed. The work had commenced during the summer of 1453, probably reaching the middle tier circa 1458 and the lower register in 1461.[51] It is believed that the last scene to be depicted was *The Feast of Herod*, in the lowest section. So Botticelli must have assisted, although no trace of his intervention is identifiable, with the depiction of the lower-tier scenes: the *Celebration of the Relics of St Stephen*, the *Martyrdom of St Stephen*, the *Beheading of St John* and the *Feast of Herod*, all carried out between about 1461 and 1466. As we shall see in the following chapters, many compositional formulas and figure types from this cycle would be translated and adapted into Botticelli's own inventions. The figures of St Giovanni Gualberto and St Alberto of Trapani, enclosed in trompe-l'oeil niches of multi-coloured marble, provided Botticelli with a direct model for the representation of the early popes in the Sistine Chapel. One of them, St Sixtus II, even reproduced the very same pose as St Alberto of Trapani and was perhaps copied from an old cartoon inherited from Fra Filippo's shop. It is therefore tempting to consider that Botticelli might have been responsible for the execution of these two saints.[52]

While apparently fully committed to the decoration of the apse of Prato Cathedral, Fra Filippo continued to produce easel paintings. We know, for instance, that Giovanni di Cosimo de' Medici made a special request to the Prato authorities to release Fra Filippo from his commission so that he could execute an altarpiece that he wished to send to King Alfonso of Naples, as a diplomatic gift. Extraordinarily, a letter by Fra Filippo to Giovanni, dated 20 July 1457, has survived. Below the main text in the friar's round handwriting, there features a light sketch of the painting, including its elaborate frame.[53] This altarpiece is now partially lost, but we know, thanks to this sketch, that the central panel represented an Adoration; the two wings, which have survived, depict St Anthony Abbot and St Michael (now in the Cleveland Museum of Art).[54] The painting was completed by May 1458 and it is not inconceivable that the young Botticelli had seen it. Several aspects of the figure of St Michael – its melancholic air, jewelled armour, intricate sashes and rich gilding – seem to have inspired Botticelli's first known commission. This was the allegory of Fortitude for the tribunal hall of the Mercanzia, which allowed him to make his grand entrance on the Florentine artistic scene. For the most gifted apprentices, such as Botticelli and Fra Filippo's son Filippino, the training was not only about imitating the master but rather aimed at appropriating his technique, sensibility and vision so that his artistic legacy could pass to new generations. Cennino Cennini describes this method of teaching well when he writes that the young trainee should 'bind [himself] to a master with respect for authority, undergoing an apprenticeship in order to achieve perfection' and 'submit [himself] to the direction of a master for instruction as early as [he] can and not leave the master until [he] has to'.[55]

Some have suggested that the young Botticelli could be partially responsible for the execution of the *Adoration of the Infant Jesus with St George and St Vincent Ferrer*, particularly the figure of St Joseph, which seems to differ slightly from Fra Filippo's practice.[56] Botticelli's participation in the predella now in Palazzo Pretorio was also considered. In the light of such a culture of collaboration, though, these attributions are difficult to assess. It is therefore probably more interesting to look instead at what the young Botticelli might have seen in Prato. His observation of Fra Filippo's art there would inspire his artistic vision and fuel his innovative approach to picture making. Alongside the Prato frescoes, Botticelli had probably witnessed the execution of at least four panels datable to the 1460s: the so-called Camaldoli Adoration, which appears as a partial replica of the Medici chapel Adoration, made for a cell dedicated to John the Baptist in the mountain hermitage of Camaldoli.[57] The golden palette enlivened by honey-brown hues and highlights of pure gold against a receding dark green background must have provoked a powerful mysterious effect in situ, like a jewellery box enclosing a sparkle of divine light. The *Annunciation with Donor* (now in Corsham Court, Wiltshire), datable to about 1466, shows a more open architectural setting, whose receding formula recurs somewhat in the *Presentation in the Temple* commissioned by the Servites of Prato in 1468 (church of Santo Spirito, Prato). Finally, the so-called Bartolini tondo (mid- to late 1460s), representing the Virgin and Child with scenes from the life of St Anne, probably shaped Botticelli's vision of what would become the mainstay of his work: circular devotional pictures called *tondi* ('round', in Italian), which, as we shall see, were particularly appreciated by Florentines in the second half of the century.

From Lippi's mature style, Botticelli was able to absorb a visual repertory and a number of formulas that, though transformed, adapted and enriched, would become hallmarks of his style, a 'brand' both highly recognizable and never matched, which would guarantee the success of his own workshop. Following tradition, Fra Filippo had also handed down a repertory of common devotional types, as well as an innovative rendering of the pictorial space which includes a series of clever architectural devices and the introduction of a sophisticated wilderness. Botticelli would never forget the lessons of his master and would regularly return to these formulas throughout his career.

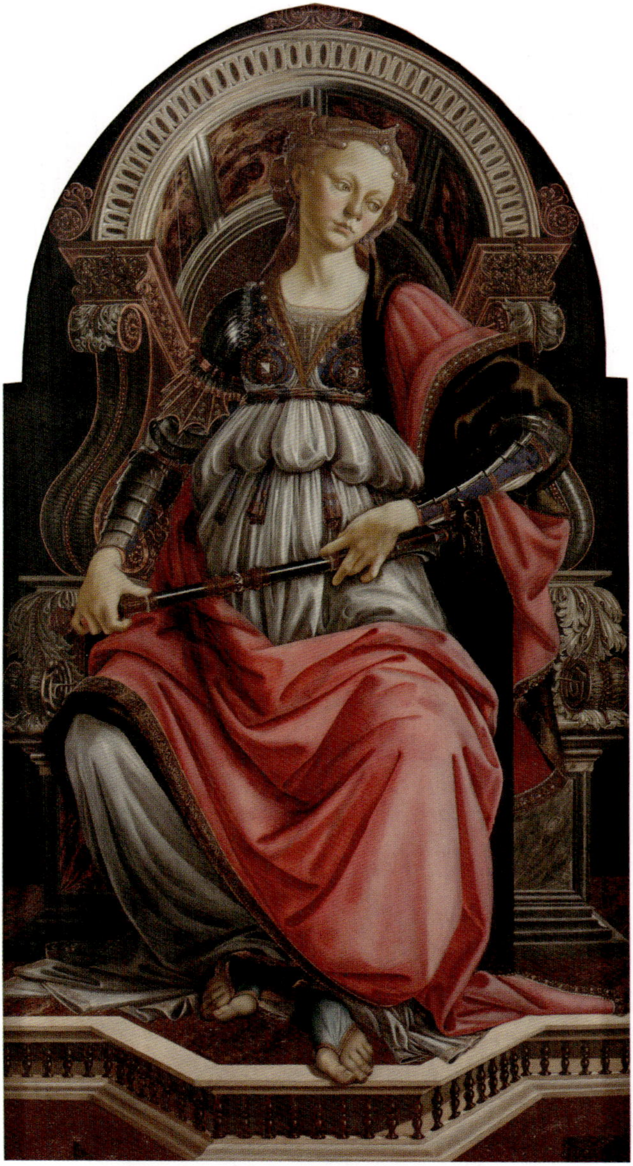

7 Botticelli, *Fortitude*, 1470, tempera on wood.

TWO

Making an Impression: The Painter's Debut in Context

The year 1469 was a decisive one for the fate of Florence; it also marked Botticelli's debut as an independent master. Piero il Gottoso, the ruler of Florence, died in December, and for a short period of time there was some uncertainty as to whether his son Lorenzo de' Medici, then only twenty years old, might succeed him as the legitimate ruler of the city. One man was instrumental in securing both Lorenzo's power and his first important commission for Botticelli. His name was Tommaso Soderini (1403–1485), an uncle by marriage to the Medici family as his wife Dianora was the elder sister of Lorenzo's mother, Lucrezia Tornabuoni (1427–1482). A long supporter of the Medici family, Tommaso Soderini fought against the anti-Medicean movement that arose at the eve of Piero's death.[1] He had strengthened his political status during Piero's last years (1466–9) and was in 1469 at the pinnacle of his power. The Florentine chronicler Francesco Guicciardini (1483–1540) recorded that Soderini played a major role in settling peace both in Florence and abroad, 'for he was the most respected citizen and perhaps the wisest'.[2] It may therefore appear quite extraordinary that such an important citizen proved instrumental in assisting Botticelli, a relatively inexperienced painter, with his first documented commission. This was a painting for the figure of Fortitude, one of the seven Virtues commissioned by the Sei della Mercanzia (the court of the merchants' guild in charge of hearing their disputes) and described in the document as a spalliera, a wooden panel probably intended to ornament the back seats of their tribunal hall.

The story of this commission is a mystery. An incomplete note dated 18 June 1470 records Soderini's intervention and a payment of forty florins to Botticelli despite the fact that the Virtues had already been allocated to another painter, Piero del Pollaiuolo (1443–1496).[3] Pollaiuolo received this important contract the preceding year on 18 August, on the basis of a presentation drawing still visible today on the back of the panel of the first Virtue, *Charity* (see illus. 8). The drawing was made in response to a contest in which the young Pollaiuolo had to compete with the considerable figure of Andrea del Verrocchio (1435–1488). Verrocchio, one of the leading and most versatile artists of Florence at the time, engaged with both painting and sculpture to avoid, as he claimed, 'boredom'. He had also supplied a presentation drawing for the figure of Faith, paid for on 21 December 1469.[4] In this context, the appointment of Piero del Pollaiolo is perhaps as extraordinary as Botticelli's involvement.

Born in 1443, Piero was around 25 years of age when contracted for the Virtues, and for him, too, this was his first documented commission as an independent master. He probably benefited from the support of his elder brother Antonio (*c.* 1432–1498), who already ran a successful polyvalent workshop and is considered by some the real author of Piero's full-scale presentation drawing. The commission itself was rather unclear from the start. It does not appear, from the surviving documents, that a full cycle of Virtues was intended from the outset.[5] In fact the records stipulate that 'Piero del Pollaiuolo had been commissioned by the six [judges] to execute a painting of the Virtue *Charity* in order to replace a similar picture in the great room on the ground floor.'[6] As often happened in those days, patricians did not hesitate to replace a picture that had fallen out of fashion or had been damaged with a new work, in order to keep up with the taste of the day. A larger cycle is explicitly mentioned on 18 December 1469, but whether the cycle should be completed in the form of a painting or in another medium (*per viam picture vel aliter*), and by one or several artists (*et cui quibus locetur tale opus*), remained open questions. It was finally decided that three theological and four cardinal Virtues should be executed in the same fashion as *Charity*, which had already been completed by Piero.[7] The full cycle was allocated to Piero, who was tasked with delivering two figures every three months, beginning 1 January 1470.[8]

The two subsequent Virtues (*Temperance* and *Faith*) were still unfinished five months later, in May 1470, when Tommaso Soderini was elected a new member of the council board of the Mercanzia.[9] Shortly after, Botticelli was commissioned to depict *Fortitude*. It is now therefore generally agreed that this intervention was a direct consequence of Piero's failure to deliver the works on time, allowing Soderini to champion another painter for this commission. But the question remains: why was Botticelli chosen over Andrea del Verrocchio, or one of the '*plures pictores*' who had participated in the contest? Verrocchio was heavily preoccupied with another

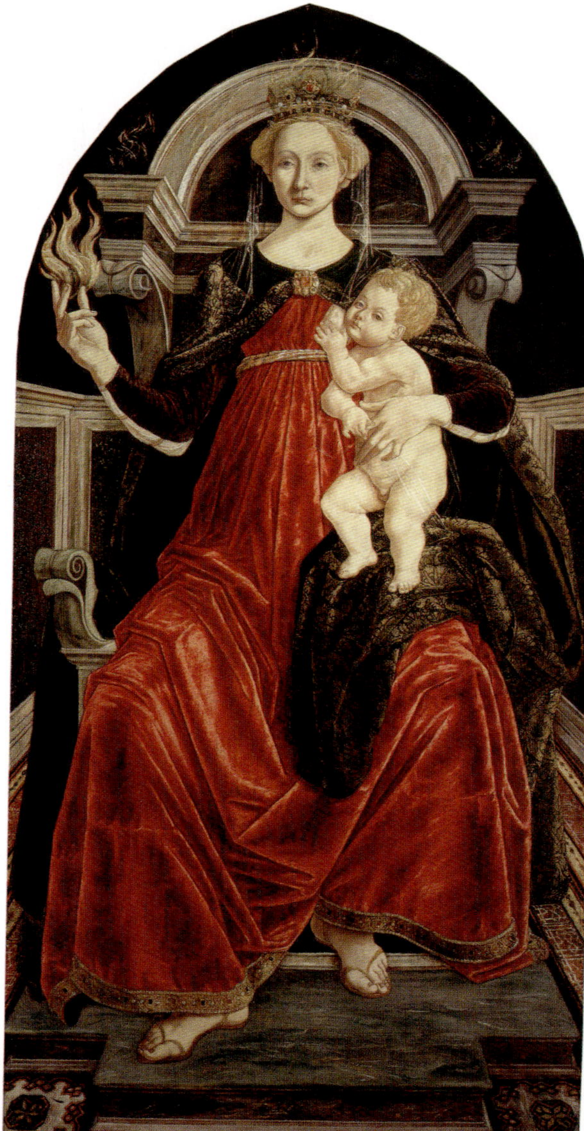

8 Piero del Pollaiolo, *Charity*, 1469–70, tempera on wood.

commission for the Mercanzia: the bronze group portraying Christ and St Thomas for the facade of Orsanmichele. Botticelli, on the other hand, might well have been one of the many painters whose proposal was retained as a reserve, thus strengthening Soderini's argument to entrust him with part of the commission. The drawing identified by consensus as Verrocchio's proposal is in fact sometimes attributed to Botticelli himself.[10]

The support of Tommaso Soderini inaugurated the patronage of Lorenzo de' Medici and his circle.[11] Soderini himself is not remembered as a talent scout apart from another important occasion a decade later, and once again he was acting on behalf of his nephew Lorenzo. This was the completion of Masaccio's frescoes in the Brancacci chapel, which provided Filippino Lippi, Botticelli's pupil, with his first commission as an independent master.[12]

Commissioning different artists to produce a full cycle was not extraordinary in Florence, or in Italy, during the Renaissance. In the same way that a master worked closely with their assistants in the workshop, there are many examples of entire rooms decorated by several artists working alongside each other, conforming their styles to produce an even and harmonious decor. The Brancacci chapel, for instance, is a good example of such a collaboration, with Masaccio and Masolino da Panicale working together. Filippo Lippi produced the altarpiece for the Medici chapel, which was decorated with frescoes by Benozzo Gozzoli, and the Chapel of the Cardinal of Portugal in San Miniato al Monte can be seen as the epitome of such practice before the completion of the Sistine Chapel's frescoes in Rome. The chapel in San Miniato was designed by Antonio Manetti (1423–1497), a disciple of Brunelleschi, and Giovanni Rossellini, while the sculptures were executed by his brothers, Antonio and Bernardo Rossellini. Alesso Baldovinetti (1425–1499) decorated the walls in the fresco technique; Luca della Robbia (1399/1400–1482) executed the extraordinary glazed terracotta ceiling while the Pollaiuolo brothers produced the altarpiece. All these many contributions resulted in the creation of a harmonious and balanced ensemble. When Botticelli was entrusted with the execution of one of the Virtues, he was therefore confronted with a twofold challenge: on the one hand, he had to adapt to the typology of the Virtues designed by Piero, but on the other, he had to create some sensation. His invention could not just blend in with the whole cycle, but had to stand out, as this was the occasion to demonstrate his artistic talent and make a name for himself. While Piero was following on with the composition of *Temperance* and *Faith*, Botticelli created his first masterpiece, *Fortitude*, which subtly broke the rules while apparently conforming to Piero's model. This was a total revolution in design which would significantly influence Piero's stylistic approach to the remaining Virtues.

Fortitude is the only figure of the whole cycle to wear a suit of armour, in the same fashion as Luca della Robbia's figure in the ceiling of the chapel of the Cardinal of Portugal mentioned above and we find further examples in manuscript illuminations. Botticelli also opted for a greater sense of three-dimensional projection by bringing the figure forward, her presence further enhanced by her shining equipment, rendered through the application of translucent glazes in successive layers so as to produce the deepest colour. This technique does not only recall Botticelli's master, Filippo Lippi, especially evident in the figure of St Michael in the surviving wing of the lost altarpiece for the king of Naples, but also the Ferrarese Cosmé Tura (before 1431–1495). Tura's warrior-dressed muse, one of the surviving elements of the decor of the Leonello d'Este 'studiolo' in Belfiore near Ferrara, dates from a decade earlier (1455–60) and displays striking similarities.[13] The *sotto in sù* perspectival effect indicates that, like the Florentine Virtues, the painting was to be hung fairly high up in the room. The pose and the bold play between the dazzling red of the cloak and more subdued colours for the underdress (black, white and ochre) emphasize the three-dimensional quality and presence of the figure, an approach that contrasts greatly with Piero's earthen and subdued palette. It is impossible to say whether Botticelli ever saw Tura's muse, or some of the many drawings he produced during his career, since lost, but we know that artists and humanists between Ferrara and Florence were often in contact.

While in Ferrara Tura designed a fantastic zoomorphic throne, Botticelli opted for more classical architectural seating, decorated with a carved palmette at the top and a baluster motif on the bottom step. This wealth of detail is nowhere to be found in Piero's works. Instead he opted for a simpler variegated marble effect. Botticelli must have taken a particular pleasure in rendering the different types of textures, which react to light differently according to their material: the steel of the armour produces a silvery reflection, while the crimson of the folding drapery retains a deep matte intensity. The artist also created a subtle network of recurring hues such as the light blush of the cheeks echoing the red mantle; the blonde hair and intricate silver headdress recall the hazelnut hue of her irises, as well as the gold and silver of her suit of armour. Great attention to the rendering of light on various materials is at the heart of the sculptor and goldsmith Lorenzo Ghiberti's treatise, known as the *Commentaries*, written in about 1447. This was a pioneering art treatise after Leon Battista Alberti's *On Painting* (*De pictura*, 1435). Ghiberti, the celebrated creator of the Gate of the Paradise for the Baptistry of San Giovanni in Florence (1425–52), also started his career as a painter. In the *Commentaries*, he devotes a long passage to the different type of colours, tonalities and hues that absorb or reflect light. His research in the rendering of coloured light reflections pertains to both goldsmithing and painting.

In the same manner, we can consider Botticelli's *Fortitude* as a tribute to his training both as a goldsmith and a painter owing to Botticelli's imitation of lustrous surfaces, precious metals and stones and use of deep colours. Furthermore, one cannot help but notice that Botticelli's choice of jewels and adornments echoes those worn by Lorenzo and his retinue during the joust held in honour of his twentieth birthday on 7 February 1469. Pearls and diamonds prevailed in Lorenzo's costume and his suit of armour was finely gilded as related by the poet Luigi Pulci and an anonymous spectator, who gave a detailed description of the event.[14] The game took place on Santa Croce square and included thirteen participants, all from important Florentine families allied to Lorenzo. Although jousts were often held in Florence, and drew from a long tradition of medieval combat and demonstrations of power in the most important cities of the Italian peninsula, this one was especially remarkable for the lavish costumes and suits of armour, which glittered in the sun. The cost of the abundant use of gold, precious stones and diamonds exceeded 200,000 ducats, according to the anonymous narrator, and the richness of the costumes of the participants and of Lorenzo in particular is given lavish attention and endless description.

Lorenzo wore a short cape (*mezza giornea*) in white and purple velvet, a crimson red beret decorated with three hundred pearls and a larger pearl in the centre. His *mazzocchio*, a traditional wooden or wicker male headdress, was decorated with three gold feathers and eleven diamonds, as well as two gold chains. More pearls and precious stones adorned the shield, itself covered in velvet and embroidered with the head of Medusa. The horse wore similar equipment fashioned in the same colour and material as the clothes of his rider. It goes without saying that during the jousting, in the heat of the action, these delicate ornaments would be damaged and torn apart and would end up in the arena sand, trampled by horses.

By using the specific colours and recreating the precious material displayed during the joust in the depiction of *Fortitude*, Botticelli might have been paying tribute to his 'true' patron (diamonds were part of the Medici's armorial devices). The painting also evokes the work of goldsmiths, with whom Botticelli had originally trained, and who excelled in combining their observation of the everyday with a considerable power of invention. The taste for lavish materials and intense colours has been described as 'a dominant goldsmith's aesthetic in Florence' at the time.[15] Lorenzo himself had a predilection for richly gilded and exquisitely finished artefacts. The philosopher Marsilio Ficino (1433–1499), for instance, manifests a similar taste in his philosophical writings.[16] Manuscripts were often adorned to resemble precious jewel-like objects and this fashion extended to paintings.[17] The two small panels showing the *Discovery of the Dead Holofernes* (illus. 9) and *Judith Returning to Bethulia* (illus. 10) that Botticelli painted in that same period were probably framed together so as to imitate a precious codex. They are often compared to the lost panels of the *Labours of Hercules* executed by Antonio del Pollaiolo and described in the posthumous inventory of the sculptor Giambologna as enclosed in a gilded frame '*a uso di libro che si serra*' ('like a bookcover one can close').[18] Another similar small painting of the same subject by the Paduan painter Francesco Squarcione (*c.* 1395–after 1468), is described in the 1492 Medici inventory as part of the *studiolo* content, together with precious stones, medals and cameos.[19] Keeping in line with this tradition of small panels akin to precious pieces of jewellery, the small paintings of the story of Judith and Holofernes are executed in the same palette as *Fortitude*. Their rich colours and the careful rendering of metals, fabric and flesh characterized Botticelli's early style, which reveals its full potential in the Mercanzia Virtue.

Botticelli's *Fortitude* is doubtless a tour de force, and reveals the master's creative process as one of the most sensitive artists of his time. Aware of the work of his fellow artists and those of the previous generation, he treasured and transformed this artistic inheritance in a highly personal manner, which would in turn have no small impact on his contemporaries. The figural formula of the Virtues was not new: first and foremost was Giotto's series of Vices and Virtues in the Scrovegni chapel in Padua (1303–6), notably *Justice* and *Injustice*, similarly enthroned; another example was the large cycle of Ambrogio Lorenzetti's *Allegory of the Bad and Good Governments* in the Sala dei Nove (Salon of the Nine) in the Palazzo Pubblico in Siena (1338–9). However, it seems that Botticelli looked at further sources of inspiration in Florence, such as the southern door of the Florence Baptistry where Andrea Pisano (*c.* 1290–1348/9) designed 28 scenes, including the four cardinal Virtues (1430). Further examples of similar enthroned figures include Domenico Veneziano's first Florentine painting for a street tabernacle once on the Canto de' Carnesecchi, near Santa Maria Novella square in Florence: the painting represents a Virgin enthroned, set in rigorous perspective enhanced by marble intarsia.[20] Fra Filippo Lippi's figure of the Virgin, in the large altarpiece produced for the Medici chapel of the Noviciate in Santa Croce, and Giuliano da Maiano's marqueted figure of St Zenobius, after a design by Maso Finiguerra, in the sacristy of the Florence cathedral might have provided further models to the young artist.

Piero would eventually produce all the remaining Virtues. *Charity* aside, they are all surmounted by an arched canopy, which is most likely a direct consequence of Botticelli's design; however, it was too late for him to reposition the figures forward. That dramatic change appears only in his remaining panels. While *Temperance* and *Faith*, the second pair delivered, still show a marble entablature and a rather distant viewpoint similar to that of *Charity*, *Hope* and *Justice* have been brought forward, conveying a sense of three-dimensionality comparable to that of *Fortitude*. Similarly, the marble entablature has disappeared. *Prudence*, however, which should have followed an equivalent repositioning, surprisingly retains the same

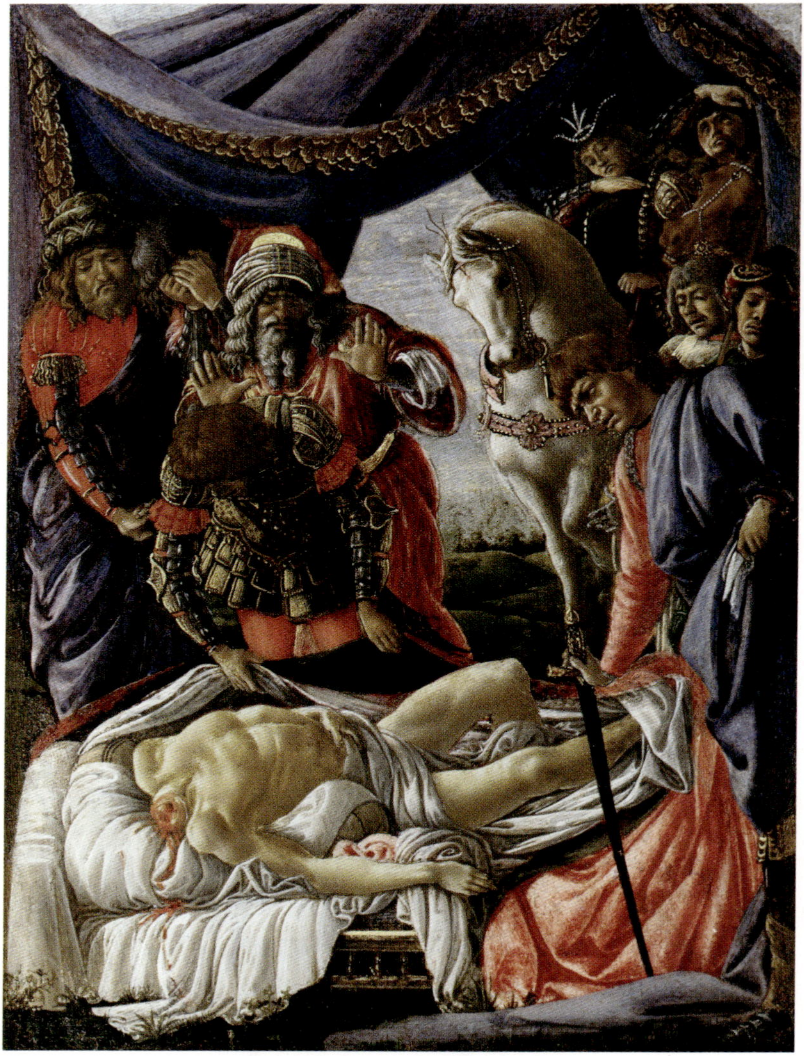

9 Botticelli, *Discovery of the Dead Holofernes*, *c.* 1470, tempera on wood.

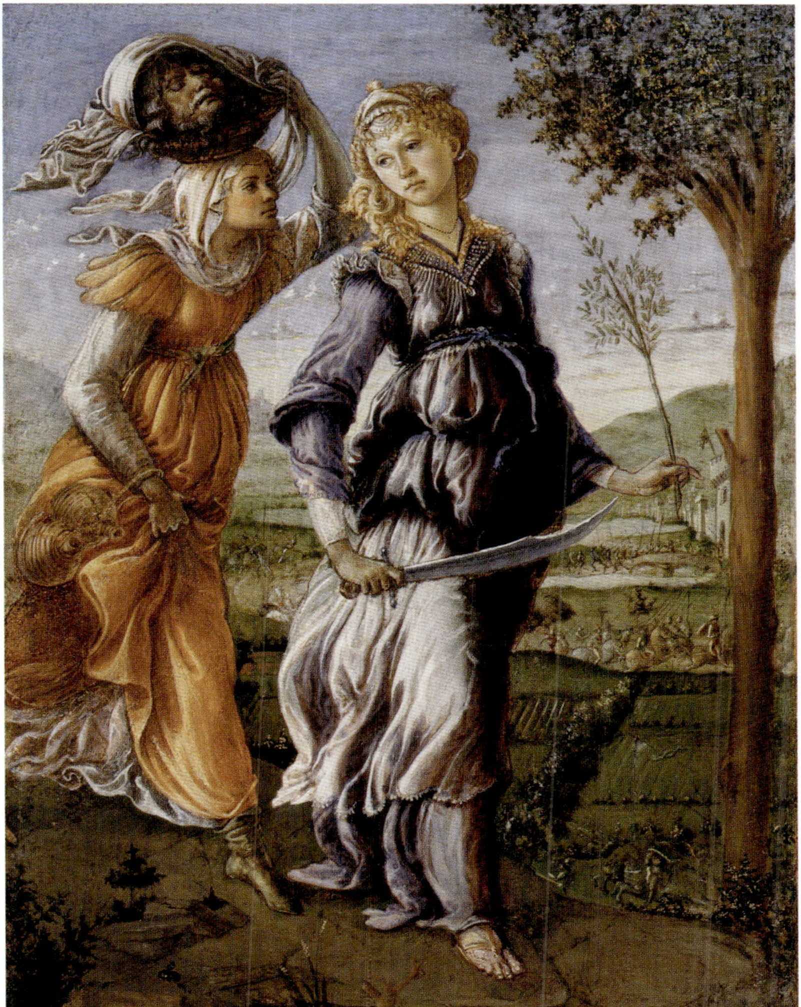

10 Botticelli, *Judith Returning to Bethulia*, *c.* 1470, tempera on wood.

format as *Charity*. To explain such a discrepancy, it has been suggested that this painting was executed by Antonio, the elder and more experienced of the Pollaiolo brothers, in order to speed up the delivery and save Piero's commission, which was seriously threatened by Botticelli. Graphic evidence and the use of a different pictorial technique observed during a campaign of restoration seem to attest to Antonio's authorship.[21]

Indeed, Botticelli had been promised the sum of forty florins, the price for two panels, but a change of plan, most likely due to Antonio's intervention, redirected the commission to Piero. Another important consequence of Botticelli's innovation on Piero's remaining Virtues is the introduction of rich brocade, fine gilding and lustrous surfaces along with a more sculptural rendering of the overmantle, which better defines the lower limbs around the knees. Time has inexorably altered the original appearance of Pollaiolo's Virtues and while it is true that *Charity* displays a crown, a large jewel clasping at her mantle, which is finely trimmed with gold, the overall visual effect is much less lavish than that of *Fortitude*. The richer ornaments of the following panels must have been introduced in an attempt to re-equilibrate this difference.[22] All these new details were doubtless inspired by Botticelli's masterpiece and one cannot but regret that Botticelli could not execute another of these Virtues.

Piero eventually executed the remaining works, and so Botticelli's contribution consists only in this unique masterpiece. Although collaborations between artists were common practice at the time, Botticelli's intervention happened after the cycle had already been assigned to Piero. This therefore must have been felt as a real intrusion, which was unusual and threatening enough to provoke a reaction by the painters' guild. In January 1471 a special regulation was published to forbid the transfer of a commission to another artist during the course of its execution.[23]

Botticelli's masterpiece opened the way to a steady stream of commissions from the Medici and their circle, a period that culminated with the execution of the Sistine Chapel frescoes in 1481–2 for Pope Sixtus IV in the Vatican in Rome. It also revealed an aspect of Botticelli's personality as a fierce entrepreneur and a creative genius.

The mainstay of his shop consisted of religious and devotional pictures, mostly images of the Madonna and Child, a long-loved formula inherited from the Byzantine icon tradition and reinvigorated by his master, Filippo Lippi. Keeping *Fortitude* in mind as a milestone in Botticelli's early production, we can infer from stylistic comparisons that he had produced around the same date a series of Madonna and Child enthroned, on a compositional formula comparable to *Fortitude*. Despite its relatively poor condition, the *Madonna of the Rosegarden* can be considered the other masterpiece of the period (illus. 11).[24] The eight-branch star atop its frame, which has lost its identifying colour code, suggests that it was intended for one of the Florentine guilds.[25] The overall formula is a perfect example of what would become one of Botticelli's main design strategies, as it appears to be an almost exact transposition of *Fortitude*, translated into a sacred context. The figure of the Virgin follows the same design: her round, delicate oval is slightly tilted towards the right, while she is now looking down at the Child, who in effect replaces the mace on her lap.

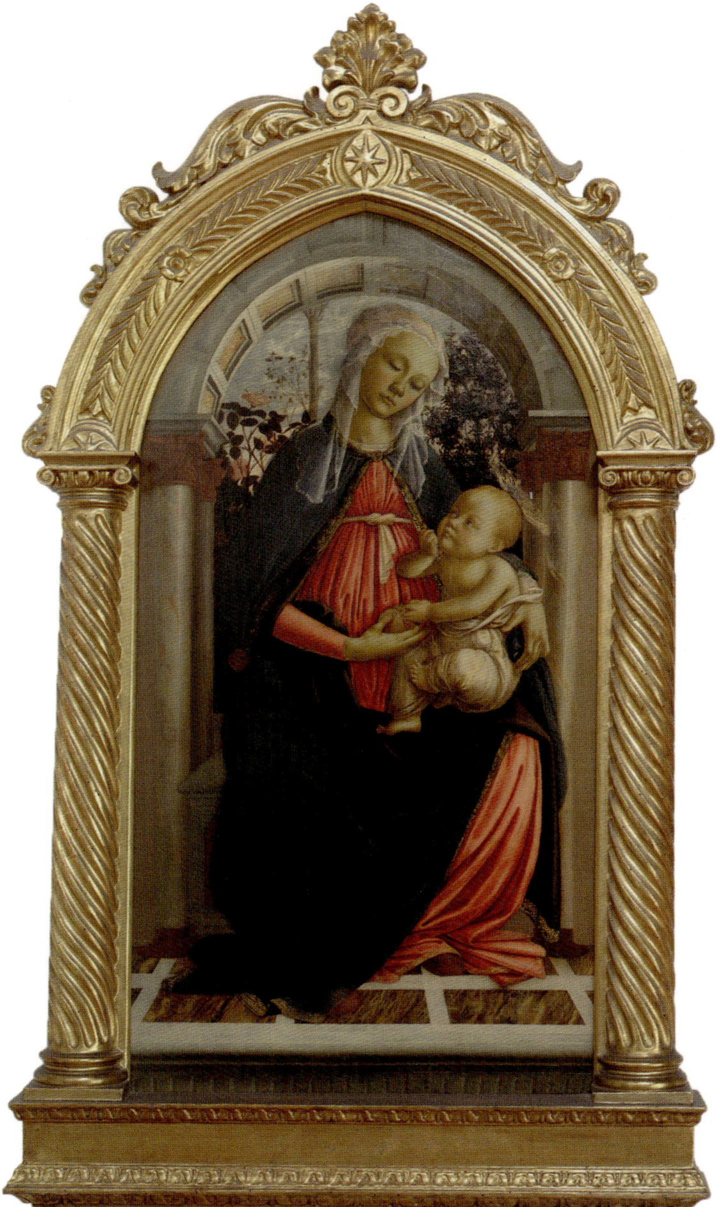

11 Botticelli, *Madonna of the Rosegarden*, *c.* 1469–70, tempera on wood.

Similarly intended to be hung high, the composition conveys a deep sense of three-dimensionality comparable to that of Botticelli's Virtue, but in a more modest fashion. The seat is simpler in form, flanked by two fluted Corinthian columns and surmounted by a canopy, while the foreground is paved with variegated marble set in receding perspective. The background opens on a sunny garden enlivened by rich vegetation, combining symbolic flowers and plants that convey specific Christian meanings. The roses refer to Mary, as she is identified in sacred texts as 'Mystical Rose'; the adjacent flowers, identifiable as stars of Bethlehem, are associated with Christ as a child, and the distant darker foliage could be myrtle, which alludes to those converted to Christianity. The Virgin Mary holds in her hand a pomegranate, which traditionally symbolizes fertility, but also announces the forthcoming sacrifice and resurrection of Christ. This wealth of detail echoes the rich apparatus of *Fortitude*, and reveals Botticelli's obsession with naturalistic features that would soon become a distinctive trait of his art. It is his capacity to depict the natural world as a veritable spectacle of marvels that made Botticelli one of the most successful translators of the Florentine devotional and mythological scenes alike.

The somewhat less rigorous perspective, mostly visible in the relationship between the throne and the figures, might indicate an earlier date of production, as this slight awkwardness is completely overcome in *Fortitude*. It is not impossible, given the similar type of commission (a merchants' corporation), that the execution of one led to the production of the other. If both were intended for a corporation's palace, a semi-public space, then they were easily accessible and visible to a large number of individuals and thus might have raised admiration and desire for a similar picture.

Looking back at Botticelli's earlier group of *Madonna and Child*, largely indebted to Fra Filippo's model, it seems that *Fortitude* and the related enthroned *Madonna of the Rosegarden* constituted a real stepping stone in his artistic development. They enabled him to find his own style, progressively distancing himself from Fra Filippo's repertory while sublimating the artistic inheritance of his old master. A small group of other works can be included in this transitional phase. A slight variation on the same design can be seen in the *Virgin in Glory of Seraphim*, which displays a much simpler setting, devoid of any architectural elements but set against an almond-shaped aureole of seraphim (*mandorla*), already a fairly archaic feature.[26] The design of the Child himself still seems heavily indebted to Fra Filippo's models. The so-called *Virgin of the Humility* reproduces a similar compositional arrangement but in a simpler fashion. The Virgin, holding the Child on the left hand-side and surrounded by five angels, is not represented on a throne but sitting or rather crouching directly on the ground, since her legs wrapped in her blue mantle awkwardly replicate the pose of the Virgin enthroned.[27]

This series of Madonnas leads us to the first surviving altarpiece for which Botticelli was commissioned, the so-called *Virgin and Child with Six Saints* (Sant'Ambrogio altarpiece) (illus. 12), whose central figure also relies on the same compositional formula as *Fortitude*.[28] Again, at the centre of the composition, the enthroned Virgin holds the Child. She displays a three-dimensionality similar to her distant model, Fra Filippo's *Madonna of the Noviciate*, and appears brought forward, closer to the viewer than Filippo's figure. This spatial projection and the architectural setting, a marble-panelled square room enhancing the overall depth of the composition, probably echo the original location of the painting, still unknown today, but possibly a Franciscan church or a chapel dedicated to St Francis, given his presence at the right-hand side of the Virgin.[29] The altarpiece's relatively small and square format suggests that it was set in a frame, possibly equipped with two shutters and a predella running at the bottom (now lost), in the same fashion as the proposed reconstruction for the altarpiece Botticelli executed years later for the church of San Paolino.[30] The commissioner probably belonged to the Medicean circle, or was in fact a Medici, given the presence of Cosmas and Damian, the family's patron saints.

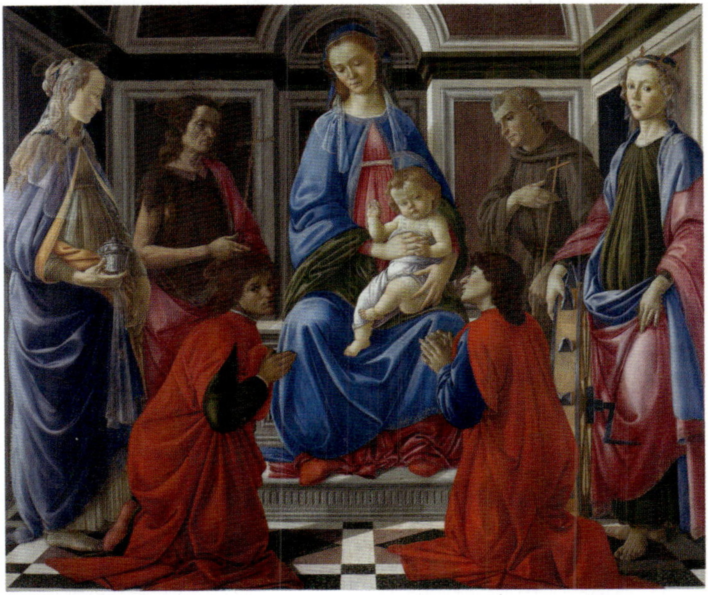

12 Botticelli, *Virgin and Child with Six Saints* (Sant'Ambrogio Altarpiece), *c.* 1470, tempera on wood.

Carefully spacing the figures around the throne, Botticelli has given them complementary gestures and expressions that breathe life and movement into this rather contemplative scene. A play between the gaze of each figure connects them to one another: St Mary Magdalen on the left-hand side looks down while her counterpart, St Catherine of Alexandria on the right, gazes at the viewer, as does St Cosmas, while St Damian stares at the Virgin and Child. St Francis and St John the Baptist in return contemplate the Child. Such a strategy would recur in later works.

The whole composition, despite its relatively simple arrangement, abounds in quotations. First and foremost, Botticelli pays homage to his old master, Fra Filippo, by borrowing the outward gaze of St Catherine from Filippo's figure of St Theophista in the *Maringhi Coronation* executed around 1439–47.[31] Yet Botticelli translates the face of the saint in his own fashion, reproducing the delicate oval and modelling of *Fortitude*, and replicating it in St Mary Magdalen on the opposite side. This specific facial type would soon become characteristic of Botticelli's style; he uses a unique but interchangeable idealized face for the Virgin and the mythological figures alike.[32] The palette, still vibrant despite the poor condition of the work, and the distribution of light coming from the left, follow the tradition emphasizing the reception of light and coloured reflections introduced by Alberti in his treatise *On Painting* (II, 30) and by Ghiberti in his *Commentaries*. Similar dramatic lighting, within a brighter palette, can be observed in Domenico Veneziano's Santa Lucia de' Magnoli altarpiece, executed in 1445–7 for a church in Florence. Botticelli seems to have borrowed not only Domenico's overall composition, which he translated in a simpler fashion and brought closer to the viewer, but specifically the figure of Santa Lucia that he used as the model for Mary Magdalen.

Botticelli certainly drew from a repertory of images, drawings made by him but also ones that were probably inherited from past masters or given by fellow artists. They provided him with a large choice of pre-established figures, set in different poses and conveying a wide spectrum of emotions, that he could use and reuse, adapt and vary in his compositions, as we shall see.

Such drawings were preciously kept in the workshops and passed on to following generations. Sometimes bound together, they could constitute comprehensive model-books, such as the fourteen volumes of drawings left by Maso Finiguerra.[33] Maso's brother, Francesco, inherited the volumes because he was a fellow goldsmith, unlike Maso's son and direct heir, who was a shoemaker. However, a clause in Maso's will forbade Francesco to sell or dismember any of the volumes. At the beginning of the following century, the sculptor Benvenuto Cellini (1500–1571), for instance, recalled that his friend Francesco Lippi, Filippino's son, a fellow goldsmith, showed him the stock of drawings his father left him as part of the contents of the studio.[34] Unfortunately Botticelli did not leave such a legacy to posterity. The unhappy end of his life led his family to turn down his inheritance and what became of the contents of the workshop is unknown. However, it can be inferred that a comparable stock of drawings must have existed, considering the posthumous inventories of Andrea del Verrocchio and Filippino Lippi, who both worked in a very similar manner. That said, the many surviving drawings by Filippino are the exception that proves the rule at such an early date (he died in 1504). Hardly any Renaissance drawings, especially those produced during the fifteenth century, have survived to the present day. For instance, only a handful of drawings by Verrocchio have come down to us, and the same is sadly true of Botticelli.

Botticelli's extant drawings can generally be connected to finished works, suggesting that the artist drew from a storehouse of motifs produced as workshop studies to be used and reused in future paintings. It is not impossible that Botticelli inherited some of Fra Filippo's studies, or benefited from them when Filippino came to work with him after 1469. The role and function of drawings within the workshop were of extreme importance. They were an aid for devising new compositions as well as ready-made motifs that assistants and collaborators could use to complete the compositions that the master had started. It was common practice to delegate more or less extensive parts of the paintings to assistants, especially in the case of well-known typologies such as representations of the Virgin and Child. This strategy freed up time for the master to create new inventions while speeding up the pace of production of a busy and successful workshop such as Botticelli's.

At this point, given the effusion of works issued by Botticelli in his early career, the question of potential collaborators active in his workshop arises. In the absence of archives documenting the beginning of Botticelli's career, we can only infer that he might have established himself as an independent master at his father's house as early as 1467–8, but not before 1464, when Mariano Filipepi bought the house where his son would spend his entire life and career.[35] Over the course of two to three years, Botticelli's shop had developed significantly enough to be mentioned as one of the principal *botteghe* of Florence in Benedetto Dei's (1418–1492) memoirs, written around 1470.[36]

THREE

Building the Picture: Invention and Delegation

Vasari mentioned that *infiniti giovani* (an endless retinue of young people) attended Botticelli's studio. His workshop must therefore have been large enough to welcome an important number of collaborators and apprentices as his success grew. The configuration of his *bottega* probably did not follow the Florentine archetype described in documents and represented for instance in the frescoes by Domenico Ghirlandaio (1448–94) in the Sassetti chapel in the basilica of Santa Trinita in Florence.[1] Because it was set in his own house, it was probably lacking any opening onto the street and was therefore without a proper vitrine-like display such as those represented in the famous print by Baccio Baldini mentioned earlier (see illus. 1). On the contrary, Botticelli's shop, set on the ground floor of his family home, must have been rather simple, comprising one or two rooms large enough to stock materials and produce the sheer amount of works (mostly medium-size paintings, as larger ones were probably executed on site) produced over the course of his forty-year career.

With the *bottega* came a number of assistants and apprentices, but not all would enjoy the same success. It is likely that one Benedetto di Domenico d'Andrea, nicknamed

Betto Pialla, who trained and worked on and off at Neri's shop, began working for Botticelli at an early stage, in the stretch of time between the termination of his contract with Neri, in March 1469, and January 1473, when he appears registered as a member of Botticelli's workshop in a document relating to a condemnation for sodomy.[2] Around the same time, Filippino Lippi (*c.* 1457–1504), the son of Botticelli's former master, might have joined the workshop shortly after Fra Filipo's death at the beginning of October 1469, and in any case before 1472 when he appears registered as a member of Botticelli's shop in the painters' guild.[3] While Filippino was about to become an extraordinary artist, Betto Pialla would remain an indistinguishable hand in Botticelli's wide output.

Filippino Lippi is the most famous of Botticelli's collaborators and former pupils. It is commonly believed that Botticelli must have treated him more like a peer than an assistant. The outstanding skills of the young Filippino, whose personal style quickly became identifiable, and the personal relationship between the two artists help us to better understand the complex inner workings and divisions of labour in Botticelli's shop. While the great majority of Botticelli's assistants subsumed their own artistic personalities in order to comply with the visual 'brand' of the *bottega*, a few works issued in these early years have been identified as collaborations between Botticelli and Filippino, thus enabling us to understand better the division of labour between the master and his collaborators.

Like Betto Pialla, other names appear in documents, but their hand cannot be identified in the workshop's products. This is how we learn, for instance, that a young boy named Raffaello di Lorenzo di Fruosino Tosi, known as il Toso

(1468–1498?), was a *garzone* (apprentice) in Botticelli's shop around 1480, while another, Giovanni di Benedetto di Giovanni Cianfanini (1470?–1542), worked for the master for more than ten years before joining the workshop of Lorenzo di Credi, without any works being firmly attributed to them.[4]

In the absence of a coherent corpus on which to base attributions, such artists effectively remain 'workless'. While it is possible to distinguish different hands at work in the paintings issued by Botticelli's *bottega*, none are clearly attributable to specific artists. Modern art historians have therefore tried to overcome this difficulty by identifying anonymous collaborators of Botticelli by means of generic appellations such as the Master of the Santo Spirito Holy Conversation (*Maestro della Conversazione di Santo Spirito*), or the Master of the Gothic Buildings. These names were inspired by the title of a work or a specific recurring feature which determines attribution. For instance, the name of the Master of the Gothic Buildings comes from this artist's habit of systematically including pointed edifices in the Gothic style in his compositions. This trend differs from Botticelli's own practice; he favoured much simpler landscape, a trait that Leonardo da Vinci himself famously reproved him for.[5] Proposals to identify the latter as Jacopo di Domenico di Papi da San Gaggio (1460–1530) and the former as the aforementioned Giovanni di Benedetto di Giovanni Cianfanini (1470?–1542), both attested collaborators of Botticelli in the surviving archives, are interesting hypotheses that require further investigations which cannot be conducted here.[6]

While it is possible to identify different categories of works in the *bottega*, ranging from autographed pieces and subsequent variations made by the master himself to collaborations and delegations, including workshop replicas, it is however extremely difficult to attribute the works themselves. How to define authorship in the Renaissance has been a recurring problem in art-historical studies. There is a dearth of relevant documents and, moreover, no works were signed.[7] These difficulties in identifying artworks and their authors have led some historians to construct new artistic personalities, relying on the identification of close groups of works.

The most exemplary case of such a construct is that of 'Amico di Sandro', literally 'friend of Sandro'. The American historian Bernard Berenson (1865–1959) saw in a group of works clearly indebted to Botticelli's style and design a personality distinct from Botticelli and Filippino, as he could not reconcile this early style with Filippino's mature manner. His reasoning was based on a 'scientific' method devised by the art historian Giovanni Morelli (1816–1891), who had grounded his attributions on the characterization of minute details inherent to a specific artist's hand.[8] Pictures were scrutinized in order to identify a specific manner of depicting hands, noses, ears and so on that was understood as the unique artistic expression of the author. Did Leonardo da Vinci himself not claim that 'every painter paints himself' ('ogni dipintore dipigne se')? Interestingly enough, Morelli's method developed as he was working on Botticelli. This technique, which has laid the base of modern connoisseurship, has had a long-lasting impact on following generations of art historians.

After years of intense debate, Berenson finally admitted that Amico di Sandro was in fact the young Filippino, and the creature was finally dismissed by its creator in 1932.[9] This episode demonstrates that such a homogenizing and trademarked workshop as Botticelli's could also foster emerging young talent whose distinct artistic personality could manifest itself already in the works designed by the master. It also shows that style evolves and that an artist could be heavily indebted to his master during his formative years, and then slowly develop his own artistic personality, to the point that his early production significantly contrasts with his mature style. Such changes can also occur at a later point within the career of an artist, as Botticelli himself demonstrates.

Going back to Botticelli and Filippino's early years, an interesting early example of collaboration can be seen in two panels, each representing five sibyls sat in niches (see illus. 13 and 14). Now in Oxford, the works are generally dated between 1472 and 1475 but were possibly made slightly earlier, closer to *Fortitude*, as they clearly derive from the same compositional formula. The panel representing the Babylonian, Libyan, Delphic, Cimmerian and Erythraean sibyls is currently attributed to Sandro while the other one is given to Filippino.[10] The latter probably followed a model made by the master so as to comply with the design, style and palette of the first panel. We cannot exclude the possibility that Botticelli might have intervened directly in Filippino's alleged panel to correct or adjust the work of his young collaborator, as was common practice in the *bottega*. The differences between the two panels are subtle. Despite their poor state of conservation, they reveal a palette close to that of *Fortitude* and the small works depicting the story of Judith and Holofernes (see illus. 9 and 10). Comparatively, one can notice that Botticelli's sibyls seem more elongated and perhaps more harmoniously shaped while a certain roundness characterizes Filippino's figures, which are furthermore not anatomically as successful as those in the first panel attributed to the master. We have no information on the commissioning of these works but it has been noted that the panels could relate to Marsilio Ficino's *De christiana religione*, published in Latin and Italian in 1474, in which two chapters are dedicated to the sybils.[11] Their format and subject therefore clearly relate to the decoration of a humanist *studiolo* – a room specially dedicated to study and generally decorated with selected works of art showcasing the erudition of their owner. In all likelihood, this anonymous commissioner belonged to the Medici circle, to which both Ficino and Botticelli gravitated.

In both panels, all the sibyls are set within niches that structure the whole composition. As with *Fortitude*, there is no landscape in the background; the composition is entirely dependent on the architecture. This attention to architectural features as a structural device was a trait of Botticelli's, and he would keep improving it as he developed his style. To better understand Botticelli's structural use of background architecture, one can compare the Oxford ensemble with an earlier example executed by Lo Scheggia (1406–1486), Masaccio's brother, and his son Antonfrancesco (1441–1476). These two works, most likely the front panels of wedding chests, similarly present a number of allegorical figures (here the Virtues and the Liberal Arts) set in niches, but with two main differences: the composition opens to a sky planted with various trees in the background, and the iconography is both more complex and more traditional, with the addition of statues,

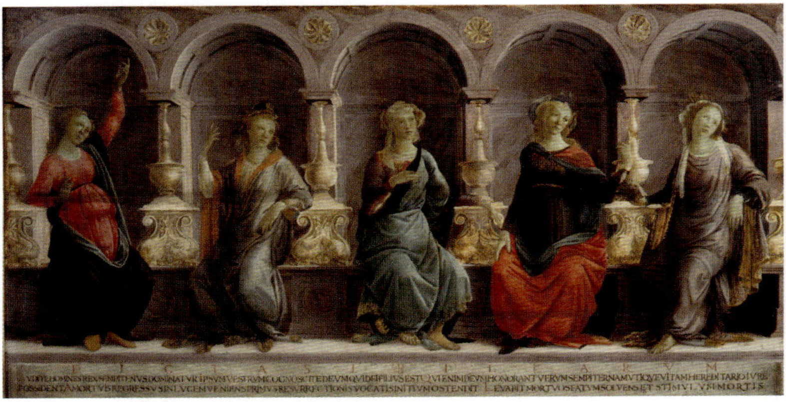

specific attributes and a row of famous men (*uomini illustri*), as well as further small ornaments.[12] These additional characteristics relate them to a late Gothic interpretation of the theme, which is completely transformed and renewed in Botticelli's version. In comparison, his relatively simple yet elegant invention conveys a lighter, more harmonious and poetic vision of the prophetesses in tune with the sacred character of their message.[13]

Alongside Botticelli, artists such as Biagio d'Antonio (1446–1516) drew inspiration from early designs. Biagio decorated the end panels of the so-called Neri-Morelli wedding chest (cassone), dated 1472, with figures of Virtues clearly derived from the Mercanzia models.[14] This is an early example of the influential nature of Botticelli's creations, which inspired artists beyond his own *bottega*. As shall be seen, the personality of Biagio d'Antonio is particularly interesting as he was an occasional collaborator of Botticelli's: he was not strictly speaking part of his workshop, but called to commissions that required an extra reliable hand when time or resources were

13 Botticelli, *Five Sibyls Seated in Niches: The Babylonian, Libyan, Delphic, Cimmerian and Erythraean*, c. 1472–5, tempera on panel.

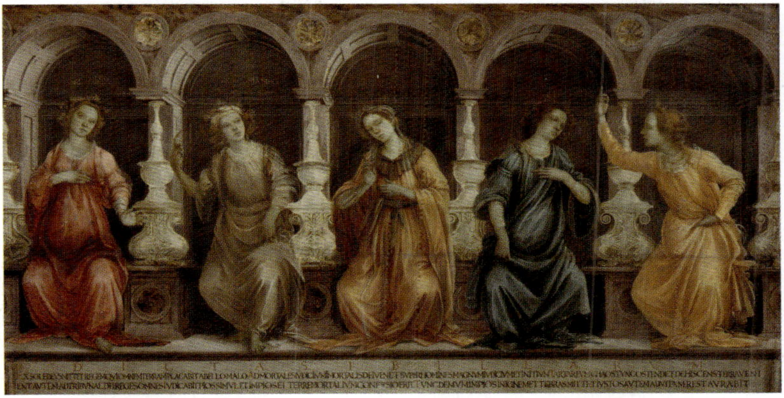

running out. He therefore had quite easy access to Botticelli's designs and inventions.

In the same period Botticelli and Filippino painted another six panels together, originally forming two cassoni depicting the story of the Old Testament heroine Esther.[15] This cycle is another key example of the complex division of labour within the *bottega*.[16] The panels were long regarded as Filippino Lippi's work, utilizing Botticelli's inventions, with the exception of two end panels: *The Despair of Mordecai* (illus. 18), formerly known as *La derelitta*, and *The Triumph of Mordecai* (illus. 19).[17] The question of these attributions appeared partly resolved during a campaign of infrared reflectography in 2010, which revealed three different types of preparatory drawing executed on the panel ground before paint was applied.[18] Invisible to the naked eye, these sketches, commonly called underdrawings, often reveal differences that betray the plurality of hands involved in the execution of a painting. For instance, the underdrawing of *Esther at the Palace Gate* (illus. 15) reveals a speediness in the design consistent with Filippino's drawing manner

14 Filippino Lippi, *Five Sibyls Seated in Niches: The Samian, Cumean, Hellespontic, Phrygian and Tiburtine*, c. 1472–5, tempera on panel.

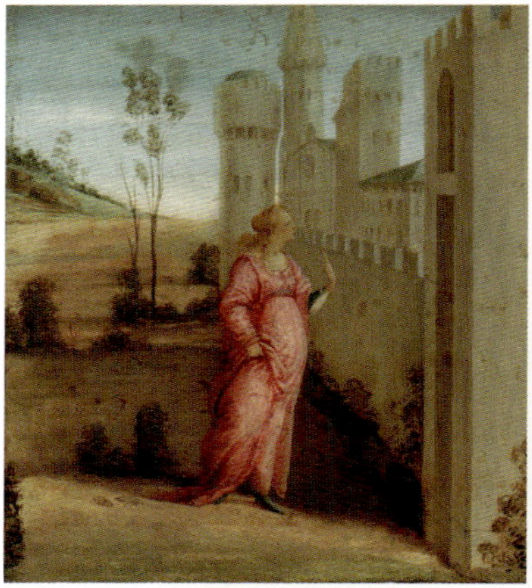

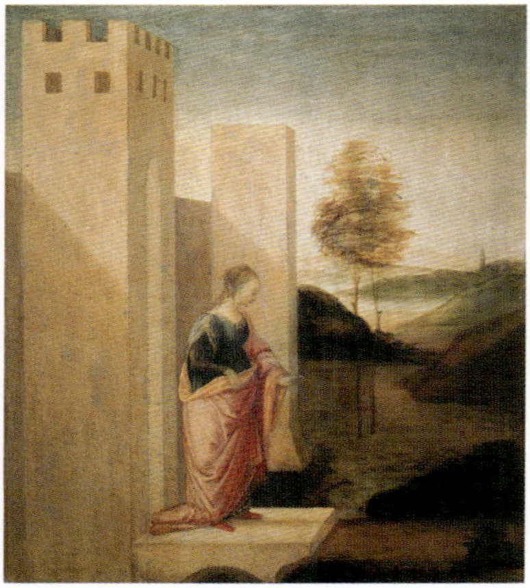

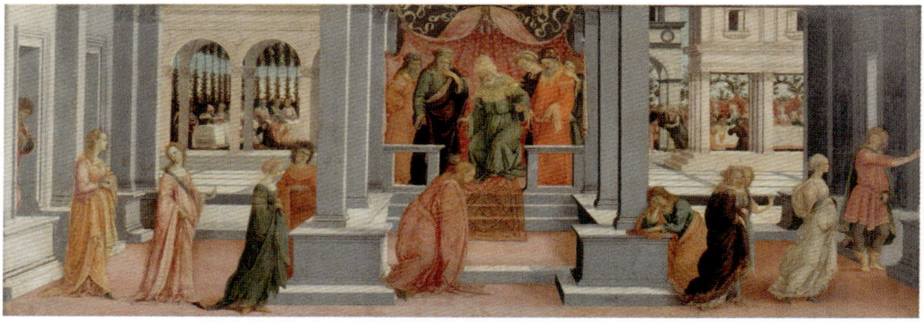

15 Botticelli, Filippino Lippi and workshop, *Esther at the Palace Gate*, first cassone, 1470–75, tempera on wood.
16 Botticelli, Filippino Lippi and workshop, *Vashti Leaving the Palace*, first cassone, 1470–75, tempera on wood.
17 Botticelli, Filippino Lippi and workshop, *Esther Before Asshuerus*, first cassone, 1470–75, tempera on wood.

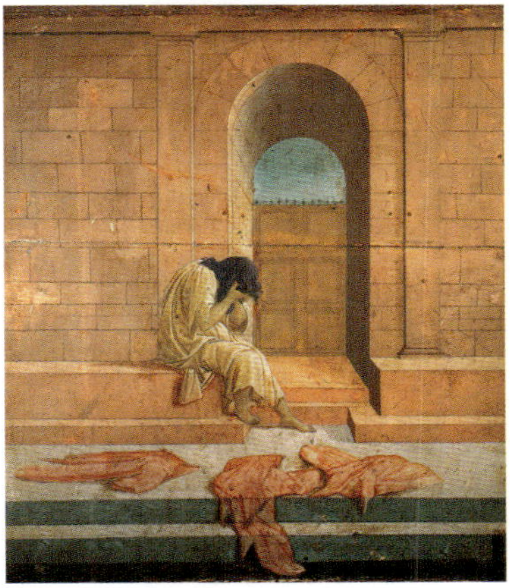

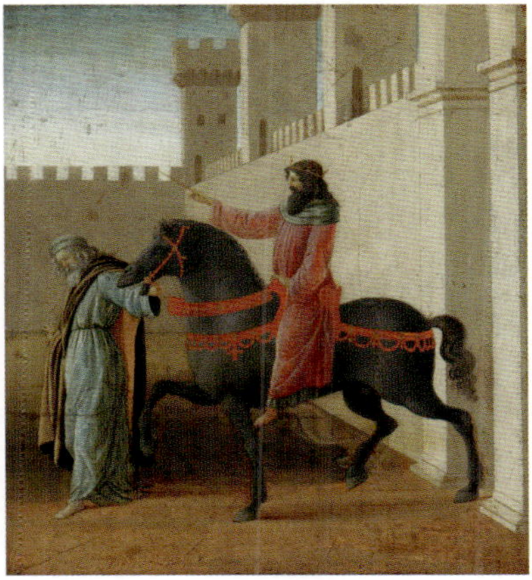

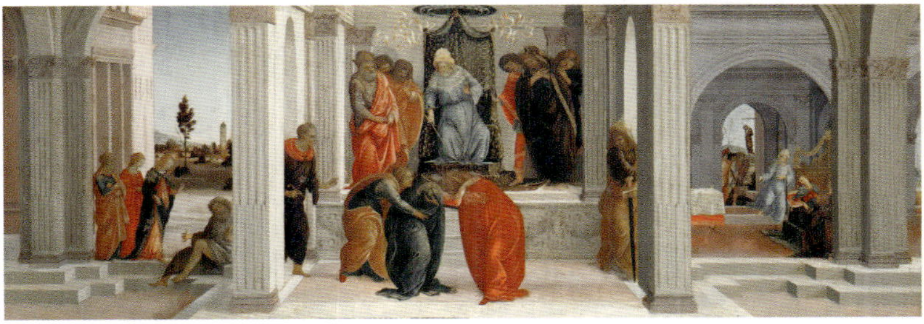

18 Botticelli, Filippino Lippi and workshop, *The Despair of Mordecai* (*La derelitta*), second cassone, 1470–75, tempera on wood.
19 Botticelli, Filippino Lippi and workshop. *The Triumph of Mordecai*, second cassone, 1470–75, tempera on wood.
20 Botticelli, Filippino Lippi and workshop, *Esther Pleading*, second cassone, 1470–75, tempera on wood.

while *The Despair of Mordecai* and his *Triumph* show the characteristic graphic style of Botticelli himself. On the other hand, *Vashti Leaving the Palace* (illus. 16) shows an underdrawing 'very different from everywhere else and unexpectedly detailed and monotonous'.[19] This suggests the contribution of another collaborator in Botticelli's workshop, less trained or talented than Filippino. He might have resorted to a cartoon, that is, a full-scale preparatory drawing that was transferred directly on the panel in order to reproduce the model as faithfully as possible. Cartoons were generally drawn by the master and then used by his assistants to transfer his designs onto the final substrate as if he had drawn it himself. Graphic evidence therefore points towards the identification of three different contributions, starting with the master himself, then the gifted pupil, Filippino, down to an assistant not talented enough or too inexperienced to draw freehand.

Various reasons can explain such extensive collaboration: Botticelli's own workload, or a short lapse of time between the commission and the delivery date, in all likelihood an imminent wedding. Unfortunately, no documents about this commission have survived.[20] Stylistically datable to the 1470s, the cassoni were produced during an intense period of work for the artist. In those years, it is likely that Botticelli produced two major altarpieces: one for Guasparre Del Lama, which includes a series of Medicean portraits and an alleged self-portrait, and another Adoration, identified as the Pucci tondo, whose design derives from the former, as we shall see. In 1475 Botticelli was also entrusted with designing the standard of Giuliano de' Medici on the occasion of the joust given in his honour.

Filippino certainly contributed extensively to the execution of the panels, but the design indubitably shows the masterly vision of Botticelli and his highly personal use of architecture as a structural device. Reading these panels may be difficult for the modern spectator, but followed a quite straightforward construction: left to right and with a low viewpoint, as these paintings were meant to be placed close to the ground and seen from above. The six panels are conceived as sequences of the same story, but do not read chronologically. Although the story comes from the Book of Esther, a late addition to the Old Testament – together with the Book of Tobias and the Book of Judith, also illustrated by Botticelli – it was the subject of a religious drama (*sacra rappresentazione*) that was performed several times in Florence throughout the second half of the fifteenth century. It seems in this instance that the panels follow the religious drama rather than the biblical text. One *Representation of Queen Esther* (*La rappresentazione della Regina Ester*) long circulated in manuscript form before being published.[21]

The story takes place in Susa, capital of Persia, where reigned King Ahasuerus (also known as Xerxes I). The reading starts in the background of the first cassone's front panel (now in Chantilly) where Ahasuerus is giving a banquet in honour of some distinguished guests to whom he wants to introduce his wife, Vashti. She, however, refuses to attend, and the offended king decides to punish her publicly. On the right, Vashti is shown as her crown is taken away from her. These two scenes constitute the background of the story of Esther and are distanced from the foreground by a patterned marble pavement and a series of loggias. Vashti is represented leaving the scene in the end right-hand panel (illus. 16). After

Vashti's repudiation, the king summons all the women in Persia in order to choose another wife. The story of Esther then commences on the left-hand end panel, with the heroine approaching the palace gate (illus. 15). In the foreground of the front panel (illus. 17), the women are passing before the king, who then is stricken with admiration as Esther kneels before him.

Painted cassoni were typical wedding gifts destined to adorn the bedchamber, and their illustrations often entwined moral and political messages. This first cassone provides a lesson for the future bride, a true *exemplum virtutis*, as Vashti's misfortune illustrates what fate a disobedient wife might endure. Indeed, the play reads:

> The queen should be deprived from any honour, as she disobeyed, and banned from the country. This will be an example for all the people, and all women should learn to love and honour their husband, and their honour will be safe and sound.
>
> *La reina del regno sia private / E d'ogni onor, come disubbediente, / E del paese . . . sbandeggiata: / Questo sarà esempio a ogni gente, / Et ogni donna fia amaestrata / D'amare et onorare il suo marito, / E il [suo] onor fie salvo et stabilito.*[22]

In contrast, Esther's humility and beauty won the king's heart: 'because, as you should know, the woman is all to the glorious crown if she is virtuous and good' (*perchè è ogni cosa, sappi, alta corona, / La donna s'ell'è virtuosa e buona*).[23] Her final reward is illustrated in the second cassone, which turns the tale of the 'good wife' into a political fable.

The second cassone follows a much simpler construction. On the end panel to the left (illus. 18), Mordecai, Esther's uncle, is shown in despair at the king's decision to exterminate them and their fellow Jews.[24] On the left-hand side of the front panel, Esther, accompanied by two companions, meets Mordecai who tells her their misfortune. In the centre, she appears before the king and implores him to spare their people. On the right-hand side, in the background, the king visits Esther, who has fainted on her bed.[25] Esther wins over the king and quashes his cruel scheme, plotted by his chief minister Haman, who is shown hanging by the neck in the distant background.[26] In the end panel to the right (illus. 19), Mordecai rides triumphantly on the king's horse, led by Haman, an earlier episode which triggered the chief minister's anger towards the Jews.[27] The second cassone therefore provides a political reading of the biblical story: Esther is celebrated as a female heroine whose dedication saved her people. This story had a great resonance for the Florentines, who were especially receptive to high examples of civic virtues. Heroines' tales were popular subjects in art: the story of Judith, another civic saviour, was celebrated in several paintings, frescoes and sculptures.[28] Such subjects would furthermore provide the starting point for interesting debates within the *famiglia*, meaning immediate family and close relatives and friends. Sometimes a complicated reading was even more desirable than a simple, transparent one, as it prompted intense debates. The Riminese humanist Giovanni Aurelio Augurelli, for instance, wrote a Latin epigram to Bernardo Bembo about Botticelli's standard for Giuliano's joust, concluding that much pleasure can come from trying to decipher an image, as 'no opinion is the same;

and this is prettier than any painted images.'[29] Furthermore, Leon Battista Alberti had already established in his treatise *On Painting* that

> a 'historia' [narrative composition] you can justifiably praised and admire will be one that reveals itself to be so charming and attractive as to hold the eye of the learned and the unlearned spectator for a long while with a certain sense of pleasure and emotion. The first thing that gives pleasure in a 'historia' is a plentiful variety.[30]

Nonetheless, the artists had to provide some clues to the viewers in order for them to understand these compositions. Botticelli relied heavily on architectural framework to clarify the development of this multi-layered story, which the public knew well through the religious drama. Like the *sacra rappresentazione*, the cassoni omit key episodes, and distribute the events onto different 'stages'. Often performed in churches, these religious dramas would be set up on several stages contemporaneously to maintain the public in a state of surprise and wonder. There are few accounts of these plays, but one given by a Russian bishop called Abraham is highly instructive, and reveals that these spectacles provided genuine entertainment. He attended the *sacra rappresentazione* of the Annunciation, performed in the church of the Santissima Annunziata on 26 March 1439. Several stages had been set up in the church, including one in the middle of the nave, and the performance moved from one to the other unexpectedly. A complex engineering system allowed for the angel Gabriel to fly into the air above the audience, while God the Father would suddenly emerge from a blaze of light. The representation of paradise in the church of S. Felice, engineered by the great architect Filippo Brunelleschi (1377–1446), must have been similarly admired. It is reported by Vasari as 'truly marvellous, and a heaven full of living and moving figures, and a quantity of light which flashes in and out'.[31] Large painted cloth featuring architectural decor would complement the staging. It was therefore a true *son et lumière* show *avant la lettre*.

This theatrical arrangement described by Abraham strongly echoes the spatial articulation of the first cassone and its complex architectural structure, organized around a dais in central position and a multi-scenic setting. It is possible that Botticelli derived his spatial construction from observations as a spectator of sacred plays and probably also as a supplier of painted decor, since Vasari praised him as especially gifted in executing painted cloths.[32] On the other hand, the second cassone, which shows a much more linear structure that focuses on the foreground scene and a tripartite organization of the space, may have resulted from greater intervention by Filippino in the design. In both panels, however, groups of figures are clearly modelled on Botticelli's inventions, as they appear in earlier and later works by the artist. These were probably based on Botticelli's stock of drawings, which was unfortunately lost after his death. For instance, Ahasuerus echoes the type of white-bearded men developed for the small panel of *Discovery of Holofernes*: Esther follows the same design as Judith, while Vashti is modelled on St Mary Magdalen in the Sant' Ambrogio altarpiece.

As previously noted, these two panels significantly depart from the tradition and can be construed as a true turning point.

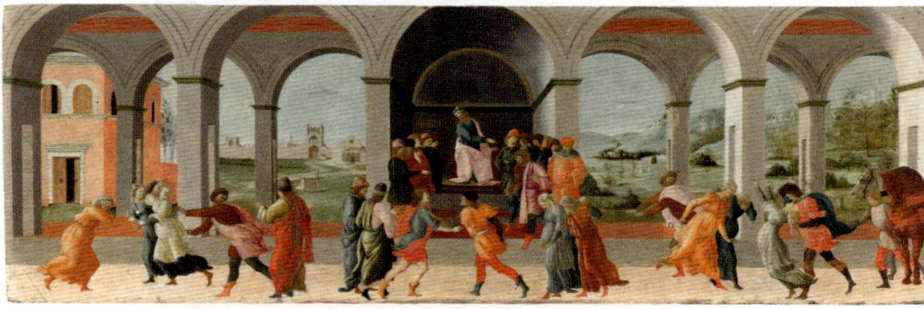

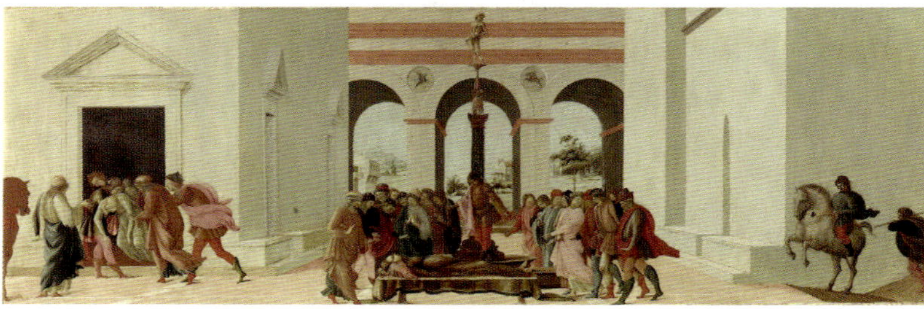

Previously, the narrative in cassone panels would unfold following a tapestry-like structure, in which groups of figures are repeated across the picture, sometimes stacked one above the other, with no sense of perspective projection.[33] Botticelli elevated the genre to the new definition of painting provided by Leon Battista Alberti, who recommended in his treatise that the artist base the pictorial construction on the 'principles of nature', implying that the painting should replicate what can be seen through an open window.[34]

A similar approach to spatial construction can be seen in Filippino's versions of another heroine's story executed shortly after that of Esther: two cassoni fronts depicting the stories of Virginia and Lucrezia (illus. 21 and 22), generally dated circa 1475–80. In his *Story of Virginia*, Filippino echoes the theatrical organization of the second Esther cassone with

21 Filippino Lippi, *Story of Virginia*, *c.* 1475–80, tempera on panel.
22 Filippino Lippi, *Story of Lucrezia*, *c.* 1475–80, tempera on wood.

a dais in the central position, but he significantly reduces the architectural features and spreads out his figures in the immediate foreground. The long loggia in the middle ground opens onto a bucolic landscape with a distant city wall. The second panel, depicting the story of Lucrezia, shows a stronger tripartite structure, but again concentrates the action in the immediate foreground. It has been suggested that this difference in construction may refer to the transition from the sacred play, inherited from the medieval tradition, to classical theatre, which was revived in Florence in those years.[35] With these works an interesting artistic and lifelong dialogue between

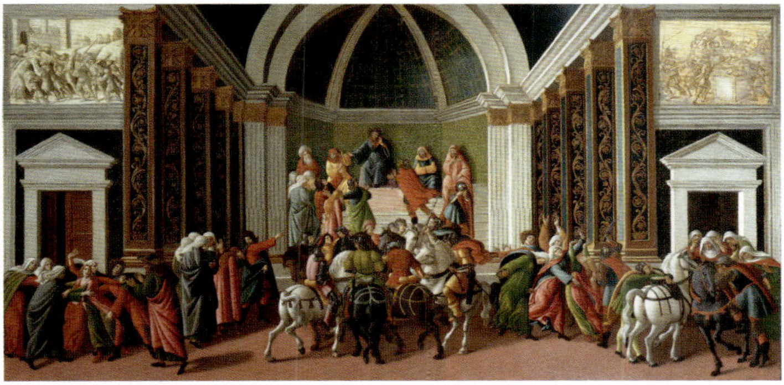

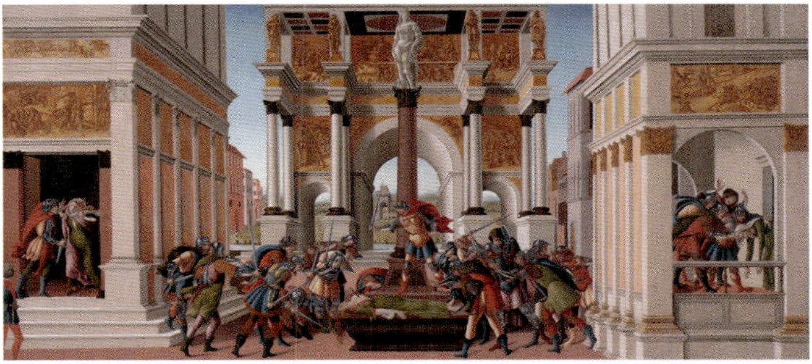

23 Botticelli, *Story of Virginia*, 1496–1504, tempera on panel.
24 Botticelli, *Story of Lucrezia*, c. 1500, tempera and oil on panel.

the two artists begins, as Botticelli would later echo Filippino's panels in his own interpretation of the stories, probably executed around 1500 – two large spalliere now divided between Bergamo and Boston (see illus. 23 and 24) – unless, of course, Filippino had based his panels on now-lost drawings by Botticelli, to which the latter might have returned twenty years later.[36] The main difference between the two approaches is that Botticelli introduces a greater sense of depth, while Filippino opts for a compositional formula that reflects the immediacy of a theatrical stage, with less receding background.

Similar structural developments on the parts of Botticelli appear in a group of Adorations executed in the same period, which may well explain his need to delegate the execution of the Esther cassoni paintings. Four Adorations attest to another revolution in design. A painting commissioned around 1475 by Guasparre di Zanobi Del Lama for his funerary chapel in the church of Santa Maria Novella appears to be the earliest of the series. In this work Botticelli departs from the traditional representation of the subject, as exemplified by his master, Filippo Lippi, in the Cook tondo, which places the main characters on the left while the rest of the figures are unevenly scattered across the picture plane.[37]

In the Del Lama Adoration, Botticelli repositioned and slightly raised the main group of figures (the Virgin and Child) at the centre of his composition. Already a master of the art of linear perspective in this early stage of his career, Botticelli completely transformed the vision of this traditional theme by making the Virgin and Child the true focal point of the whole composition. This new formula (probably inspired by the structure of the sacra conversazione, which were produced in that same period), allowed him to distribute secondary figures all around this focal point in a harmonious and symmetrical, yet lively, ensemble. Ruined arches and walls function as structural outlines to this central stage, enhancing the illusion of depth on the flat surface. With the Del Lama altarpiece (illus. 25), Botticelli achieved another feat of design, which provided the viewer with a new visual experience of the Adoration type. As a probable token of allegiance on the part of the commissioner, who appears in the painting as the man clothed in blue and looking towards the viewer in the right middle ground, key members of the Medici family (Cosimo de' Medici, with his sons Piero and Giovanni and his grandsons Lorenzo and Giuliano) are portrayed in the

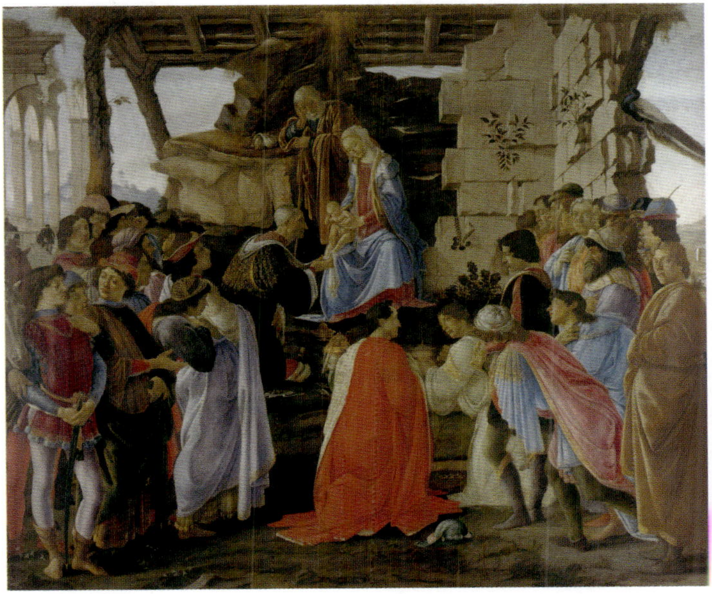

25 Botticelli, *Adoration of the Magi* (Del Lama altarpiece), 1475, tempera on wood.

guise of the Magi and their retinue.[38] The man wrapped in a yellow cloak on the far right is believed to be the only self-portrait that Botticelli left to posterity. Should this hypothesis be true, Botticelli seized the opportunity to claim his status as a member of the Medicean circle and somehow 'sign' this revolutionary composition.

Botticelli's subsequent paintings of the Adoration are all variations of the Del Lama altarpiece, whose formula appeared especially successful for tondi. This is particularly apparent for instance in the Pucci tondo (now in the National Gallery, London).[39] Botticelli would carry on developing and adapting this new perspectival arrangement to other formats.

A similar strategy prevails in the four spalliere depicting the story of Nastagio degli Onesti, based on Boccaccio's well-known story in the *Decameron*.[40] Set in Ravenna, the story tells of the misfortune of a young gentleman whose love for the daughter of Paolo Traversari is not reciprocated. Nastagio wanders in despair in a pine forest when he suddenly sees a naked woman chased by a knight on horseback accompanied by two mastiffs. The knight dismounts in front of Nastagio and reveals the reason for this cruel apparition. His name is Guido degli Anastagi. He committed suicide after he was refused by his beloved. Both were subsequently punished: the knight forced to chase her and rip her heart out of her chest, the lady to endure such a brutal fate for eternity. Turning this event to his advantage, Nastagio organizes a banquet for Paolo Traversari and his family in the forest, and waits for the ghosts to appear. As expected, the guests react with horror at the sight of the damned couple. The moral of the story can be seen in the fourth panel of the series, which depicts the nuptial banquet after the wedding of Nastagio and his beloved, won over by the spectacle that she has witnessed.

Once again, the narrative is complex and combines two different temporalities: Nastagio's present and the eternity of the damned couple, which acts as the moral exemplum of the story. The cycle was commissioned for the wedding of Gianozzo di Antonio Pucci and Lucrezia di Piero Bini in 1483 and was probably meant to adorn the walls of their bedchamber, inserted into the wainscoting panelling and to be seen at shoulder level (*spalliera* comes from *spalla*, 'shoulder'). In the first three panels (illus. 26, 27, 28), the trees form a natural loggia, with trunks for columns and foliage for a vault, while the last panel substitutes the trees for a loggia with Corinthian columns, under which is the wedding feast. This overtly Renaissance architecture modifies the temporality of the tale and introduces the present: the real wedding for which the cycle had been commissioned. The scene also includes a gallery of portraits from the Pucci family, while the arms of the Pucci and the Bini arms depicted on the top of the first columns transform Nastagio's wedding into the Pucci-Bini nuptial celebration. The exemplum fuses with a political allegory, which stresses the importance of dynastic alliances for the peace of the city. The inclusion of the Medici coat of arms reminds the viewer of their role as protectors of Florence, and likely negotiators of the wedding. The distant arch in the background is reminiscent of the ancient arch of the Roman emperor Constantine, a powerful symbol identified by some as an image of the idealized Pucci-Bini lineage, stretching from Roman antiquity to fifteenth-century Florence,[41] but it may also be construed as the allusion of the prestigious ancient origins of the city of Florence, grown out of the Roman Florentia under the protection of the god Mars, the first patron of the city. More importantly, it records Botticelli's stay in Rome and is another example of reuse of motifs.

However prestigious this series was, Botticelli did not hesitate to delegate its final execution, which makes this cycle another informative example of collaborative effort. The execution differs from one panel to the other, leading to the conclusion that more than one collaborator contributed to the series. The composition and design of the four panels are consensually attributed to Botticelli himself, who seems to have personally contributed to the last panel given the quality of its gallery of portraits. The execution of the other panels, on the other hand, clearly shows the involvement of several collaborators. Hypotheses range from members of the workshop, including Jacopo di Domenico di Papi, to external occasional collaborators such as Bartolomeo di Giovanni (panel 3 in particular), who had his own workshop in Florence. Bartolomeo was a specialist of small figures for contained formats such as cassoni, predelle and spalliere.[42] He would offer his services to other fellow artists such as Domenico Ghirlandaio, for whom he executed not only the predella of the Innocenti altarpiece in 1488, but the Massacre of the Innocents in the background of the main panel on the left. Bartolomeo must have been close enough to Botticelli to make use of his designs independently. For instance, his painting of three angels is clearly copied from a drawing by Botticelli.[43]

The four panels depicting the story of Nastagio degli Onesti (illus. 26–9) recall the early cassone fronts depicting the Story of Esther, as they develop further and improve the multi-scenic compositional approach.

The relatively small panel showing the *Calumny of Apelles* (illus. 30), generally dated between 1494 and 1497, constitutes the apex of this phase in Botticelli's oeuvre. The main scene replicates a subject depicted by the ancient painter Apelles, long lost but described by the Greek author Lucian, whom Alberti quotes in his treatise *On Painting*. Lucian, in his discourse *On Slander*, describes how Apelles himself had been falsely accused of treason in front of Emperor Ptolemy IV by a rival artist, Antiphilos. Apelles then composed a painting,

> [in which] there was a figure with enormous ears sticking out, attended on each side by two women, Ignorance and Suspicion; from one side Calumny was approaching in the form of an attractive woman, but whose face seemed too well and versed in cunning, and she was holding in her left hand a lighted torch, while with her right she was dragging by the hair a youth with his arms outstretched towards heaven. Leading her was another man, pale, ugly and fierce to look upon, whom you would rightly compare to those exhausted by long service in the field. They identified him correctly as Envy. There are two other women attendant on Calumny and busy arranging their mistress's dress; they are Treachery and Deceit. Behind them comes Repentance clad in mourning and rending her hair, and in her train chaste and modest Truth.[44]

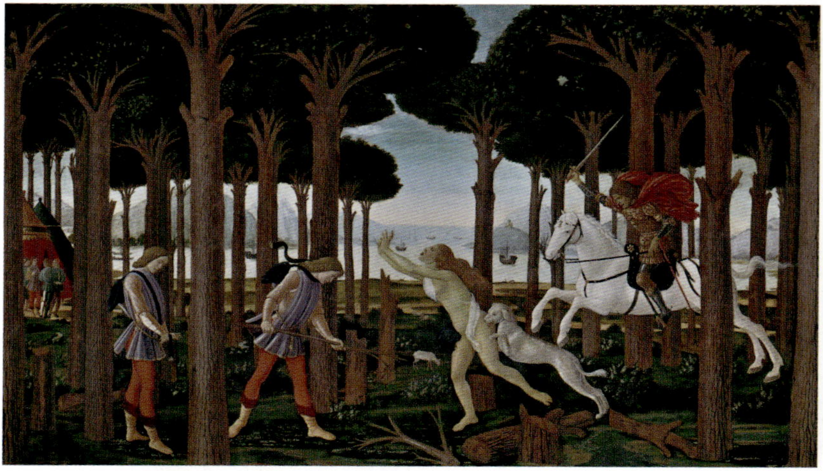

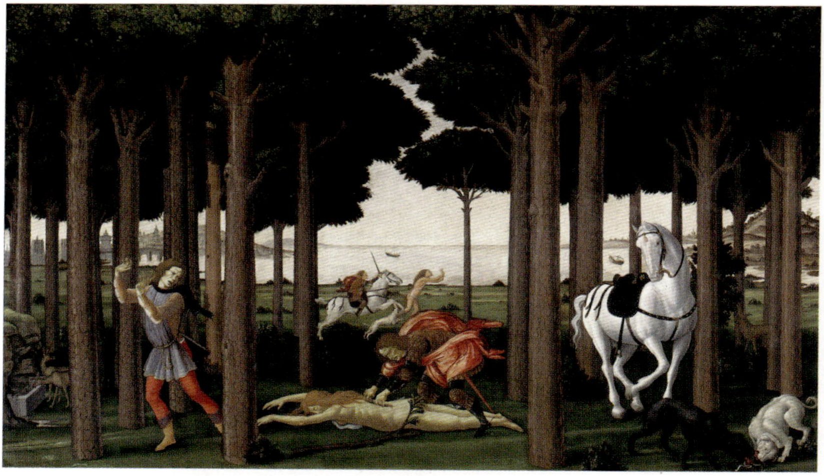

26, 27, 28, 29 Botticelli and collaborators, *Story of Nastagio degli Onesti*, parts I–IV, *c.* 1483, tempera on panel.

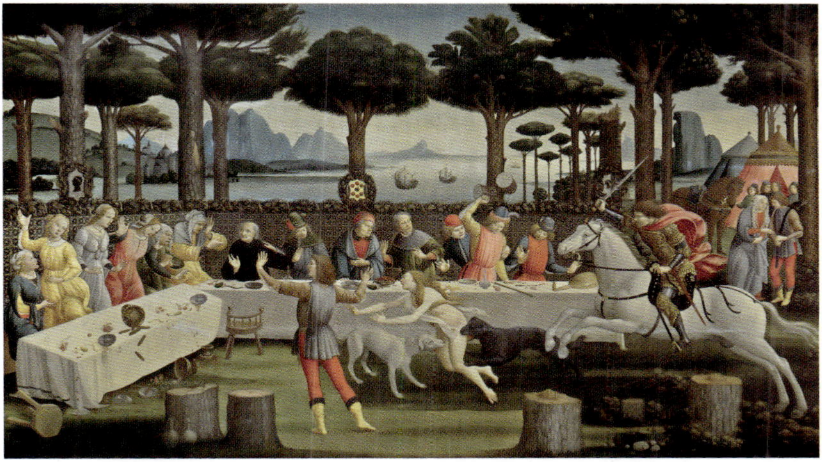

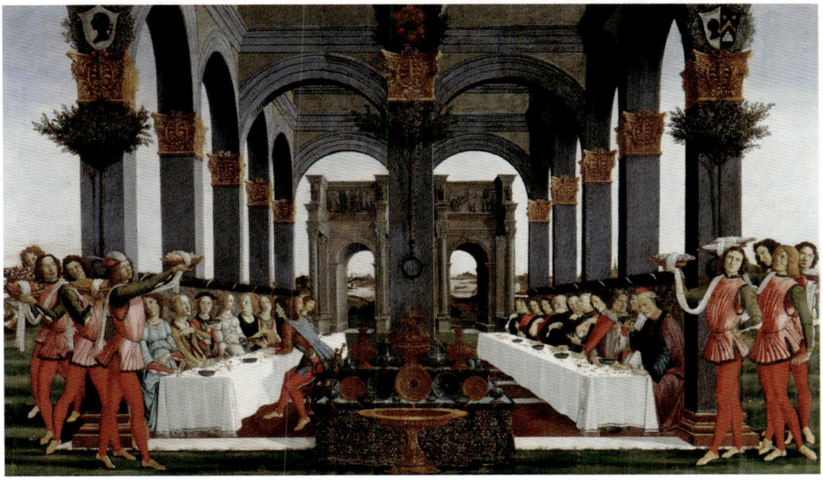

There was in Apelles' enterprise an implicit political agenda, which does not appear in Alberti's text since he uses this example to praise what makes a good invention, a good *istoria*: 'if the "historia" seizes the imagination when described in words, how much beauty and pleasure do you think it presented in the actual painting of that excellent artist?'[45]

Botticelli sets the scene in a fanciful antique loggia, opening onto a calm sea (according to some reminiscent of the Sala dei Gigli in the Palazzo Vecchio),[46] while every aspect of this complex architectural framework is decorated with small illusory low reliefs: 72 scenes are depicted, an outstanding tour de force in such a small format.[47] The relationship between the multiple scenes, painted in gilded grisaille, and the main subject has long puzzled art historians: are they interrelated or independent?[48] These trompe l'oeil scenes draw from various sources, ranging from the Old and New Testament, to ancient mythology and the two pillars of Italian literature – Boccaccio's vernacular tales and Dante's poem of *The Divine Comedy* – bridging the gap between the time of myths and the Renaissance. The main scene was probably very fresh in everybody's mind at the time, since a 'triumph' (*trionfo*) – that is, a pageantry procession of floats elaborately decorated with figures – based on Lucian's story was performed in the streets of Florence in 1491. This triumph was accompanied by a *canto carnascialesco*, a descriptive poem, titled *Triumph of Calumny* (*Trionfo della Calunnia*), written by Bernardo Rucellai, Lorenzo's brother-in-law.[49]

It cannot go unnoticed that Botticelli's highly dramatic translation of the tale reflects in many aspects this processional performance up to the detail of presenting Truth, the last figure on the left, *nuda e pura* (naked and pure), a detail omitted

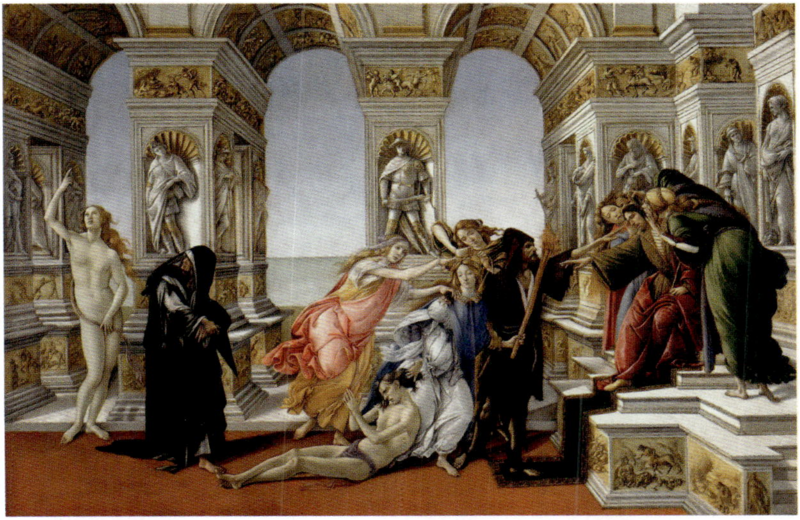

by Alberti and Lucian but present in the canto. Botticelli equally took great care in balancing his composition with a great variety of movements, pose and gestures in the main group of figures, in accordance with Alberti's precepts.

The relationship between the literary source of the Calumny and the pageant version seems to have inspired Botticelli in his choice of the scenes illustrated in the fictive reliefs in the background. There Botticelli intertwined representations of classical myths with a selection of his own inventions, or those borrowed from fellow artists, thus combining literary sources with figural quotations. For instance, the series of Nastagio degli Onesti is reproduced on the far-left vault; meanwhile at the extreme opposite of the painting, Minerva, already represented in a series of drawings and paintings by the artist, appears on the far-right step of the platform's low relief, in prominent position. A group of putti

30 Botticelli, *Calumny of Apelles*, c. 1494–7, tempera on panel.

dragging the heavy spear of Mars and hiding his helmet is reminiscent of the *spalliera* titled *Mars and Venus*, now in the National Gallery in London. Variations of this composition can be observed in another two fictive reliefs showing Jupiter and Antiope on the base next to Minerva, and Cimon and Iphigenia in the frieze above. Behind King Midas is a statue of Judith, holding a sword with the head of Holofernes at her feet; above this figure is a frieze showing the heroine at the entrance of Holofernes' tent, and again, in the relief below the niche, Judith and her maid are shown returning to Bethulia. These scenes connect not only with the theme developed by Botticelli in the 1470s, but with Donatello's famous bronze sculpture of Judith and Holofernes installed on Piazza della Signoria in 1494, around the same time as the execution of the *Calumny*. Another celebrated statue by Donatello representing David with the head of Goliath appears in the fictive relief on the left-hand side of Envy, below the statue of St George. Last but not least, the *Fall of the Titans*, depicted on the right vault, recalls Botticelli's own drawings for the *Divine Comedy*. Although Botticelli was most likely responsible for the design of these small scenes, some of them show a slightly different stylistic approach, tentatively attributed to Bartolomeo di Giovanni.[50] Many of these scenes allude to the idea of the Florentine *libertas* and the battle for freedom against a tyrannical ruler. Botticelli thus introduced a political agenda to what was for Alberti just an excellent *historia*.

We know nothing about the commission of Botticelli's *Calumny*, but Vasari informs us that it was a gift to his 'close friend, Antonio Segni' (1457–1502).[51] When Vasari saw it in the home of Antonio's son, Fabio, the panel bore an inscription which reads as an admonition to abusive rulers, and was used by the author as an epitaph to his biography of the artist.[52] It is impossible to say whether the subject of the painting alludes to Antonio's suffering from a similar accusation, or if it reflects the agitated period in Florence after the return of the apocalyptic preacher Savonarola, who rapidly installed a climate of terror and a culture of denunciation in the city. No doubt Botticelli succeeded in this picture in having 'the spectators dwelling in observing all the details' as Alberti recommends.[53] Botticelli's quotations of previous compositions interwoven with new inventions were certainly intended to act as further 'entertainment' for the spectator, but also reflect his own artistic practice and approach to picture making. In any case, this pool of motifs allowed the painter to reinvent himself each time and fuelled his imagination. This compositional strategy and these outstanding skills would serve him well in the major part of his production: religious pictures including representations of the Madonna and Child and the Holy Family, repetitive by nature.

Botticelli's *Calumny* demonstrates, in any case, the painter's outstanding power of invention and its origins in a strong sense of spatial construction. Such ability was praised in the mathematician Luca Pacioli's first book *Summa de arithmetica, geometria, proportioni et proportionalita*, published in 1494, in which Botticelli is ranked among the leading masters of perspective in his time: 'In Florence, Alessandro Botticelli, Filippino and Domenico Ghirlandaio . . . always scaled their works to perfection with the ruler and compass so that they appear to us not human but divine. In all, it seems that only life is missing.'[54]

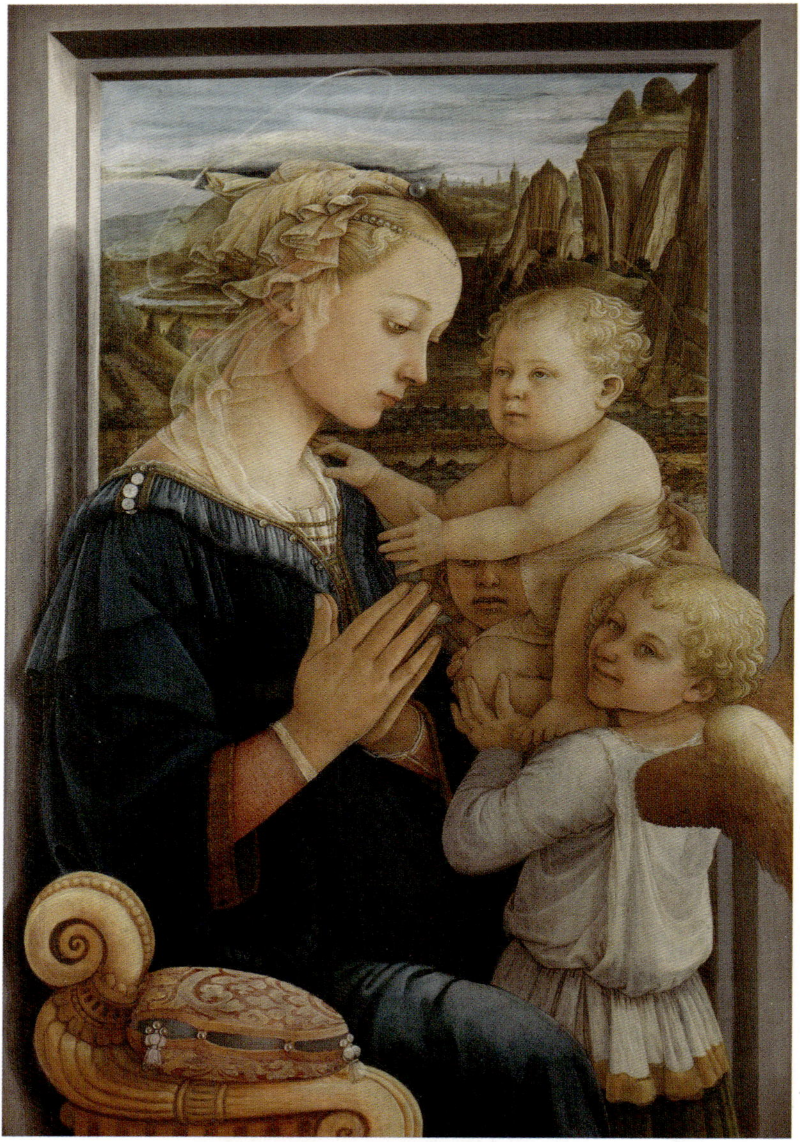

31 Fra Filippo Lippi, *Madonna and Child with Two Angels*, 1460–65, tempera on wood.

FOUR

The Original Multiple and the Wandering Motif

Although Botticelli is better known today for his mythological paintings, the majority of his production was devotional pictures, mostly, but not exclusively, images of the Virgin and Child. It was as a painter of such subjects that he had been best remembered before the dramatic rediscovery of the breadth of his work over the course of the nineteenth century.[1] Relying on and borrowing from a stock of images was profitable, but it also required a great power of invention in order to avoid tedious repetition. The artist had to successfully adapt motifs and ideas to renewed contexts in order to provide the visual experience expected by the customers. Levels of originality and complexity were often determined by the type of clientele, who either specially commissioned a specific subject or opted for a workshop variation or replica.

The many unhappy replicas of famous formulae attest to the difficulty of devising new narratives when drawing from a common pool of motifs. According to Vasari, Perugino, Raphael's master, was mocked by his peers when in 1507 he unveiled the altarpiece of the *Assumption of the Virgin*, commissioned for the church of the Santissima Annunziata in Florence (still in situ), for he had reused figures employed elsewhere:[2]

> It is said that when the work was unveiled, all the new craftsmen criticised it. Particularly because Pietro had used those figures which had already occurred in other pictures; with which his friends twitted him, saying that he had taken no pains, and that he had abandoned the good method of working, either through avarice or to save time.[3]

This mockery may appear, at first, quite surprising, as the reuse of motifs was a pretty standard workshop practice throughout the fifteenth century. The main concern was in fact not so much the re-employment of such motifs but the lack of dedication and inventiveness in this re-composition. In other words, Perugino was accused of not having dedicated enough time and labour to this commission, hence considerably lowering his usually high standard. For such important and sought-after artists, who had built their reputation in creating beautifully composed images, to rely on a stock of drawings and ready-made motifs had its downsides, and did not always ease the creative process.

As mentioned, Botticelli was particularly ingenious with regard to his reuse of his designs and generally managed to avoid monotony in the many versions of the Virgin and Child (with or without additional figures) that he and his team produced over the years. The scene was already a key subject for Byzantine art and the many icons that dominated artistic production in Italy during the Middle Ages. The artistic approach to this highly codified subject progressively evolved until the fathers of modern art, Giotto (1266–1337) and later Masaccio (1401– 1428), significantly contributed to its transformation by breathing naturalism, life and intimacy into these hieratic figures. The gold background, still favoured in the first half of the century to enhance the sublime character of the holy figures, was slowly abandoned and replaced by more naturalistic architectural settings or landscapes. This reflects not only the Flemish examples then available in Florence, which favoured such realistic backgrounds, but Alberti's advocacy of natural settings and warning against the excessive use of gold.[4]

Workshop practice and ad hoc artistic training, implying the imitation of the master, led to the development and enhancement of this iconography throughout the fifteenth century.[5] By gaining more and more naturalism and vitality, the Virgin eventually transformed into a more human character, effectively departing from what Vasari perceived as the Byzantine 'clumsy' type ('ugly Greek manner') and evolving into a more natural figure with which Florentine mothers and housewives could better identify. The Virgin was indeed presented as a role model, embodying the duties of mother and spouse. Dante, following St Augustine, records in the opening of the last canto of the *Divine Comedy*: 'Virgin mother, daughter of your son' ('Vergine madre, figlia del tuo figlio', *Paradiso*, XXXIII, 1) and this epithet would be reproduced by Botticelli on the base of the Virgin's throne in the San Barnaba altarpiece. Masaccio's personal rendering of the Virgin and Child represents a turning point in the treatment of this iconography, subsequently developed by his artistic heirs, notably Filippo Lippi. Botticelli took over his master's vision, internalized it and transformed it into the ideal model of ethereal beauty for which he is still famous today.

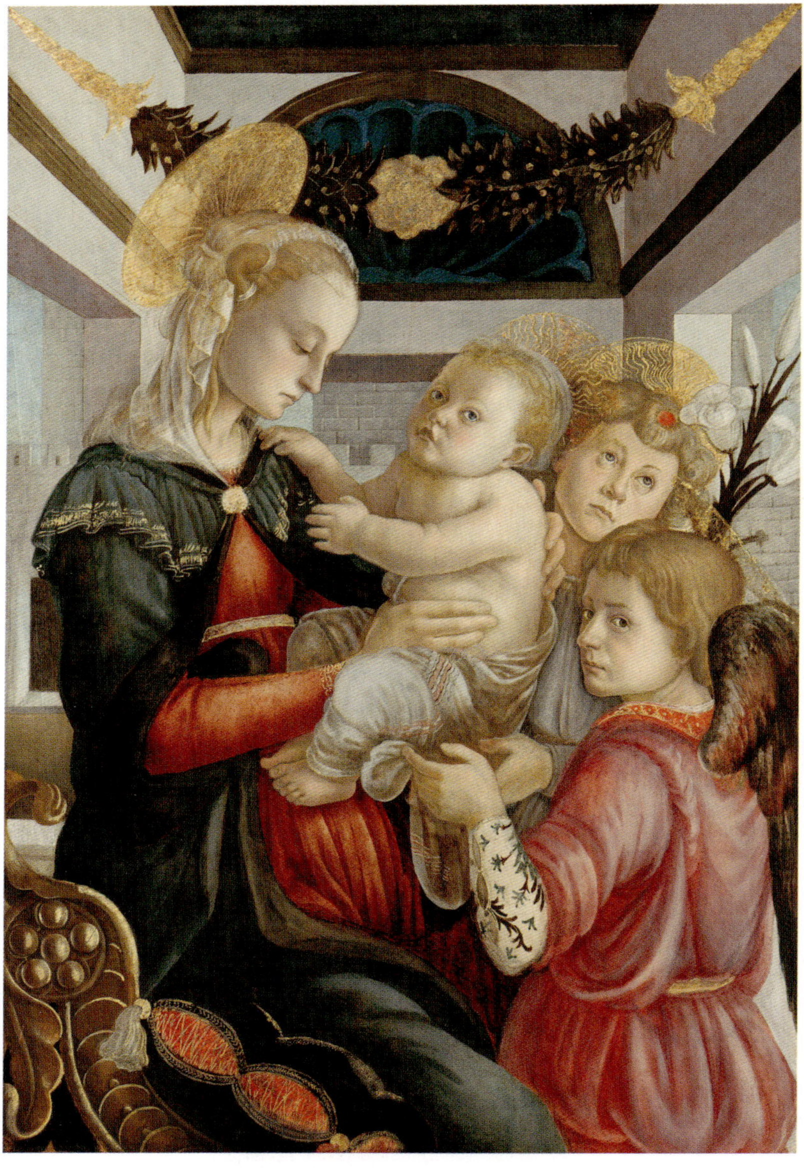

32 Botticelli, *Madonna and Child with Angels*, 1465–70, tempera on poplar panel.

Botticelli's early production of Madonnas is heavily indebted to Fra Filippo's models. Two works in particular, which date from his late career and stand out as particularly innovative, inspired the young painter. These are the *Virgin and Child with Two Angels* (illus. 31) in the Uffizi, and *Madonna and Child* (illus. 34), now in Munich, both dating from about 1460–65. Botticelli reproduced Filippo's compositions in a way that cannot be described as a straightforward exercise in copying because he added subtle variations to his master's inventions. In his own interpretation of Filippo's panel (illus. 33), Botticelli receded the figures in space, placing them at a greater distance from the viewer, and added a parapet behind them to isolate the figures from the landscape and provide a better articulation between the two picture planes. In doing so, Botticelli assents to Alberti's key idea of the painting being similar to a window that opens onto the world. He also lowered the horizon line to allow for the head of the Virgin to stand out against the light blue sky. While working on this replica, called *Madonna Guidi da Faenza*, Botticelli most likely elaborated some preparatory drawings that he would reuse in later compositions. For instance, the ornament of the seat reappears in the throne of *Fortitude*, while the design of the Virgin's silhouette, with her head slightly bent and turned in three-quarter profile, inaugurates a type that would recur several times in this early phase.[6]

The second example is an interesting case, as three different versions (in poor states of conservation) have survived and their chronology is still subject to debate: one is a particularly faithful version, while the other two show significant discrepancies. Filippo's prototype shows a different approach

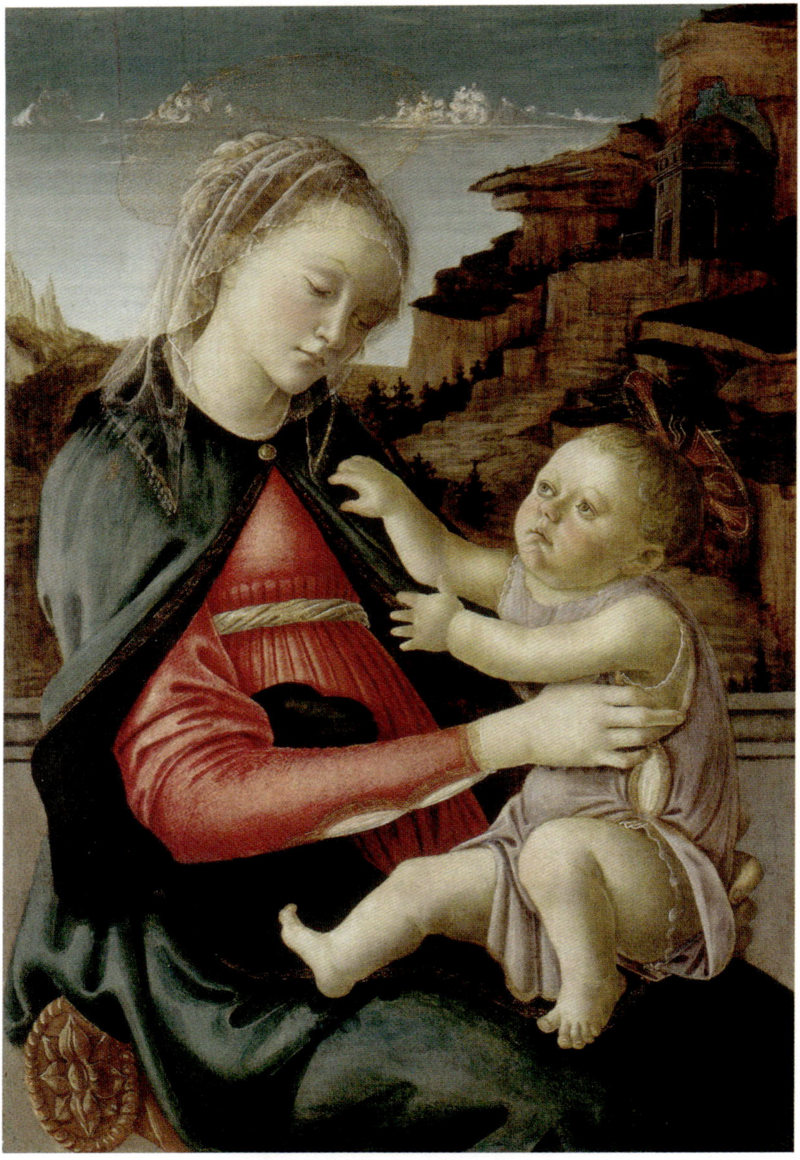

33 Botticelli, *Virgin and Child* (*Madonna Guidi da Faenza*), late 1460s, tempera on panel.

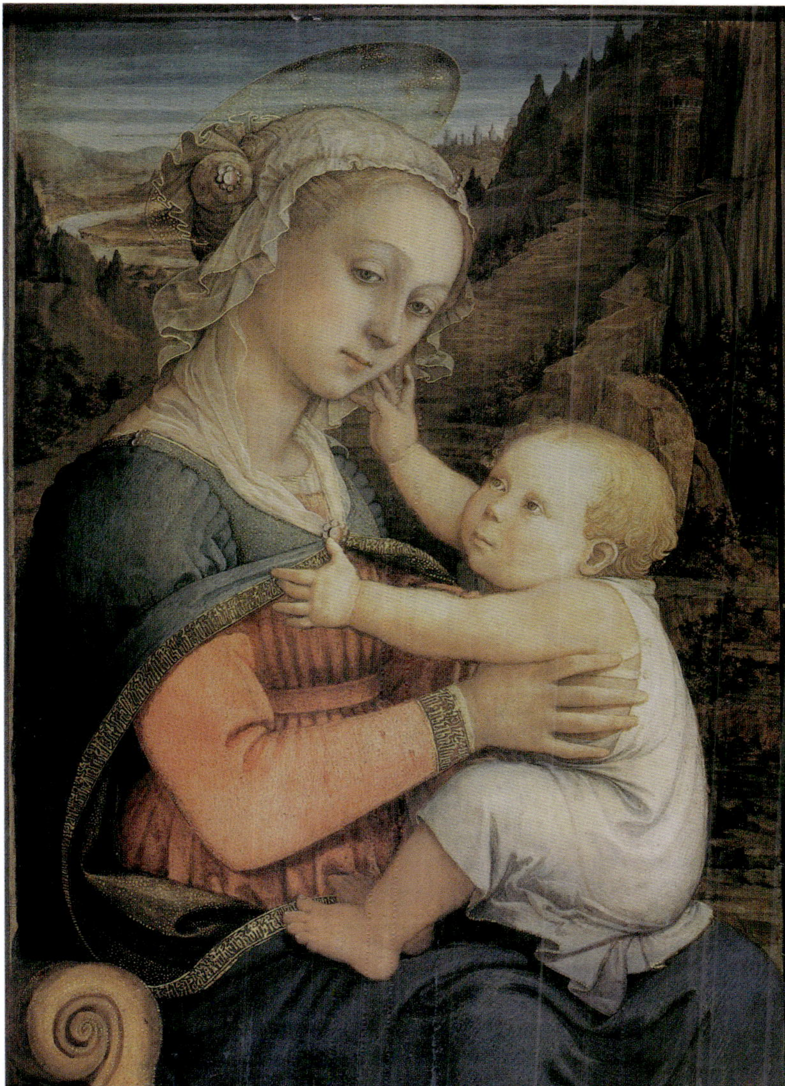

34 Fra Filippo Lippi, *Virgin and Child*, late 1460s, tempera on panel.

to the articulation of space, by introducing a window frame that delineates and effectively connects foreground and background. In Botticelli's version (illus. 32), today in the National Gallery of Art in Washington, which is sometimes considered as the first of the series, the young painter only partially carries over Filippo's original composition, which had quickly become extremely popular among both artists and customers. Botticelli adopts a greater receding effect and opts for a more ambitious background than Filippo by introducing a narrow interior decorated with a scallop-shell lunette and a garland, though not very successfully rendered, as Botticelli was still experimenting with the rules of linear perspective. The background of another version, today in the Museo degli Innocenti in Florence, is even more incongruous, while a third one, in the Metropolitan Museum in New York, reproduces Lippi's original landscape fairly faithfully.[7] In these three works, in addition to notable changes in the background, Botticelli introduced subtle variations in the group of the angels, none reproducing Filippo's original arrangement. Botticelli redirected their gaze, modified their pose and even removed one of them (in the Museo degli Innocenti version), compositional strategies that would become a key feature of his art when producing variations of the same theme.[8] In all, the Virgin appears absorbed in her thoughts while the angel in the foreground looks out, engaging the attention of the spectator, but he has lost the smile he wore in Filippo's original. The Child and the angel next to him look up (to the divine realm?), inviting the viewer to do the same. This group of early works offers a good example of variations on a prototype developed by the master. Neither straightforward copies nor workshop replicas, these pictures show Botticelli's artistic development and slow emulation of his master, even as he capitalized on his teaching.[9]

A further variation of Lippi's prototype, which denotes a new maturity, can be seen in Botticelli's *Madonna and Child with Angels* (illus. 35), now at the Capodimonte Museum in Naples, which reversed the original composition and displays the characteristic features of Botticelli's Virgin's head, whose prototype can be found in *Fortitude*. The search for idealized, beautiful heads also developed among artists such as Verrocchio, Ghirlandaio and Leonardo. Verrocchio's studies and cartoons of graceful female faces are a good example of this trend.[10] One of Verrocchio's paintings also follows the same scheme as the Capodimonte picture, with a variant: the Madonna unveils her breast to nurse the Child (illus. 36), a detail that Botticelli appropriated in another simplified variant of the same composition, now in Avignon (illus. 37). It is impossible to say with certainty which painting came first, Botticelli's or Verrocchio's, but this competitive dialogue between artists over the depiction of beautiful Virgins reflects a preoccupation of the time. Over the course of the fifteenth century, beauty rapidly became an important feature of devotional paintings and almost a requisite in iconography; this reached its full development in Botticelli. It is difficult to say whether Filippo Lippi's vision of beautiful Madonnas was dependent on his love for Lucrezia Buti, his alleged model (and mother of Filippino Lippi), or if its development followed a line encouraged by courtly love poetry promoted by Dante (*c.* 1265–1321) and Petrarch (1304–1374). Dante in the *Divine Comedy* and Petrarch in the *Rerum vulgarium fragmenta* (better known as *Canzoniere*) claimed to have

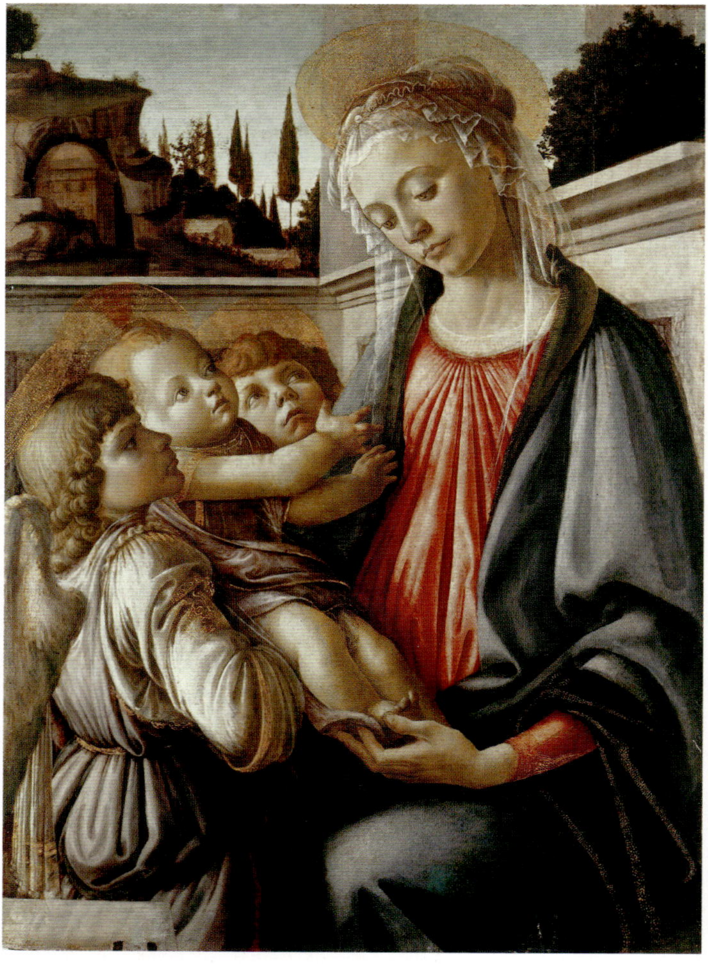

35 Botticelli, *Madonna and Child with Angels, c.* 1470, tempera on wood.

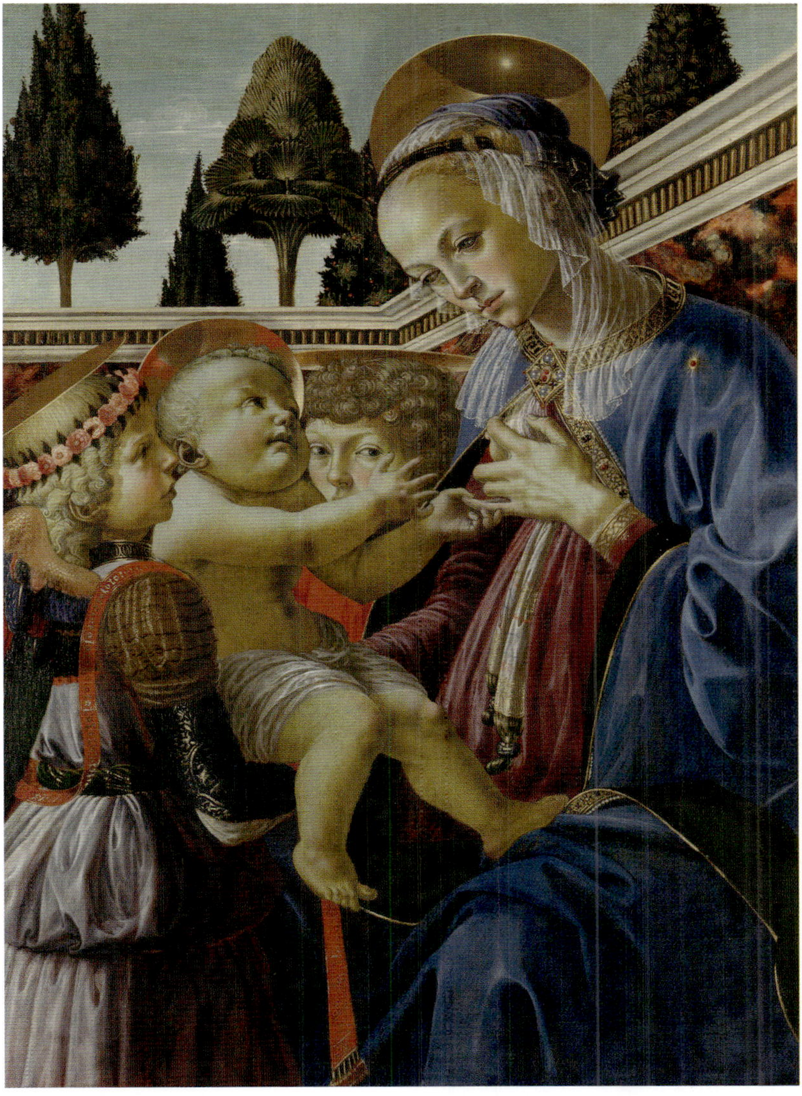

36 Andrea del Verrocchio, *Madonna and Child with Angels*, c. 1467–9, tempera on wood.

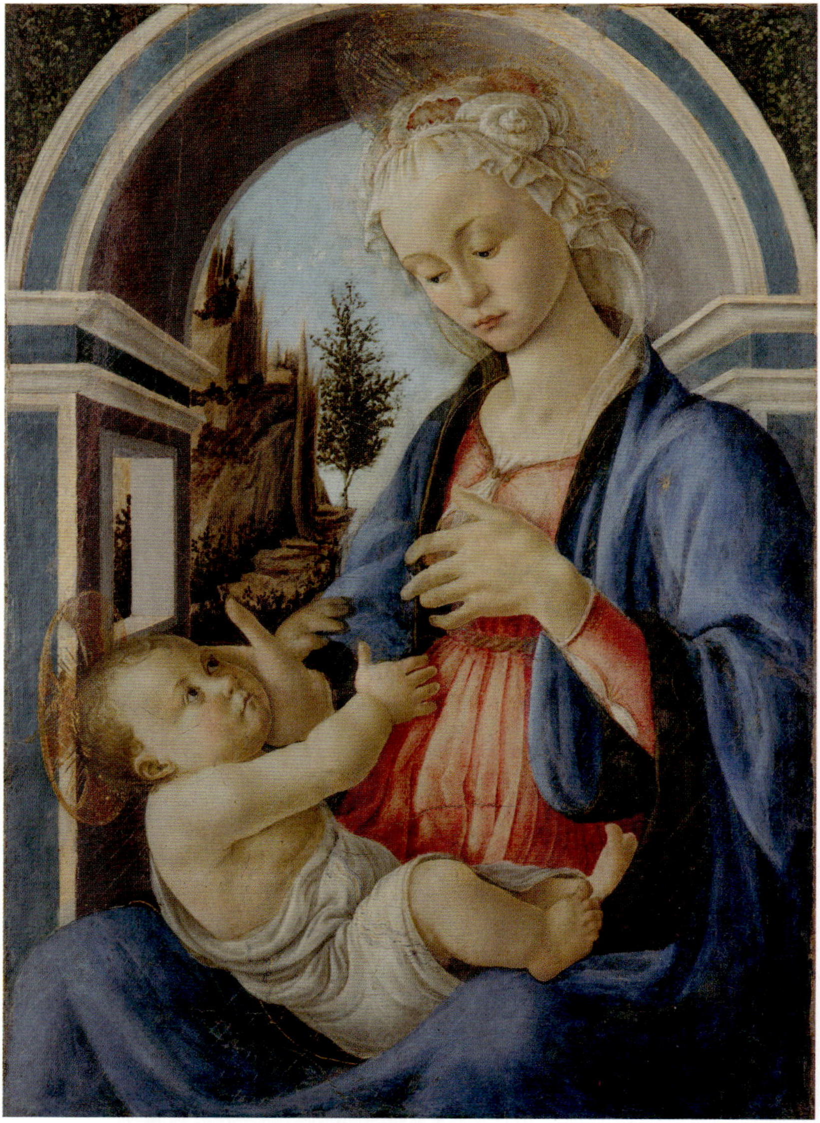

37 Botticelli, *Madonna and Child* (*Campana Madonna*), *c.* 1470, tempera on wood.

been led to divine love through their terrestrial attraction for the beautiful Beatrice and Laura, respectively. In their work, the beloved earthly women give way to the Virgin, the celestial woman who appears, resplendent, at the culmination of their literary journey, and announces a new entirely spiritual experience to come, beyond speech.

The idea that divine love is first stirred in human hearts by terrestrial beauty, which through desire takes the soul to the celestial realm, was a major poetic theme in the Renaissance. It was Petrarch's main legacy. This literary movement was revivified in the second half of the fifteenth century when the philosopher Marsilio Ficino (1433–1499) reintroduced Neoplatonist philosophy to the Western world. Neoplatonism developed a similar concept.[11] To Ficino, in the footsteps of Plato and his early commentators, beauty leads to the divine, likened to the supreme good. Thus beauty is good in its origins since goodness *is* beauty. At the same time, Ficino also used poetical metaphors to illustrate his arguments. In his most important text on the subject, *De amore* (*On Love*, first written in 1467 and re-elaborated at Lorenzo de' Medici's behest in 1474), the image of the beloved, passing through the eyes of the lover, imprints itself on his heart and generates love.[12] This terrestrial love is not the end but the beginning of a journey towards the divine.[13] Ficino's conception of love greatly influenced his contemporaries, and the next generation. Lorenzo de' Medici himself, as well as his protégé, the poet and humanist Poliziano, who was one of the foremost classical scholars of the Renaissance, developed a similar concept in their poems. This perhaps culminates in Michelangelo's own poems nearly forty years after Ficino's death, while it influenced most of the sixteenth-century commentators on Petrarch's *Canzoniere*.[14]

It is therefore not surprising that such a conception similarly developed in art. Botticelli in particular quickly made a speciality of beautiful Virgins, and carried over this Neoplatonist idea of beauty to every single figure of his compositions, regardless of gender. The St Sebastian commissioned to stand against a column in the church of Santa Maria Maggiore in Florence is, in this respect, a good example.[15] Executed as early as January 1474 (perhaps for the saint's feast day on 20 January), the painting depicts a muscular young man, traditionally pierced by several arrows, set in a slightly *contrapposto* pose, with a beautiful, tilted head – a type that would recur throughout Botticelli's oeuvre. St Sebastian can be construed as the male pendant of *Fortitude* for a series of reasons, including the existence of a later painting of the same subject made by the Pollaiolos for the Pucci Chapel in the church of the Santissima Annunziata, hence reactivating their artistic rivalry.[16] He prefigures the many beautiful young men, pagan gods and angels that would populate Botticelli's future compositions. Botticelli probably created some preparatory drawings for this composition, similar to two head studies which still survive today (illus. 38).[17] The type inaugurated by St Sebastian reappears under the guise of the god Mercury in the *Primavera*, but also in the many adolescent young men (angels) who accompany the Virgin and Child, already allowing for a certain permeability between sacred and profane themes.[18]

There was only a limited variety of types that could inform the theme of the Virgin and Child in high demand in Renaissance Florence. Botticelli favoured about four types of composition, three inherited from the Byzantine tradition, and a fourth derived from the accounts of the vision of a nun, St Bridget of Sweden (*c.* 1303–1373). The first three types correspond to the Eleusa or 'Virgin of Tenderness', the Hodegetria, when the Virgin rests her child on her hand and points at him, and the Panachranta, or Virgin enthroned. The fourth type was exemplified by Filippo Lippi in the altarpiece

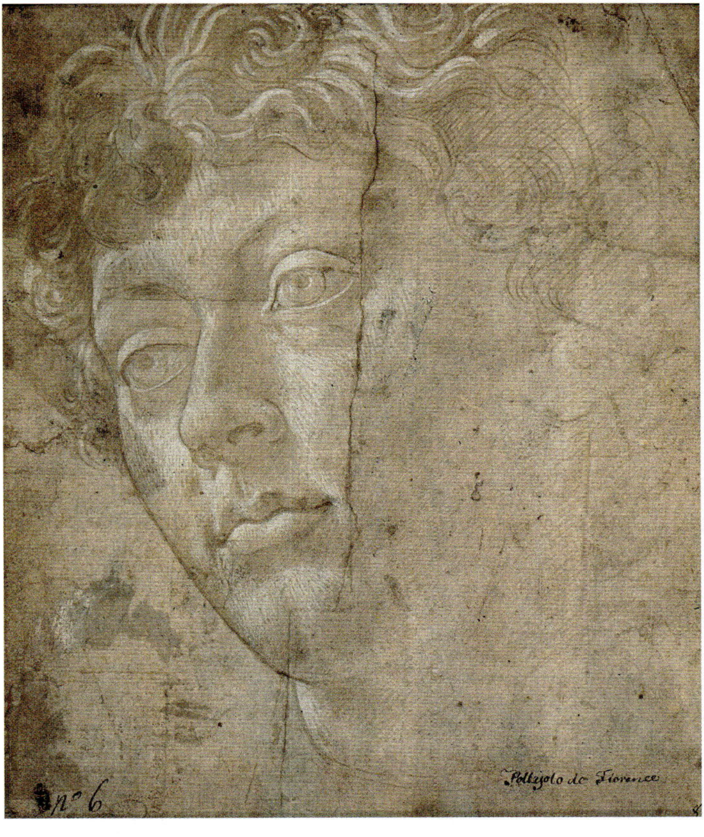

38 Botticelli, *Head of an Angel*, *c.* 1480, metalpoint highlighted with white on brown paper.

for the Medici chapel in the family's palace in via Larga and shows a kneeling Virgin in adoration before the Child resting on the ground.[19] For better clarity, we can subcategorize these devotional pictures into two groups: innovative compositions that constitute important milestones within the painter's artistic development, and less ambitious devotional works, often made for private devotions in domestic settings (usually the bedchamber), derived from the former and usually produced in series at different levels of quality.

Botticelli's outstanding power of invention shows in his ability not only to devise innovative designs within this strictly codified iconography, but to create a highly personal style that is almost immediately recognizable. Drawing inspiration from his master, the young painter continued to improve his designs by relying on his previous compositions to fuel his imagination and gradually to create more innovative formulae by following the exact same modus operandi as in his youth, when drawing upon his master's models. This is especially apparent in the *Chigi Madonna* (illus. 39), a painting that derives from the Capodimonte panel (see illus. 35), itself inspired by Filippo's masterpiece in the Uffizi (illus. 31). Botticelli introduced here a notable change by flipping the position of the Child and showing him resting on his mother's hand, an iconography that at first seems to correspond to the Byzantine Hodegetria type.[20] However, instead of pointing to her Child as the source of redemption for humankind, the Virgin delicately selects an ear of wheat that an angel presents on a plate laden with grapes. By introducing the admirable still-life motif, Botticelli revivified this traditional iconography (wheat and grapes being eucharistic symbols, allusive to the future Passion

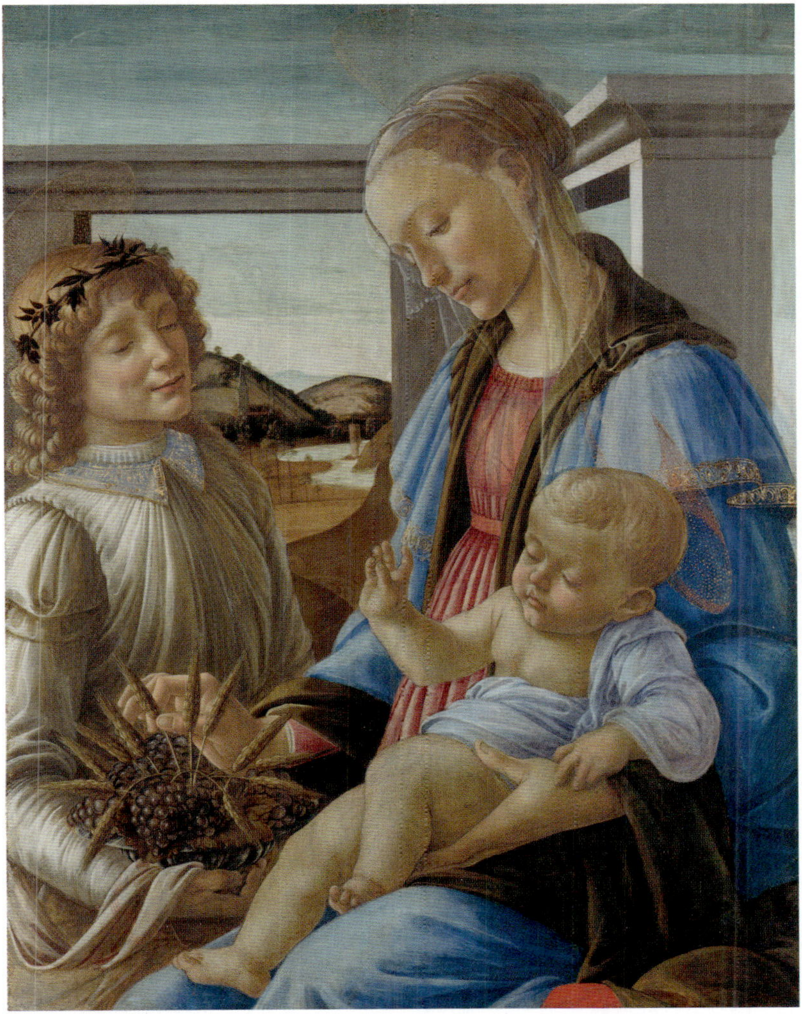

39 Botticelli, *Madonna and Child with an Angel* (*Chigi Madonna*), 1470–74, tempera on panel.

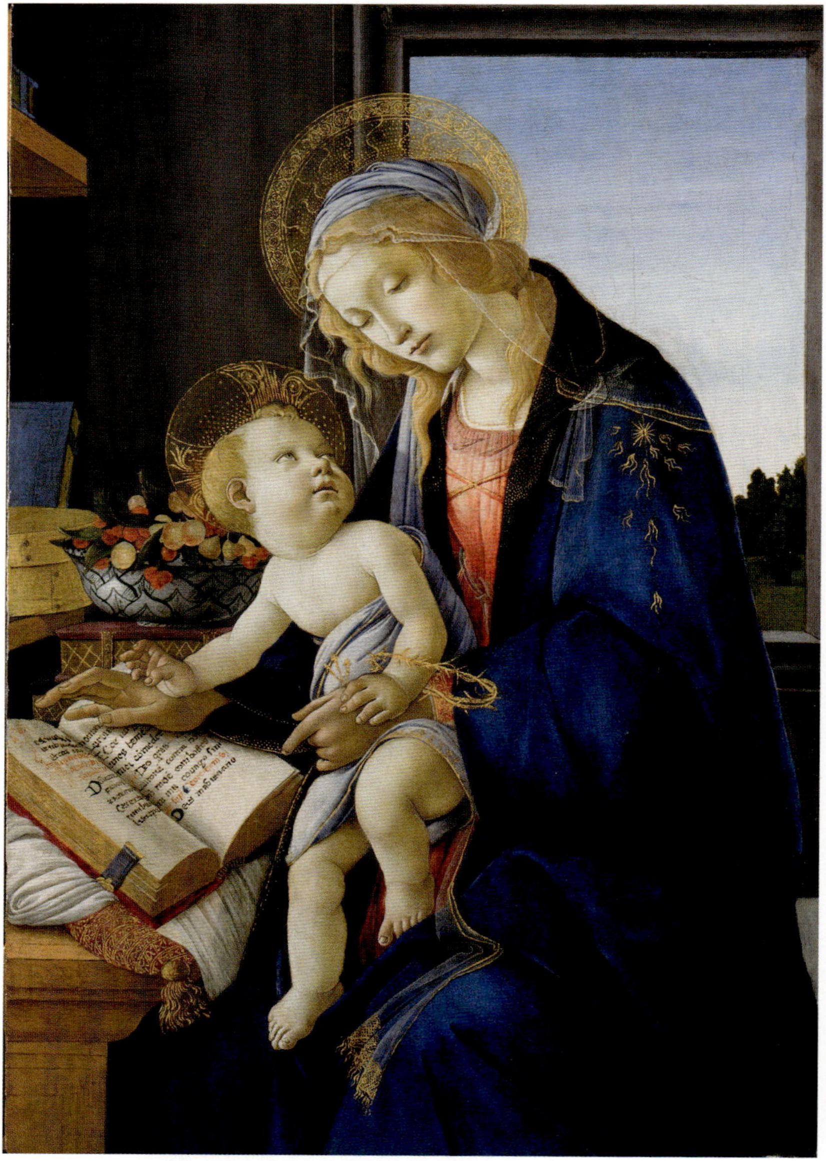

40 Botticelli, *Madonna of the Book*, *c*. 1482–3, tempera on panel.

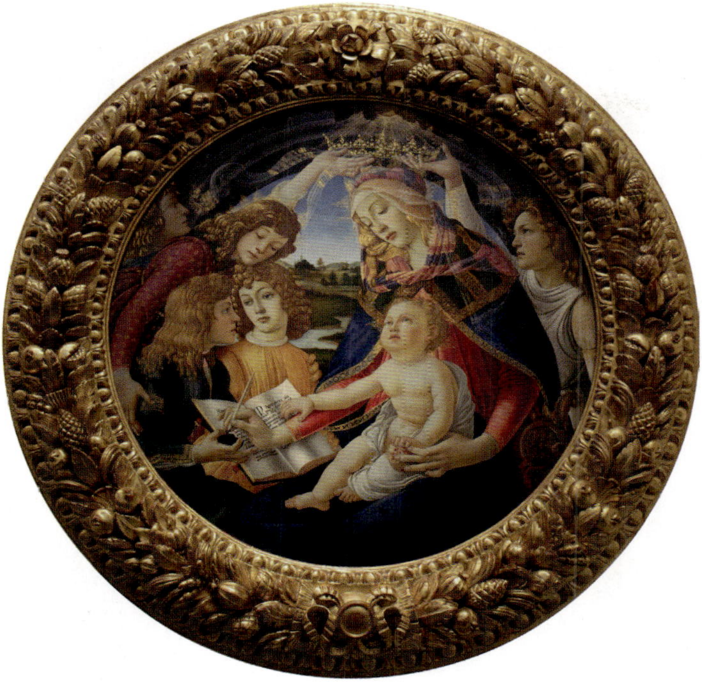

of Christ). This composition constitutes a true turning point in Botticelli's early oeuvre, as he reaches stylistic maturity and displays a highly personal conception of this holy subject. Generally dated about or after 1470, the *Chigi Madonna* opens up a twenty-year season of masterpieces springing from the reuse and adaptation of his own motifs, at first barely noticeable given the ingenuity of their redeployment. This series includes, though is not restricted to, the *Madonna of the Book* (illus. 40), chronologically followed by *Madonna of the Magnificat* (illus. 41) and the so-called *Rockefeller Madonna* (illus. 42). These works clearly adapt the pose and specific gesture of the Virgin to different iconographical contexts. The design of

41 Botticelli, *Madonna of the Magnificat*, c. 1483, tempera on wood.

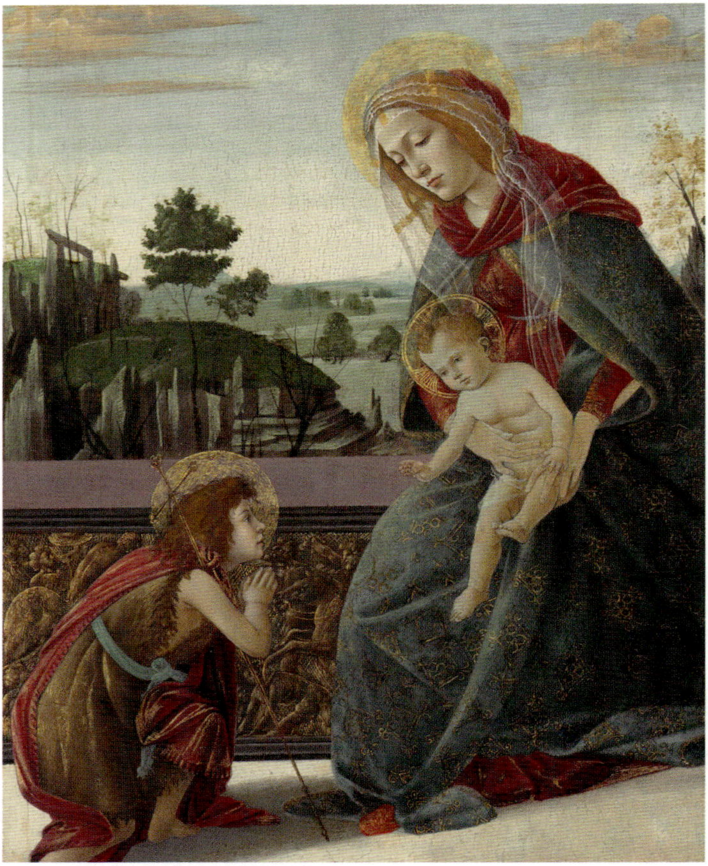

the Virgin derives from the same model and she essentially remains unchanged from one painting to the next, the only subtle difference being in her face, which is shown in three-quarter profile in the three subsequent works, following the Capodimonte type.

Botticelli therefore playfully reused a specific model but substituted and swapped head types and body parts in order

42 Botticelli, *Rockefeller Madonna*, early 1490s, tempera on panel.

to breathe life into this rigid, but not inflexible, subject. To do so, Botticelli did not mechanically transfer a preparatory drawing or cartoon directly onto the panel, though this method became more and more customary in the second half of the fifteenth century. On the contrary, he probably copied freehand from a specific model type, rearranging some details such as the hands and finally adjusting the whole design to different scales and formats. Such a process is further attested to by the many pentimenti (changes of mind), alterations and corrections in the underdrawing of the *Virgin of the Magnificat*, revealed by infrared reflectography. In addition, none of the paintings discussed here that share the same model-type have similar dimensions, which suggests Botticelli drew from a repertory of motifs that he adapted each time to the specific format of his commissions. However, as we shall see, this does not exclude the possibility that he might have used cartoons from time to time.

In three of the images the Virgin's left hand is identical (illus. 39, 40 and 41), but the setting provides a sense of novelty. Her right hand varies slightly in each, showing different arrangements of the fingers. The design of the Child in illustrations 40 and 42 differs only in His position, which has been slightly rotated anticlockwise (see illus. 39 and 40). Illustrations 41 and 42 add a small variant to the mantle of the Virgin: a shawl is wrapped over her shoulders. Thus Botticelli takes full advantage of permutational sections (head, limbs, elements of garments and so on) while the sense of novelty is provided by small amended details and more apparent changes in the background. As already discussed, architectural settings play a major role in Botticelli's personal conception of space, and these four examples are no exception, as each offers a different point of view over the Tuscan countryside. In addition, the highly refined depictions of the still-life (wheat, fruits and a book, substituted in the last example by a remarkable low relief on the parapet) enrich the iconography and conceal the reuse of common models. Besides conveying the quietness and elegance necessary for the devotional practice these works were meant to encourage, a further incentive for the devout may lie in the identification of the many symbols hidden in these compositions. These include the aforementioned wheat and grapes, symbols of the Eucharist, but also the fruits depicted in the maiolica bowl above the book, itself legible enough for the viewer to recognize a passage from Isaiah (7:14–15) announcing the birth of the Saviour (illus. 40).[21] The nails and the crown of thorns allude to Jesus' sacrifice, the cherries to His blood, the plums to the Virgin's tenderness and the figs to His resurrection. Once again, Botticelli encourages the spectator to linger in the contemplation of the painting by offering him *varietas* (as Alberti puts it) through a wealth of meaningful details. This compositional strategy is typical of Botticelli, who followed a similar process of review and refinement throughout his career.

Another important group of works, following a similar line of development, depicts the Mother and Child enthroned with saints, a type better known as Holy Conversation (*sacra conversazione*), which derives from the Byzantine Panachranta, and whose Italian prototype may be found in Fra Angelico's oeuvre, for instance the Annalena altarpiece (dated about 1435 and today in the San Marco Museum in Florence). Botticelli also probably had in mind his master's example in the so-called Medici Novitiate altarpiece, now in the Uffizi.[22] Botticelli's first recorded altarpiece for the church of Sant'Ambrogio in Florence, executed around 1475 (illus. 12), appears to provide a template for his own series. A campaign of restoration carried out in 2018–19 on this early altarpiece revealed an impressive amount of pentimenti in the underdrawing, even at a late stage of execution. Most notable is the late inclusion of a platform in order to raise the Virgin's central and dominant position, covering another type of (flat) pavement that had originally been drawn.[23] These many hesitations suggest that it was most likely Botticelli's first attempt to produce an altarpiece on such a scale. It therefore explains the amount of care and reworking to obtain a satisfactory solution, yet this work would set in stone the compositional formula that the artist would follow throughout his career. Only minor changes and variations (notably in the number and identity of the attending figures) distinguished at least five surviving important altarpieces (*pala* in Italian) executed over a period of thirty years. These are, in chronological order, the so-called Bardi (1484–5), San Barnaba (*c.* 1488–90), Trebbio (1495–6) and Montelupo (1499) altarpieces (illus. 43–6). They all reproduce the same compositional formula, with some variations in the accompanying standing figures, as well as in the background setting. The Virgin in frontal position derived from the type developed for the earlier *Fortitude* while the Child borrows from a pool of motifs that recur in other compositions. For instance, the Child in the Sant'Ambrogio altarpiece seems identical to the Child in the *Chigi Madonna* (illus. 39), the latter being represented upright, while the former is depicted

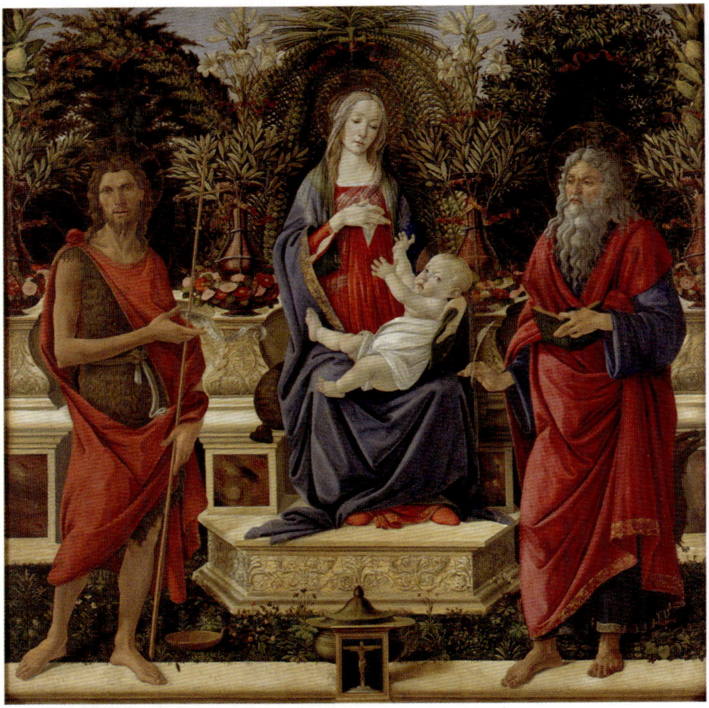

lying on his mother's lap. The same design is used here and rotated 45 degrees so as to give the illusion of a child lying down. The torso, legs and raised arm are almost identical, while the head has been changed slightly. Inclining, reversing and swapping over a model-type was common practice in Quattrocento workshops to avoid too obvious repetitions. Unfortunately, as already mentioned, none of the model-books that were doubtless in use in Botticelli's *bottega* has survived.[24]

Unlike private devotional works, which were often confined within the domestic setting and only accessible to a limited public, altarpieces were on show in churches and

43 Botticelli, Bardi altarpiece, 1484–5, tempera on wood.

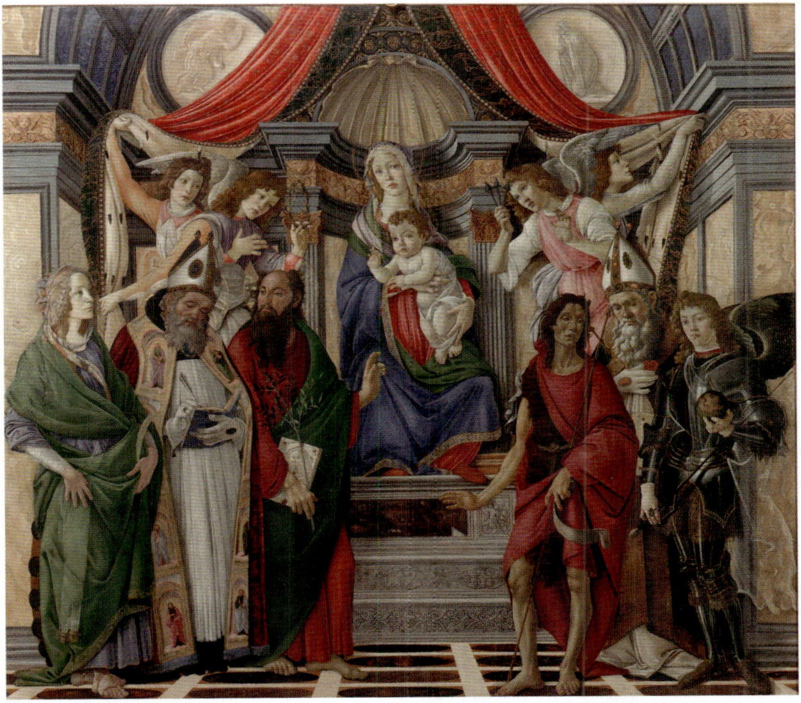

therefore exposed to a wider audience. Artists certainly took advantage of such exposure, which provided them with an ad hoc marketing campaign. The extraordinary background of the Bardi altarpiece (illus. 43), for instance, which stands out from the series, might be explained by its original setting in the church of Santo Spirito, which had just reopened in 1481/2 after a fire had consumed it ten years earlier. A number of altarpieces were commissioned around the same time to furnish the several 'new' chapels, hence the level of competition rising between artists whose work would be inevitably compared.[25] Botticelli's altarpiece, commissioned by Giovanni

44 Botticelli, San Barnaba altarpiece, *c.* 1488–90, tempera on wood.

de' Bardi (*c.* 1431–1488), a partner of the Medici bank in London in the 1460s, recorded as 'the great merchant of England', follows the same structure as the other altarpieces in the church but significantly increases the presence of the vegetation to the point that it forms the principal feature of the composition.[26] Following a compositional strategy he had already employed in the Nastagio degli Onesti series, Botticelli transformed the natural setting behind the parapet in order to form three niches, which acted as an architectural device to structure the composition, increased the sense of recession

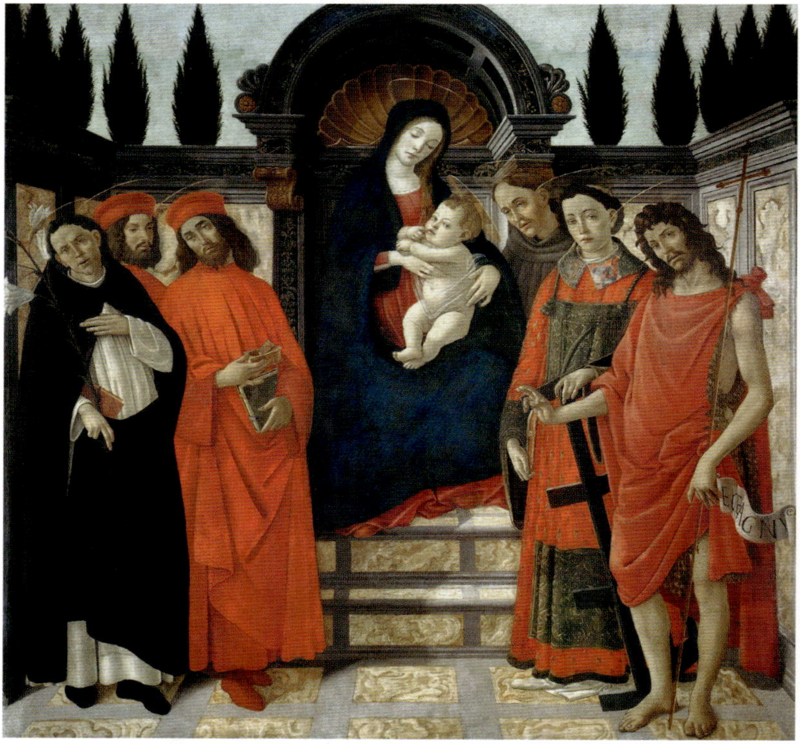

45 Botticelli, Trebbio altarpiece, 1495–6, tempera on wood, transferred onto canvas.

in space and framed the three main sections of the painting occupied by the Virgin and Child at the centre, with St John the Baptist on the left and St John the Evangelist on the right. The composition is lit from the left-hand side, as shown in the projected shadow of the small crucifixion on the ledge. This carefully planned orientation of light follows the setting of the painting, originally to be placed on an altar located on the extreme left of the rear of the apse (extant today).[27] As the spectator walked towards the chapel, the painting would shine as if lit by a special light, which would have been enhanced

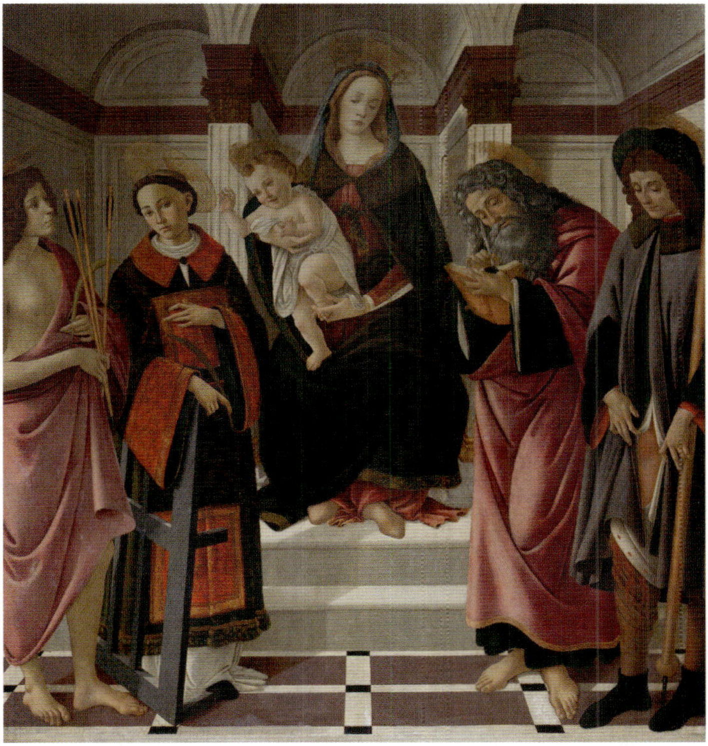

46 Botticelli, Montelupo altarpiece, 1499, tempera on wood.

by the candles that would have picked up the delicate gilding carefully distributed throughout the composition.

The Child, as the focal point of the composition, looking out at the beholder, would invite him into the picture. A similar invitation is extended by St John the Baptist, who can be construed as a mediator between the divine realm represented by the Child and that of the beholder, while the Virgin and the older saint John seem absorbed in their thoughts, like worshippers at prayer. As is customary with Botticelli, the richness of the details, which include an astonishing number of plants and flowers (alluding to the Virgin's epithet as an enclosed garden, 'hortus conclusus', in the Song of Songs (4:12) and echoing the *Primavera*), acts as a further meditative trigger for the learned and unlearned beholder, who could start interpreting the painting on several levels according to the extent of their own knowledge and competence.[28] It was still possible for Vasari to admire the care Botticelli took in devising this composition. He records the altarpiece as 'diligently executed and well finished, containing some olives and palms made with the greatest love'.[29] Following the same modus operandi at work in the execution of *Fortitude*, his youthful masterpiece, Botticelli carefully planned the effect of his painting on the spectator by relying entirely on the design, since the subject was shared by most of the other altarpieces commissioned for the church. It most likely allowed him to cast a new light on his work in the mid-1480s and renew not only interest from patrons but his own creative vein.

The execution of such large altarpieces, even if brought to completion with the help of assistants, was labour-intensive and time-consuming. It seems that Botticelli was paid a good price for these works, but no more than his contemporaries.[30] In such a competitive market, it was therefore necessary to answer the high demand for medium-size devotional works. A number of partial replicas of these prestigious commissions have survived. In the absence of direct testimony, it is difficult to say whether these were specially requested or whether it was, for the painter and his assistants, a financially shrewd decision to reuse ready-made designs in much simpler versions; more likely, it was a combination of both. For example, the Madonna and Child from the Bardi and San Barnaba altarpieces were extracted from their Holy Conversation context and reproduced in smaller devotional panels with a different background. An example currently in a private collection shows a faithful reproduction of the Madonna and Child from the Bardi altarpiece, while the background has been changed into an arched window opening onto a sunny landscape. The arched window recurs in other previous works, for instance in the aforementioned *Campana Madonna* and the *Madonna and Child with Angels* in the Museo degli Innocenti (see illus. 37). The San Barnaba altarpiece has inspired at least five replicas of the two central figures following the same principle: they repeat the same design of the Madonna, with variations in that of the Child, while the concept of the niche behind them is reproduced in simpler form. The background depicts either an arched window, a column or a curved parapet, all opening onto a sunny landscape.[31] The Child, on the other hand, echoes several well-known Botticellian types and introduces additional variety to this repetitive image.

Meanwhile, full replicas of much-admired paintings were issued by Botticelli's workshop, most likely in order to respond to a specific demand in Florence. For example, at least five replicas after the celebrated tondo of the *Madonna of the Magnificat* have survived in various dimensions.[32] Particularly in vogue in Florence in the fifteenth century, the tondo format died out in the first quarter of the sixteenth century. The circle was viewed since antiquity as the perfect geometrical form, and therefore most appropriate to represent foundational scenes of the Christian faith, such as the Virgin and Child, the Nativity and the Adoration of the Magi – the shape was also used in different media such as glazed terracotta, stucco and papier-mâché (*cartapesta*). Tondi were typically made for private or semi-public devotion and predominantly installed in lay or domestic settings such as the bedchamber. For instance, a tondo depicting the Virgin and Child, now identified as *Madonna of the Pomegranate*, was commissioned from Botticelli for the audience hall of the Massai della Camera in the Palazzo Vecchio in 1486.[33] The other only two recorded payments to Botticelli came from private citizens.[34] To judge from the more than sixty surviving tondi issued by his workshop, Botticelli was especially prolific and ingenious in creating successful designs for this complex circular format.

The closest copy of the *Magnificat*, in terms of dimensions, is now in the Musée Fabre in Montpellier, but the design has been significantly altered in the group of the angels on the left, one of which is missing, while the abundant use of gold that characterizes the original is missing entirely. The most faithful design, on the other hand, has been reproduced in a smaller version, now in New York. These replicas were typically produced by the workshop. Vasari reports an anecdote that illustrates the conditions of execution and sale. One of

Botticelli's assistants, called Biagio, produced a reduced copy of a tondo, possibly the Raczynski tondo, for which he was paid six florins. It is possible that this copy is the version now in the Lindenau Museum, which has lost its bottom half. Vasari's story allows us to better understand Botticelli's relationship with his collaborators, as it is said that he himself had arranged for the sale of the reduced replica, the proceedings of which were paid to Biagio directly. Vasari also implies that the picture was produced without a proper commission and appeared on offer 'off the shelf'.

> Finding Biagio, Sandro said, 'I have sold your picture at last, but the purchaser wants it set up this evening to have a better view of it. Go to the citizen's house tomorrow, taking it with you, so that he has seen it well placed he may pay you the price'. Biagio was delighted, and thanked his master, and hastened to the workshop, setting the picture fairly high up, and departed.[35]

This sale provided a good opportunity for Botticelli to play a joke on his assistant, as was customary practice in workshops at the time. Botticelli then called another assistant and one Jacopo to place small red hats of paper on the heads of each figure.

> The next morning Biagio arrived with the citizen who had bought this picture, and who was aware of the joke. When Biagio entered the shop and looked up, he saw his Madonna seated not in the midst of angels, but of the Signoria of Florence, with their hoods. He

> was about to excuse himself to his patron, but as the latter said nothing but praise of the picture, he kept his counsel. Finally, Biagio went home with the citizen and received the payment of six florins as settled by his master. Meanwhile Sandro and Jacopo had removed the paper hoods, and on Biagio's return he saw his angels as they should be and no longer hooded citizens. Lost in amazement, he knew not what to say. At length he turned to Sandro and said, 'Master, I do not know if I am dreaming or awake. When I came here these angels had red hoods on their head and now they have none; what does it mean?' 'You must be mad, Biagio,' said Sandro; 'this money has turned your brain. If they had been like that do you think the citizen would have bought it?'[36]

This type of joke is in keeping with workshop habits and customs attested by the literature of the time, which is full of similar anecdotes.[37] We do not know how much Botticelli's tondo fetched, as very few documented prices remain, but the highest registered price was one hundred florins for the San Marco altarpiece, while simpler tondi showing a Madonna and Child with or without additional figures ranged between nineteen (for example for the so-called Martelli tondo – presumed lost) and forty florins (for the tondo identified as the one now in Piacenza).[38]

At this point, questions arise about the workshop technique used to reproduce Sandro's compositions. It appears that Botticelli used different methods of transfer to copy his original designs, according to the anticipated final appearance of the replica. A quick survey of Botticelli's most important series such as the six surviving replicas after the *Madonna of the Magnificat* shows us that Botticelli and his assistants most likely reproduced the design freehand, copying the composition by eye rather than being guided by a full-size cartoon applied directly onto the panel. The use of cartoons would have meant that all the replicas have similar dimensions, while they actually vary in size. The Lindenau Museum copy of the so-called Raczinski tondo, for instance, is half the size of the original.

Another method for transferring the design without the help of full-size cartoons, which would let Botticelli and his assistants play more freely across a wide range of scales and formats, is one described as 'squaring', as shown in a drawing in the Uffizi.[39] This design, which represents the goddess Minerva (Pallas, in Greek) holding her customary helmet in her right hand and a branch of olive in her left, was used in a series of works executed in different sizes and media over a period of at least ten years. A grid was drawn across the small preparatory design while another of the same relative proportions was made on the panel or final substrate. The drawing was then reproduced freehand by eye, taking as a guide the relationship between the outlines and the squares. This technique allows for a relatively easy change of scale and adaptation to various formats. The design was used to represent the goddess in the marquetry technique (inlaid work made from small pieces of coloured wood or other materials, usually used for the decoration of furniture) on a door that delimits the so-called 'Sala degli Angeli' from the 'Salone d'onore' in the Palazzo Ducale, Urbino. Its pendant, a figure of Apollo, was also supplied by Botticelli.

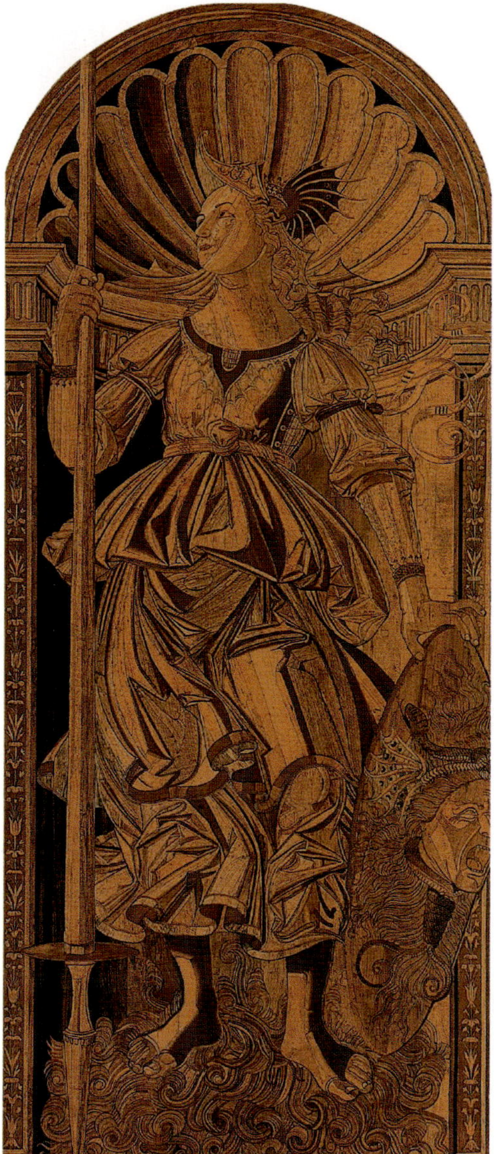

47 Benedetto da Maiano after Botticelli, *Minerva* (detail), 1480s, inlaid wood.

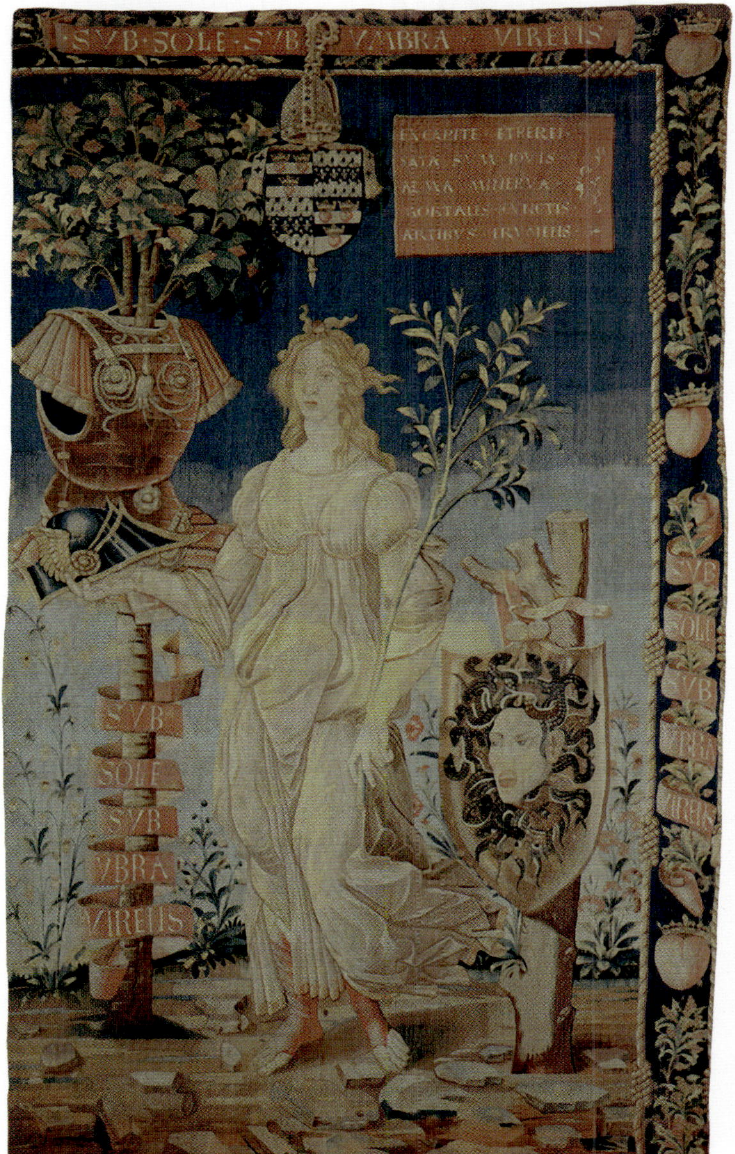

48 French manufacture, *Minerva pacifica*, *c.* 1490, fragment of a tapestry, wool and silk.

An important aspect of Botticelli's quality as a designer is his involvement in the decorative arts. On a much lesser scale than the celebrated multidisciplinary workshops of the Pollaiolo brothers and Andrea Verrocchio, who worked as goldsmiths, painters and sculptors, Botticelli collaborated with such craftsmen as wood carvers, embroiderers and engravers on a regular basis throughout his career. This little-known and still under-studied activity goes hand in hand with Botticelli's involvement in designing the (lost) banner for Giuliano's joust in 1475, and possibly, as mentioned before, ephemeral decor that has not survived. Vasari informs us that Botticelli 'was one of the first to find a way of making standards and other draperies in commesso . . . He also did the *baldacchino* of Or San Michele, full of Madonnas, all different and beautiful.'[40]

The works mentioned by Vasari did not survive but the technique of *commesso* consists in creating figures and motifs with small pieces of materials, in this case fabric, assembled together with a final appearance resembling appliqué work. Botticelli's supply of designs for the decorative arts probably started as early as the late 1470s when he collaborated with the woodcarvers Francione and Giuliano da Maiano, who were paid in 1480 for two marquetry doors for the so-called 'Sala dei Gigli' in the Palazzo Vecchio, the town hall of Florence, still in situ. The doors respectively portrayed the two fathers of Italian poetry, Dante and Petrarch, executed after Botticelli's designs – one of which, representing Petrarch, is recorded in a drawing attributed to Filippino Lippi, who possibly competed for this commission.[41] The figure of Dante would reappear in a later portrait painted by Botticelli, probably in connection with his interest in the *Divine Comedy*, the poet's magnum opus.

Providing designs for the decorative arts probably appealed to Botticelli as a challenge to his creativity and power of invention. The translation into different materials, from inlaid woods using various substances and textures to textiles with wool, silk and metal threads, must also have raised his curiosity and interest. His specific linear style, which has been commented on at length, was especially congenial to translation into various materials using a range of different techniques. Several drawings and finished works document this activity, which took chiefly place in the 1480s and '90s.

The figure of Minerva, for instance, reappears with more or less variations in several further works. It is found in the painting representing Minerva and the Centaur (illus. 49), possibly commissioned for the marriage of Lorenzo di Pierfrancesco de' Medici and Seramide Appiani in 1482,[42] and again in a tapestry woven about 1490 (illus. 48) for Guy de Baudreuil, abbot of Saint-Martin-aux-Bois, in the French region of Picardy, whose coat of arms appears at the top centre. The tapestry was probably created from a small presentation drawing similar to the workshop record drawing now in Oxford, which displays a more mechanical and stiff manner.[43] In addition to squaring, the Uffizi drawing was also pricked along the outlines, allowing for a secondary drawing to be mechanically produced by pouncing. Charcoal would have been dusted through the holes with a 'pounce bag' (hence the name 'pouncing', *spolvero* in Italian), creating a map of dots to be joined up to recreate the design on the secondary substrate.

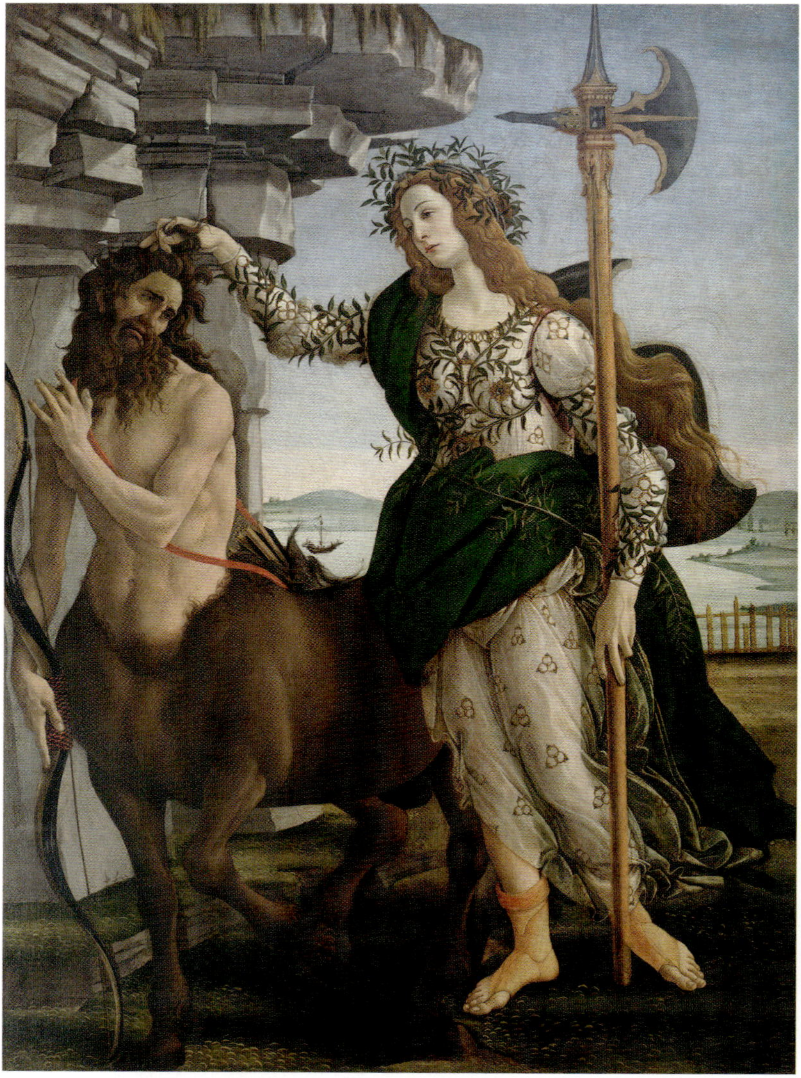

49 Botticelli, *Minerva and the Centaur*, *c.* 1482, tempera on canvas.

A Miracle by St John the Evangelist, a drawing on silk that is now in the Louvre, illustrates the technique described by Cennino Cennini in his *Libro dell'arte* in which a chapter explains 'how to draw on canvas or silk for the embroiderers'.[44] This delicate drawing is executed in a purely linear manner, and appears very close in style and composition to another, on paper this time, kept in the Uffizi, which represents a separate miracle of the same saint.[45] The two drawings, devised most likely for the same ensemble, therefore present two consecutive stages in the making process: first the design was drawn on paper to fix the composition (and probably kept in the workshop for later reuse); then it was transposed onto silk

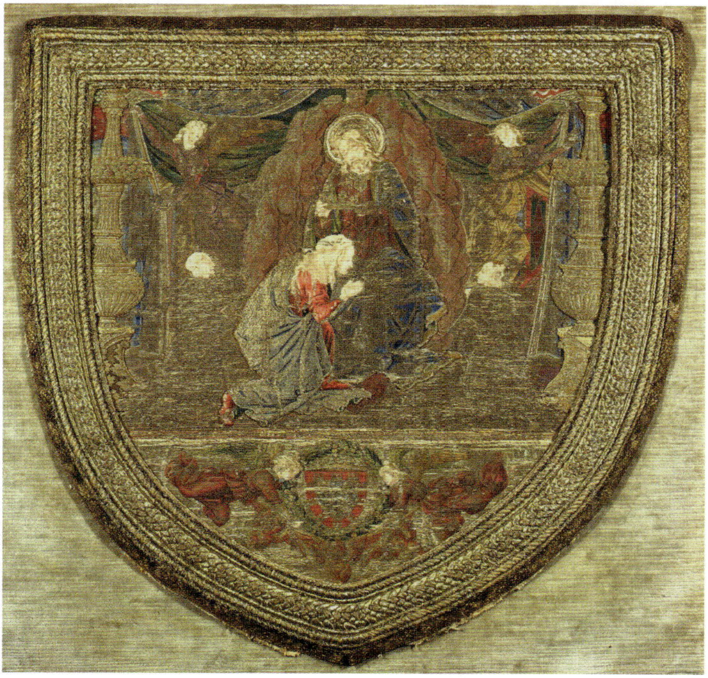

50 Italian manufacture after Botticelli, *Hood of a Liturgical Cope Showing the Coronation of the Virgin*, 1490–95, gold and linen on silk.

ready to be embroidered. What the end result would have looked like can be seen in two surviving liturgical vestments: a chasuble and the hood of a cope. The chasuble is made of lavish pomegranate-patterned velvet and bears a scene of the Annunciation, which relates to a design Botticelli had already employed, for example in the predella of the San Marco altarpiece and in the two small Annunciations now in Glasgow and New York.[46] On the chasuble, Botticelli most likely designed the saints enthroned, reminiscent of the sibyls series – themselves derived from *Fortitude*.[47]

The dialogue of motifs within Botticelli's oeuvre is characteristic of his creative process. The lavish chasuble itself appears to be the source of inspiration for the robe of St Justus in the altarpiece now in Miami and originally made for a Camaldolese abbey in Volterra (illus. 52). The upper part of that same altarpiece shows a Coronation of the Virgin, following a design that Botticelli used several times in similar large works, namely the San Marco altarpiece and another for the church of San Francesco in Montevarchi (now at Villa La Quiete, see illus. 53). A rare preparatory drawing for this upper section has survived and, as customary with Botticelli, does not fully correspond to the finished compositions but provides another interesting insight into his artistic process. Taking this sketch as a starting point, Botticelli reworked his composition directly on the final support, adapting it to the two-tier composition and adding a double row of cherubs and seraphim, while pushing the dancing angels further away. The Montevarchi altarpiece presents a more faithful reproduction of the drawing, which suggests the work of an assistant who needed to rely more heavily on the master's model.

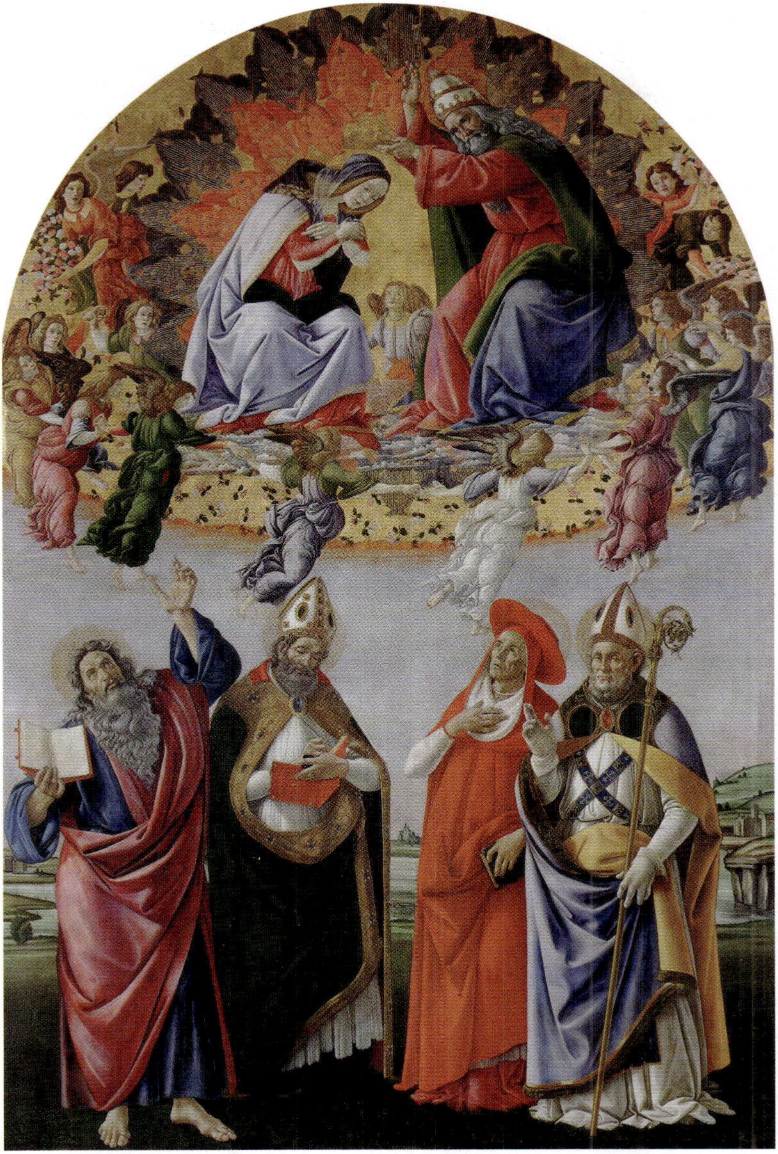

51 Botticelli, *Coronation of the Virgin with Saints and Angels* (San Marco altarpiece), *c.* 1490, tempera on wood.

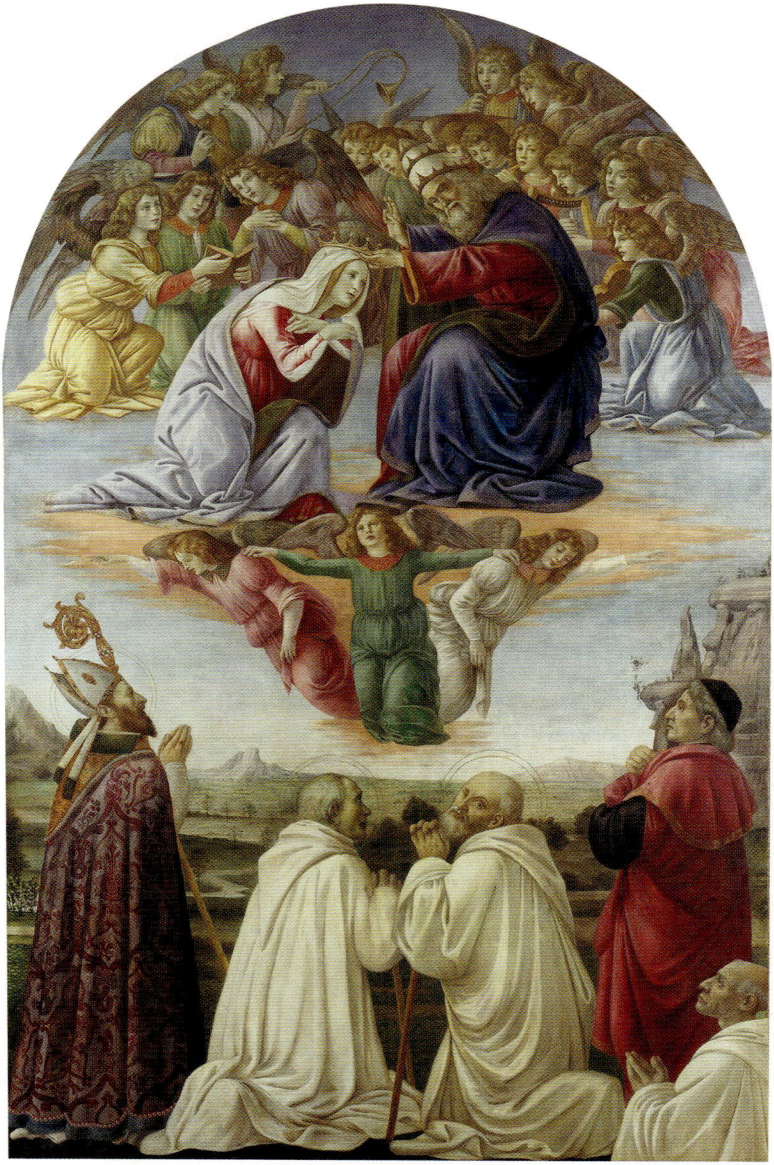

52 Botticelli and workshop, *Coronation of the Virgin with Saints and Angels*, *c.* 1492, tempera and oil transferred on canvas.

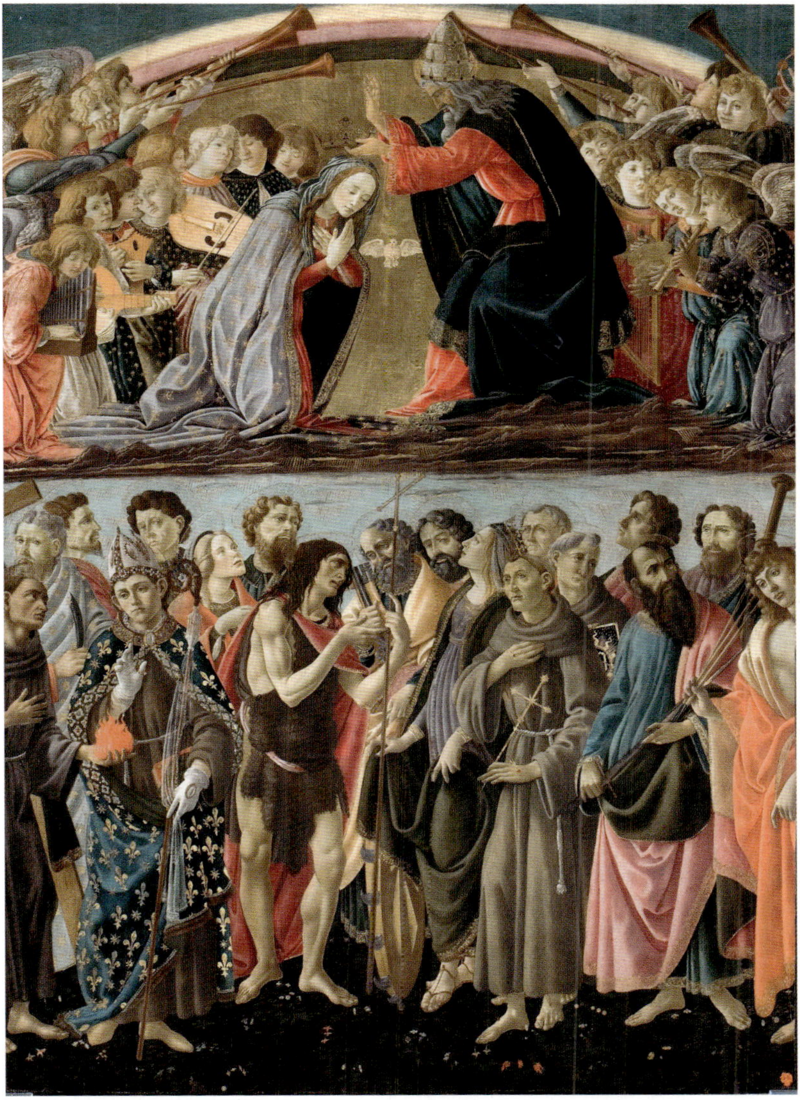

53 Botticelli and workshop, *Coronation of the Virgin with Saints and Angels*, 1490s, oil on wood.

Indisputably, Botticelli intervened in the execution of this work, as demonstrated by the quality of certain figures, notably St Lawrence in the lower section.

The hood of a cope similarly shows a coronation of the Virgin but in a slightly different arrangement (illus. 50).[48] It includes the coat of arms of King John II of Portugal (*r.* 1481–95), nephew of the Cardinal of Portugal whose funerary chapel is in the church of San Miniato al Monte in Florence. The high quality of this embroidery, executed in a complex technique, goes hand in hand with the refinement of the preparatory design apparent under the stitches, which is stylistically comparable to a drawing on silk.[49] The same design was reproduced in another hood of a cope while the arrangement of the two figures and their poses are reminiscent of the central motif of the so-called *Maringhi Coronation* by Filippo Lippi, a work to which Botticelli paid tribute on a few occasions.[50] Borrowing motifs from a wider repertory, including his former master's and those of his contemporaries, was another of Botticelli's compositional strategies, and it is significant that he not only borrowed but completely absorbed these motifs, never failing to make them his own.

A further example of such a trend followed one of the most dramatic events of the late Quattrocento: the assassination of Giuliano de' Medici, Lorenzo's younger brother, by members of the Pazzi family and their allies, who had conspired with Pope Sixtus IV. This crisis, commonly known as the Pazzi Conspiracy, took place during the Mass that was celebrated on 26 April 1478 in the cathedral of Florence, Santa Maria del Fiore. Giuliano was killed; Lorenzo escaped but was badly wounded. Of course, this was not unusual. The

Italian states were constantly on the verge of war; individual rivalries between their rulers and sudden changes of alliances meant that peace was never established for long.

The calling of Tuscan artists, including Botticelli, to the papal court in Rome only two years after this major political crisis is a clear example of such political vacillations. The strong reaction of the people of Florence, who immediately turned against the conspirators, began a two-year period of great tension.[51] The Medici's reaction was brutal: the Pazzi and their accomplices were immediately pursued, arrested, tortured and sentenced to death.[52] Those who managed to escape were condemned *in absentia* by means of a painted representation called 'images of infamy' (*pittura infamante*). Botticelli was commissioned to depict these figures above the Porta della Dogana of Palazzo Vecchio. The images were painted out in 1494 following the banishment of the eldest branch of the Medici family from the city.[53] A drawing by Leonardo da Vinci records what these effigies might have looked like.[54]

Contemporaneously, Botticelli was commissioned to create a series of portraits of Giuliano, all executed according to the same model with changes in the background, following a habitual practice that he rapidly mastered to near perfection.[55] This serial production, an exception within Renaissance portraiture, relates to a campaign of commemoration and mourning orchestrated by Lorenzo and his supporters following the tragic loss of Giuliano. Botticelli's portrait might have been based on Bertoldo di Giovanni's medal, itself possibly derived from a death mask, which bears on the obverse a portrait of Lorenzo with the inscription 'Salus publica', alluding to his salvation, and on the reverse a portrait of Giuliano

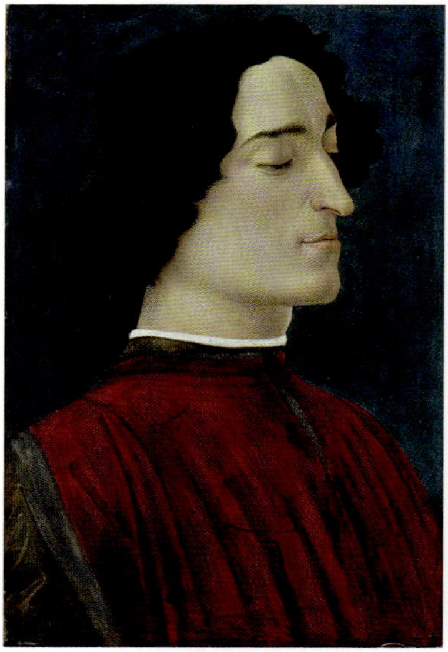 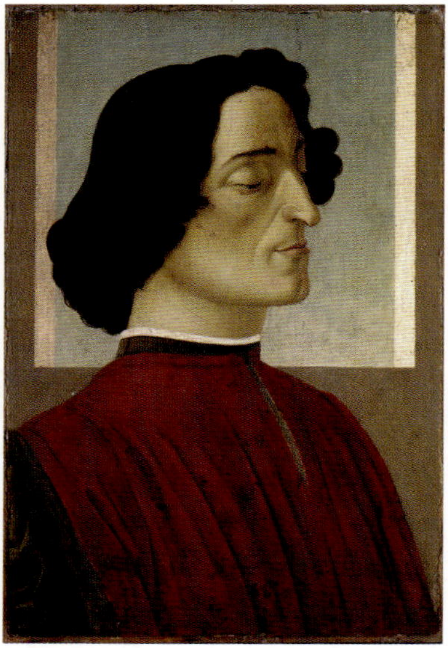

inscribed with 'Luctus publicus' (public mourning).[56] Despite the different dimensions of the three panels, the profiles are almost identical, with minute variations in the underdrawing. It is therefore probable that Botticelli and his collaborators used a more mechanical method to transfer the original design than freehand copying.[57] Since no *spolvero* has yet been identified in any of Botticelli's paintings, it is most likely that he used the *calco* method described by Vasari, similar to the modern (now outdated) use of carbon paper, which transfers marks made by the pressure of a tool. In the Renaissance either the reverse of the cartoon or a second sheet of paper was blackened with powered charcoal and used face down on the panel so the outlines could be transferred to the panel by tracing over with a stylus. This method had the advantage of preserving the integrity of the cartoon itself (so it could be

54 Botticelli, *Giuliano de' Medici*, *c.* 1478, tempera on wood.
55 Botticelli, *Giuliano de' Medici*, *c.* 1478, tempera on wood.

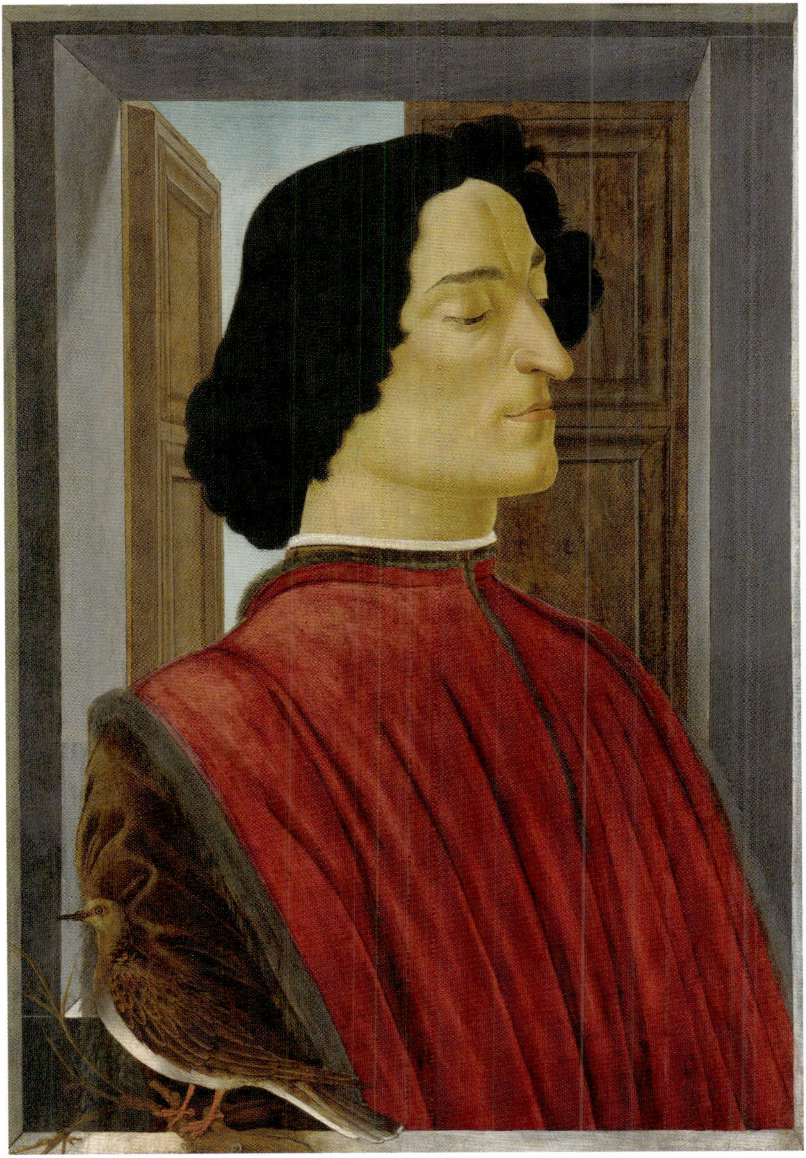

56 Botticelli, *Giuliano de' Medici*, *c.* 1478, tempera on wood.

reused) and left almost no perceptible signs on the panel. Furthermore, the practice was to brush away any indications of tracing, which in any case were then largely covered by free-hand reworking of the design.[58] This 'second underdrawing' explains why two similar designs never match perfectly: some elements of the figure always stand out when the rest of the design aligns, whether the length of a nose or locks of hair, as in the present series.[59]

Furthermore, the differences in the panels' size and iconographic details might have been the result of the original commission. Indeed, the largest and most complex composition, the version now in the National Gallery of Art in Washington, came from the Grand Duke Ferdinando I de' Medici and was perhaps the painting listed in 1503 in the inventory of Lorenzo di Pierfrancesco de' Medici.[60] The prestige of the commission probably led Botticelli and/or his advisers to provide a more composed image that exhibits clear mourning symbols, such as the dried branch, the turtledove on the windowsill and the half-open shutter suggesting, in this instance, the threshold of the afterlife. The possibility that the other, simpler settings, which all seem to have originally included a window, might result from a less prestigious commission remains an open question until new archival evidence can shed light on their early provenance. The chosen method of replication of the design raises questions about the participation of the workshop in the execution of the three versions. It is undeniable that Botticelli designed and partially executed all of them, especially the modelling of the face and such details as the turtledove; he might have left less crucial features for his team to finish. The sitter's vest, for instance (a type called *giornea* in Italian) was, unlike the head, probably not reproduced from a cartoon but drawn freehand. It could have been completed by assistants, as the modelling approach varies in all three examples.[61]

For this campaign of political recuperation, Botticelli's talents as a designer were probably most sought-after – and with good reason, to judge from the resurgence of this image in later paintings and prints, such as a woodcut illustration which derived from Botticelli's formula and was published a century later in Paolo Giovio's *Elogia virorum bellica virtute illustrium*.[62] With this image Botticelli had achieved yet another tour de force, which established the official and highly political image of the deceased Giuliano.[63] In this light, the portraits of Giuliano could be construed as the counterpart of another revolutionary portrait, of a lady called Smeralda Brandini (illus. 57), which shows for the first time a woman gazing directly out to the viewer.[64] This was extraordinary because in the Renaissance women were expected to act humbly and keep their gaze low in public. While semi-closed eyes are unusual in individual portraits, Botticelli had already represented Giuliano with similar hooded eyes a few years earlier as one of the figures attending the Adoration of the Magi, commissioned by Guasparre Del Lama in 1475 for his chapel in the church of Santa Maria Novella (see illus. 25). Botticelli knew the young Medici well and it is possible that Botticelli deliberately transformed his usual facial expression, his distinctive attribute.

Recovering figures and re-employing them in different settings became a profitable practice for Botticelli, to judge from the number of motifs wandering from one composition

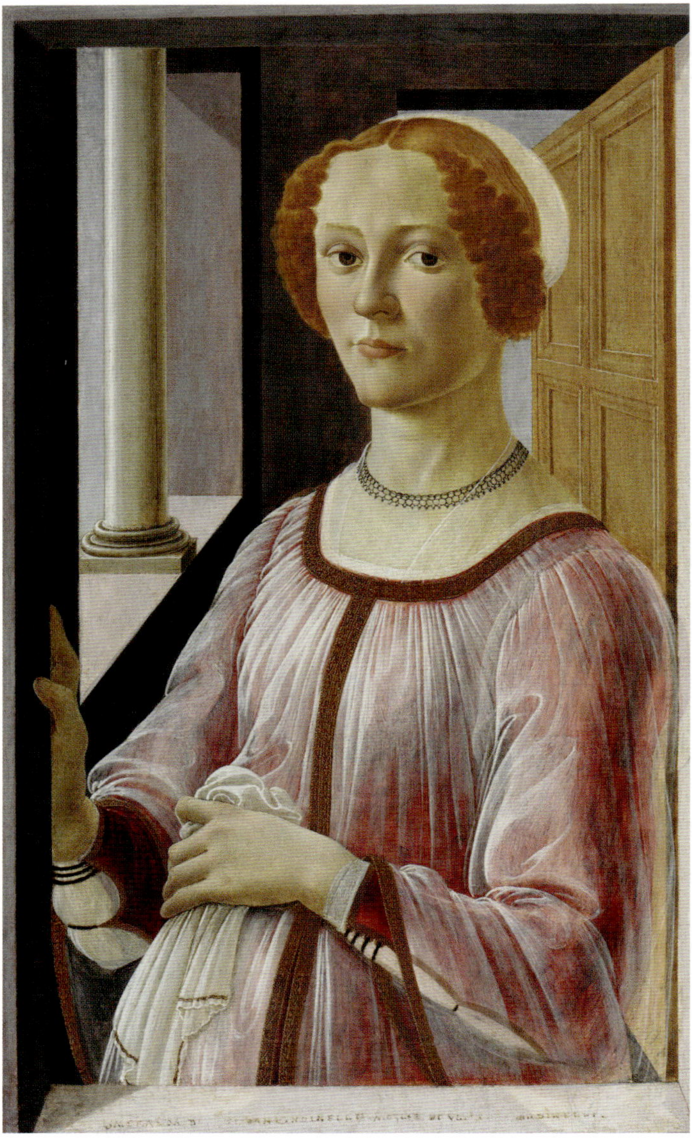

57 Botticelli, *Portrait of a Lady called Smeralda Bandinelli*, *c.* 1470–75, tempera on panel.

to another and across a wide range of media. Botticelli was far from unique in resorting to representational formulae. He was exceptionally gifted, however, in his capacity to adapt one figure to different context without conveying a sense of repetition.

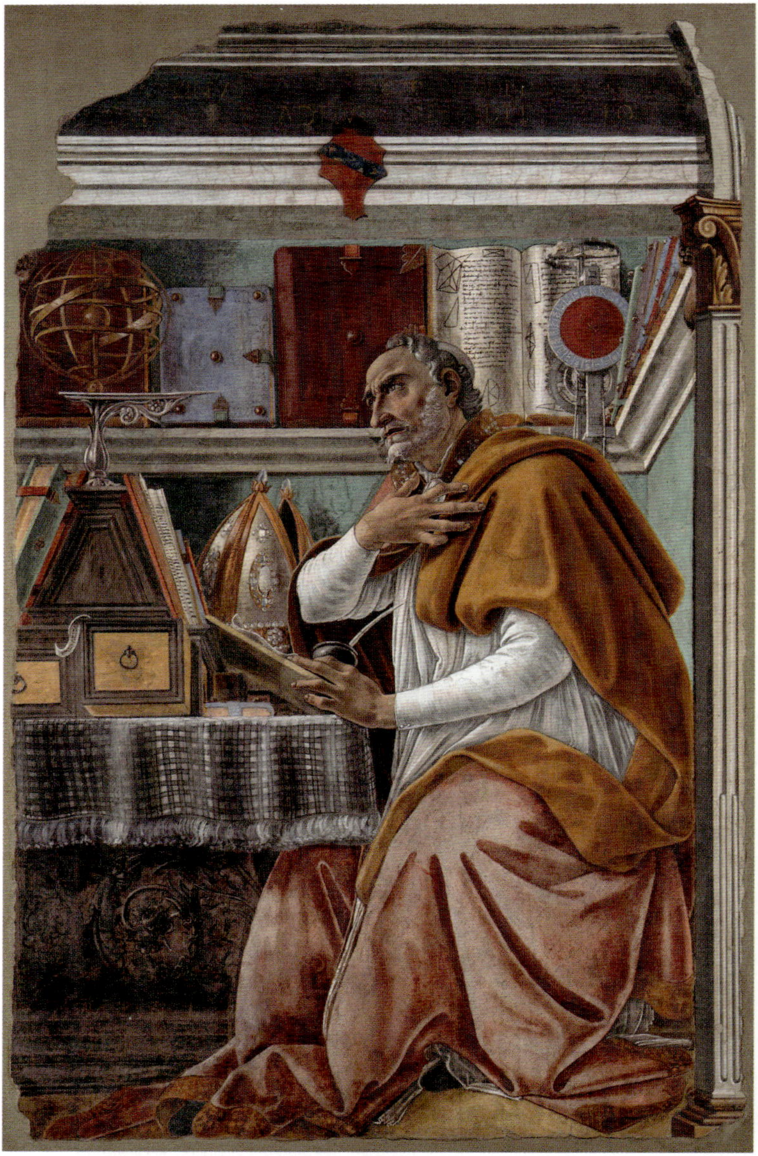

58 Botticelli, *St Augustine*, 1480, fresco in the Chiesa di Ognissanti, Florence.

FIVE

Changing Style, Adapting to the Market

It is often rehearsed that Botticelli's artistic development saw a brutal and dramatic change that coincided with the beginning of the violent and apocalyptic preaching of Girolamo Savonarola, from the monk's return to Florence in 1489 until his death in 1498. Although this observation is undeniable, it cannot go unnoticed that Botticelli changed his style several times before this dark period. When he reached his stylistic maturity, in the late 1470s, Botticelli had developed in parallel a great versatility and capacity to adapt to a changing market. His powerful inventiveness and attention to demand doubtless helped Botticelli to widen and enrich his visual vocabulary while enabling him to diversify his output. It is therefore possible to identify four main groups within Botticelli's oeuvre that respond to different tastes developed by clientele at different moments. This journey starts with the most prestigious commission of Botticelli's whole career: the decoration of the Sistine Chapel, the papal private chapel in the Vatican, a palace-state within the city of Rome.

Sometime before October 1481, Botticelli set forth to Rome. His summons there resulted from an array of circumstances and confirmed his status as one of the leading artists in Florence, especially close to the Medici household. It was quite customary at the time to send artists on diplomatic and political missions in order to reassess an alliance or ease underlying tensions between antagonist rulers and Lorenzo de' Medici rapidly became an expert in this specific strategy of persuasion.[1] When Botticelli and his fellow artists, namely Domenico Ghirlandaio, Cosimo Rosselli and Pietro Perugino, arrived in Rome, the new papal chapel, later known as the Sistine Chapel (from the name of the Pope Sixtus IV, who commissioned it), had been entirely rebuilt between 1475 and 1481. The space was therefore devoid of any decoration, apart from a starry sky depicted on the ceiling. This decoration was covered in 1508–12 by Michelangelo's celebrated scenes of the Book of the Genesis, with figures of prophets and sybils, but a drawing in the Uffizi is believed to record the original decoration. It is attributed to Piermatteo d'Amelia (*c.* 1445–1509), who had trained together with Botticelli in Filippo Lippi's workshop.[2] Michelangelo's monumental *Last Judgement*, which covers the altar wall, was completed much later, in 1541, replacing Perugino's fifteenth-century frescoed altarpiece as well as two narrative scenes. The programme of the decorations was devised by the pope and his court, and was meant to glorify and justify the pope's spiritual authority under the divine aegis of Moses and Christ.[3] Eight scenes from the life of Moses were to be represented on the middle-left register of the altar wall, the left wall and the right side of the entrance wall, while corresponding stories from the life of Christ were to be painted on the opposite sides. Each scene bears at the bottom an inscription in Latin identifying the specific episode represented. In addition, the painters were asked to depict the first thirty popes in the upper register, and large illusionary plain hangings in the lower register under each scene, somewhat saturating the whole chapel with images.

As we have already seen, it was not uncommon for a team of artists to collaborate on the decoration of a dedicated space. Yet in the case of the Sistine Chapel, the scale of the task and speediness of its completion (the original delivery date was set on 15 March 1482) raises questions about the harmonization of their styles and the sequential organization of the work itself, which could have been either done concomitantly or in consecutive sessions. The two surviving contracts (dated 27 October 1481 and 17 January 1482) do not really help to resolve this enigma. Recent research and the latest campaign of restoration have suggested that each artist and his team actually painted their allocated scenes consecutively, following the order of the narrative.[4] While the scenes are firmly attributed to specific artists, the attribution of the figures of the popes is more problematic and still subject to debate owing to the overall stylistic harmonization and given that the artists were not necessarily made responsible for the popes sitting above the frescoes they were allocated. The depiction of the upper register where the popes were to be represented was instead probably dependent on the availability of the scaffolding, which was erected at various heights at different time.[5] In total, Botticelli was entrusted with the execution of three scenes, including the curtains below them, and between nine and eleven figures of popes.[6]

The work seems to have begun with the life of Christ on the south wall (right-hand side of the altar). The first scene to be completed was Perugino's *Baptism of Christ*. Botticelli

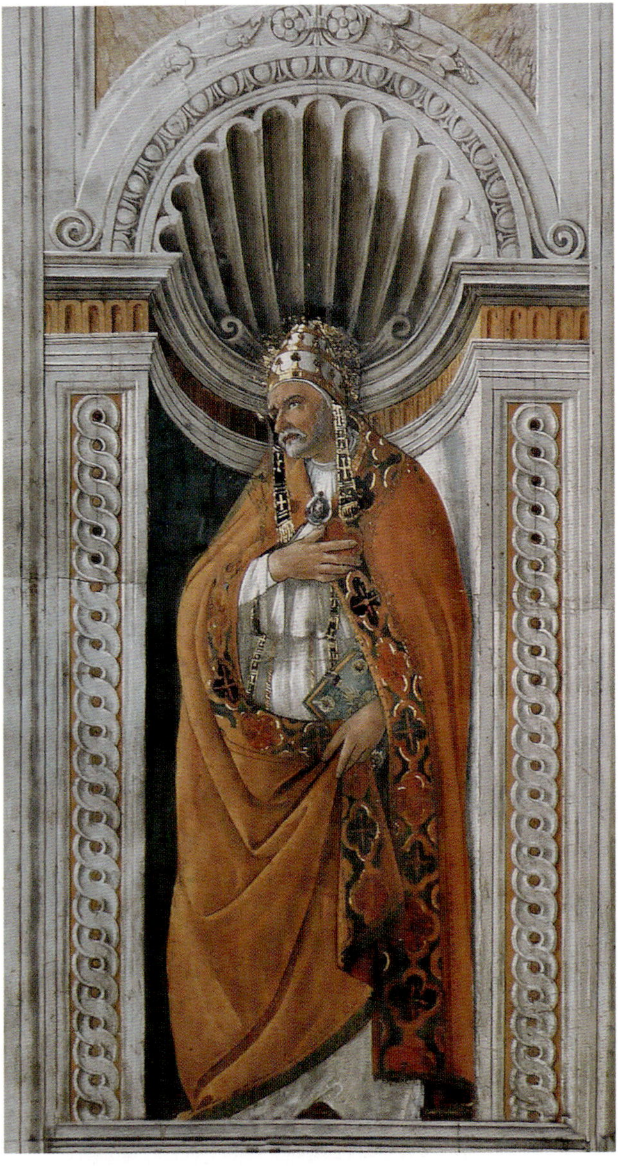

59 Botticelli, *St Sixtus II*, 1481, fresco in the Sistine Chapel.

followed this with the *Temptation of Christ*; after that came the *Calling of the Apostles* by Ghirlandaio, the *Sermon on the Mount* by Rosselli, the *Charge to Peter* by Perugino and the *Last Supper* by Rosselli. Although this was not Botticelli's first attempt at fresco painting, this initial scene took him the longest to complete. He had spent some of his years in training assisting Filippo Lippi with the frescoes in Prato's cathedral, and had already provided, in competition with Ghirlandaio, a *St Augustine in His Study* (illus. 58) for the church of Ognissanti (the same cartoon would be reused to execute the portrait of Pope Sixtus II, illus. 59),[7] as well as an *Annunciation* for the loggia to the front of the church of San Martino in the hospital of Santa Maria della Scala in Florence.[8] 'Fresco' painting implies that the wall should remain wet all the time: the painter therefore has to work in sections, each of which must be completed in one single day. As Vasari explains, '[the painting] must not be left till the day's portion is finished.'[9] This apportioning is called *giornata* ('day' in English) and was used to calculate the amount of time spent to complete a fresco.

Botticelli needed 63 *giornate* (compare to the average 45 *giornate* spent by the other painters on each of their respective scenes) to complete his first scene, the *Temptation of Christ*. This suggests that he put a significant care into the design, which was articulated over three planes: a foreground that depicts the sacrifice, set in front of the altar; the Temple in the middle ground; and the three temptations of Christ (recognizable by his red dress and blue mantle) relegated to the distant background and upper register following a compositional strategy already employed by the artist in previous years. The sacrifice is depicted here as a thankful ritual, during

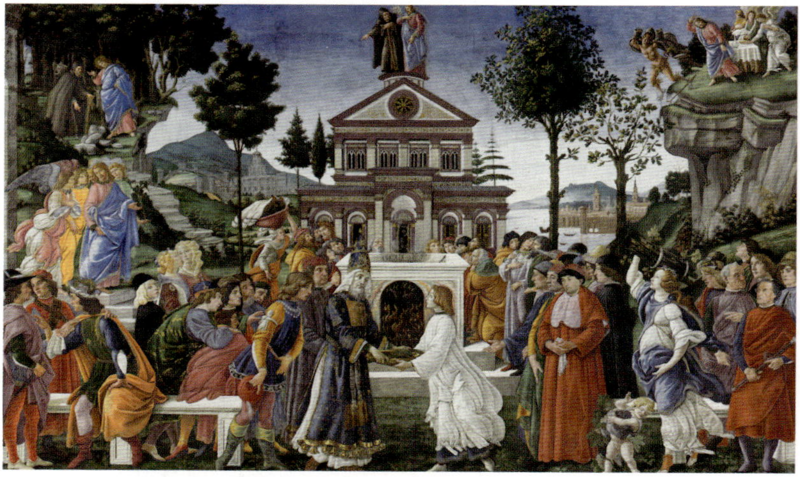

which a young boy, miraculously healed of leprosy by Christ, makes an offering to God. Such scenes typically involve a high priest, an altar and a blazing fire and include an offering of some kind. The edifice in the centre was identified as the Hospital of Santo Spirito, near the Vatican, the facade of which was commissioned by Sixtus IV from the Florentine Baccio Pontelli (*c.* 1450–1492). A gallery of portraits completes the scenes, among which include identified members of the papal court such as Girolamo Riario and Giuliano della Rovere (Sixtus IV's nephew and future Pope Julius II, respectively). Botticelli seems to have also introduced in this scene members of his own milieu: some scholars have identified a portrait of Filippino Lippi with a self-portrait of the artist as the two standing men on the left-hand corner.[10] If this identification is correct, Botticelli was certainly responding to Filippino's concomitant work in the Brancacci chapel in Florence. There, as already mentioned, Filippino

60 Botticelli, *Temptations of Christ*, 1481–2, fresco in the Sistine Chapel.

had introduced his self-portrait in the company of his former master and lifelong friend, Botticelli.

Sandro's frescoes in the Sistine Chapel contain a few 'wandering motifs' such as the woman in the middle ground with two cocks in a basket, who echoes Judith's maid in an earlier painting (see illus. 10). The same type is shown in reverse, with the lady holding faggots on her head in the foreground. This motif, together with the child holding grapes, derives from sculptural examples. The lady is reminiscent of a statue called *Dovizia*, executed by Donatello and installed in the Mercato Vecchio in Florence around 1430. Now lost, it is known through many replicas, notably the glazed terracotta statuettes made by the workshop of the Florentine sculptor Giovanni della Robbia (1469–1529/30). The young child, on the other hand, derives from a Hellenistic prototype known through a Roman copy, which Botticelli probably saw during his stay in Rome.[11] This figure is among the known antique models that would recur in Botticelli's oeuvre hereafter. In this composition, Botticelli astutely fused his own Florentine vernacular culture with that of the papal court drawn to antiquity, a specific combination that he would carry across his compositions in the chapel.

The second scene was the quickest to achieve, requiring only 45 *giornate*. It represents the temptations of Moses and was made on the wall opposite his first scene, therefore constituting its counterpart.[12] This design is perhaps the least balanced and harmonious of the three, probably owing to the large number of episodes – seven in total – articulated within this single space. It is also possible that Botticelli was pressed for time and needed to compensate for having spent too many

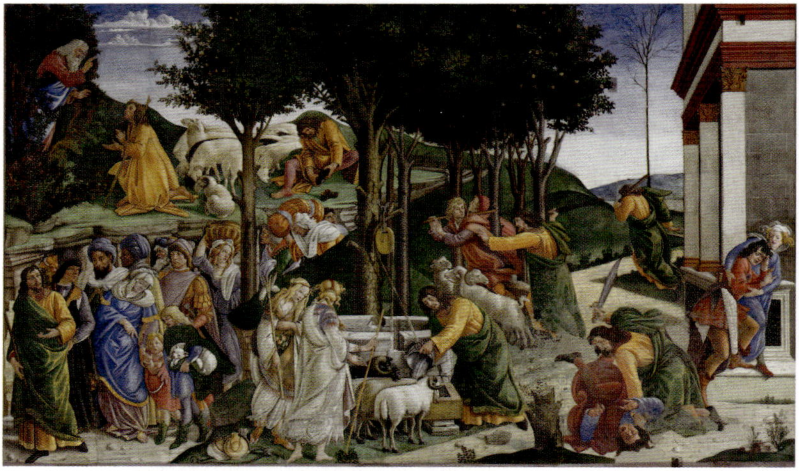

days on the previous scene while working towards a tight deadline. The figure of Moses, in his yellow robe wrapped in a green mantle, is depicted seven times around the well and its pulley, acting as a focal point at the base of a group of trees that operates as a structural device for the whole composition. The strategy of using the vegetation like an architectural device to structure the composition was perhaps inaugurated here and carried over in later works such as the series of Nastagio degli Onesti spalliere, as already seen.[13] On each side, the episodes unfold in a circular movement from right to left, while a dense group of figures is stacked on the left-hand side. The episodes depicted are the killing of the Egyptian; the fight with the shepherds to defend the daughters of Jethro; and the vision of the burning bush, as described in the Book of Exodus. Last, Moses is shown leading his people to cross the Red Sea. However, there is no real sense of perspective: all the figures, whether in the foreground or background, have pretty

61 Botticelli, *Temptations of Moses*, 1481–2, fresco in the Sistine Chapel.

much the same dimensions and the scene unfolds following a tapestry-like composition. Just off-centre are two young maidens dressed in white (the daughters of Jethro). One of them, seen in profile, is modelled on the Minerva/Pallas type but in reverse, while the lady holding a bowl on her head is another recurrence of Judith's maid. The right-hand side of the composition shows a number of exaggerated gestures, expressing intense emotions of anger and fear in anticipation of what would be the dominant feature of the last scene.

Botticelli's last fresco, the *Conturbation of Moses*, took him slightly more time, 55 *giornate*, and presents a simpler composition: this time the scene, set on one single plane, is subdivided into three groups corresponding to three episodes of the story, rarely represented in art. It shows the punishment of three high priests (Khora, Dathan and Abiram) as described in the Book of Numbers, for they had led the revolt against Moses and Abraham. Moses is still represented in a yellow robe

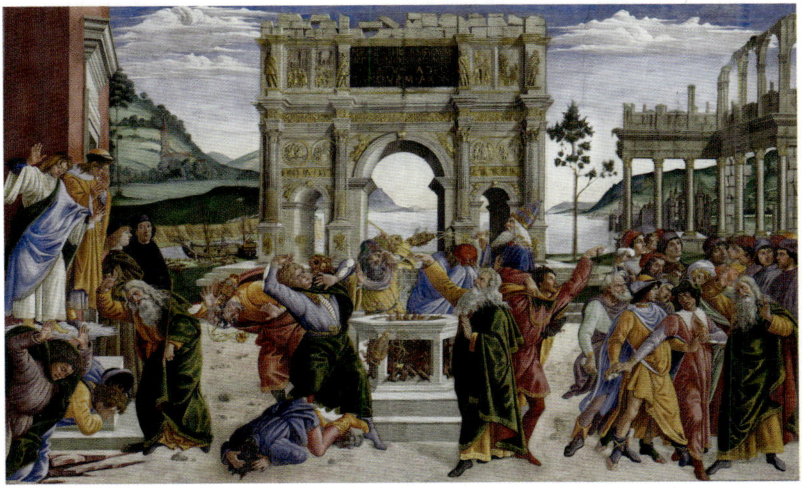

62 Botticelli, *Conturbation of Moses*, 1481–2, fresco in the Sistine Chapel.

wrapped in a green mantle, but he is now an old man with white hair and a beard, a type that Botticelli borrowed from previous compositions. One of the rebels, with his thurible (a censer traditionally suspended from chains, in which incense is burned during worship services) turned against him, appears to be a re-elaboration of the Egyptian clothed in red who was killed in the first scene; his swollen cheeks echo those of Zephyr in the *Primavera* (illus. 63) and *The Birth of Venus* (illus. 64). In the background is depicted the Arch of Constantine, which would reappear in the last panel of the Nastalgio degli Onesti series, while the classical ruins on the right recall those that structured earlier compositions, such as the Adoration of the Magi, and would be reused in later works. The Arch of Constantine, situated between the Colosseum and the Palatine Hill in Rome, was probably copied after the motif and adapted with minor variations to fit within this composition. Vasari

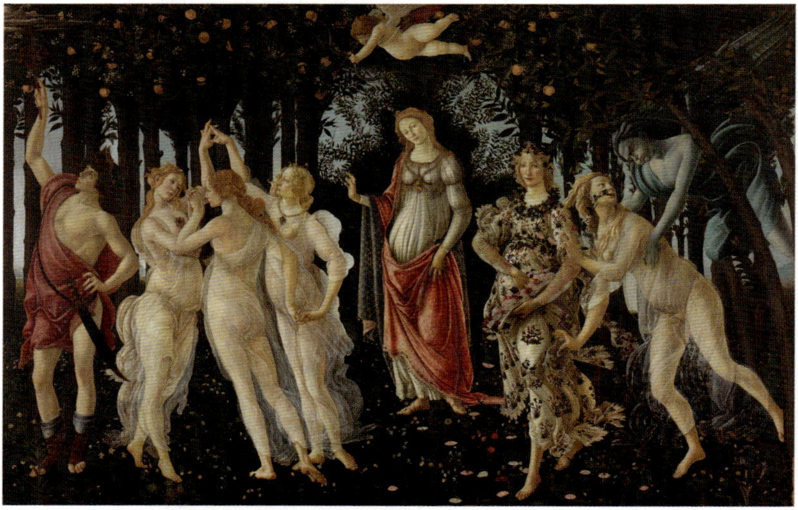

63 Botticelli, *Spring* (*Primavera*), *c.* 1480, tempera on wood.

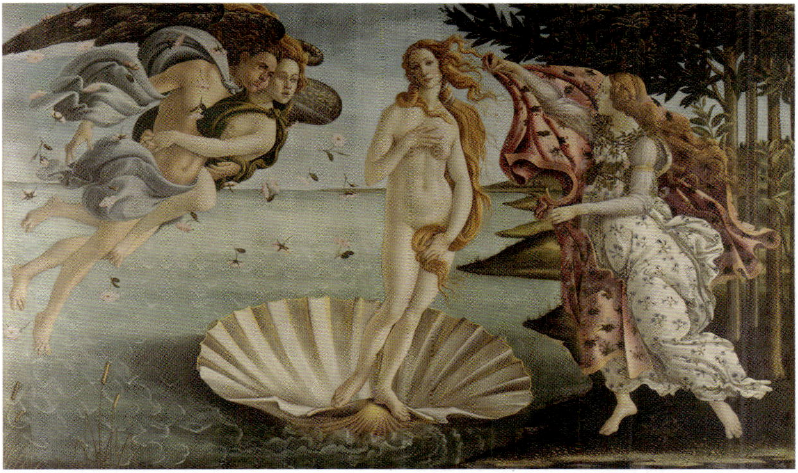

reports that during his stay in Rome, Domenico Ghirlandaio went through the city and sketched all the monuments and vestiges.[14] There is no reason to believe that Botticelli did not do the same, especially since it was during his stay in Rome that he started enriching his visual repertory with antique motifs. In this last scene, Botticelli completed his evocation of ancient Rome by including visual references to his own time, first the Renaissance palace on the left and then a second series of portraits, among which has been recognized another self-portrait, and possibly further members of the papal court.[15]

From the original ensemble, which comprised sixteen large scenes (eight for each cycle), only twelve have survived, distributed on each side of the altar wall. While looking at these remaining scenes, one is bewitched by the harmonious spectacle they convey. Their common format, with figures designed at the same scale, is further enhanced by the continuous horizon

64 Botticelli, *Birth of Venus*, 1478–82, tempera on canvas.

line between each fresco, while the overall palette, with its Quattrocento characteristic of cool and acidic hues pervaded by fine gilding, has regained its original splendour during the latest campaign of restoration. Some elements and figure-types even recur in each of the other scenes. For instance, the Arch of Constantine is reproduced in Perugino's *Charge to Peter*, located on the opposite wall to the *Conturbation of Moses*, while the lady holding a basket on her head wanders around. All the scenes illustrating the life of Christ follow a centralized plan based on two to three figures standing out in the middle of the foreground, while the rest of the compositions unfold symmetrically around them. On the north wall, while the same format is followed by Botticelli in his two scenes, this overall harmonization is less obvious, perhaps owing to the time pressure and the last-minute arrival of Luca Signorelli and Bartolomeo della Gatta, who joined the team most likely to speed up the process.[16] The works were finally completed between April and May 1482, and Botticelli was back in Florence by the summer.

While harmonizing his style with that of his fellow artists in the Sistine Chapel, Botticelli managed to make a significant stylistic development. His first and last scenes show the transformation from a multi-scenic composition, which had been his compositional strategy in most of his previous works, to a simpler articulation of the space, likened by some to a classical stage setting.[17] Coincidently, it was during this very period that classical theatre was being rediscovered in Florence, more specifically between 1476 and 1488 at the instigations of Lorenzo de' Medici and his circle.[18] The Roman commission therefore represents an important milestone in Botticelli's stylistic development, which helps to date the execution of his two most celebrated mythological scenes: *Primavera* and the *Birth of Venus*.[19]

The second group comprises the only four mythological works Botticelli produced. Paradoxically, they are Botticelli's best-known paintings today, exclusively made for the Medici and their circle. These are the aforementioned *Primavera* and the *Birth of Venus*, *Pallas and the Centaur* and *Mars and Venus*. Botticelli also executed two fresco decorations of mythological subjects at the turn of the 1480s but these were later destroyed. The critical literature on these paintings is vast and in this instance we need only to recall that their respective iconographical programme was devised by scholars and poets working for the Medici, in particular Lorenzo di Pierfrancesco de' Medici (1463–1503). He was the second cousin and ward of Lorenzo the Magnificent, a prodigious young man who would become a refined humanist and Botticelli's most important patron during the last two decades of the fifteenth century.[20] Consequently, the mythological scenes result from a combination of Neoplatonist themes developed by Marsilio Ficino, as well as vernacular poetry and classical literature, revived in particular by Poliziano, who had been appointed professor of rhetoric at the Studio (Florence University) in 1480 after a few years spent in the Medici house as the tutor of Lorenzo's sons.[21] Based on their respective designs, *Primavera* is usually dated before Botticelli's departure to Rome and the *Birth of Venus* after his subsequent return. However, in light of Botticelli's dramatic reassessment of the spatial organization of the picture plane during his Roman stay, this dating should perhaps be reconsidered.

Both works echo some of the compositional solutions developed by the painter in the Sistine Chapel. They are enriched by a number of visual quotations pertaining to the antique, but also to Botticelli's own vernacular language. Although they were not conceived as a pair, both *Primavera* and the *Birth of Venus* unfold around the central figure of Venus, who is slightly set back in the middle ground while the rest of the figures are distributed in the immediate foreground. This specific frieze-like distribution of the figures in the foreground recalls the last scene depicted by Botticelli in the Sistine Chapel, *Conturbation of Moses*. They guide the gaze of the viewer from the right along the descending movement of Zephyr, the West Wind, about to abduct Chloris, who turns into Flora, goddess of the flowering of plants. The central, slightly elevated position of Venus acts as the focal point of the composition, while the eye is drawn down towards the Three Graces, themselves engaged in a round dance, to ascend again with Mercury, who looks up and sweeps away a light cloud with his caduceus.[22]

This unprecedented composition certainly reflects artistic debates of the period. Alberti had recommended in his treatise *On Painting* to represent the flowing movements of the body, the gentle effect of the breeze in the hair and dress, the controlled but imperatively varied gestures of figures.[23] The spectacle offered by the civic feasts, notably the one celebrating spring, is another factor that undoubtedly influenced such a sensitive and receptive mind as Botticelli.[24] Over the course of three days, between 29 April and 1 May, the Florentines celebrated Calendimaggio, a medieval feast marking the renewal season of spring as the realm of Venus, goddess of love and beauty. It included (and still does today) processions with an abundant distribution of flowers, a series of competitive events and the election of a 'Madonna Primavera' (Queen of Spring), chosen from the young maidens of the city.[25] The setting of *Primavera*, one of the most luxurious ever depicted by the artist (with about 138 plants and flowers identified) seems to recall this important ritual.[26]

In addition, the panel overflows with new quotations. The Three Graces derived from the well-known Roman sculpture group of the same name later installed in the Piccolomini library in Siena, while Mercury is reminiscent of Donatello's statue of David, then in the courtyard of the Medici Palace, itself the model of Verrocchio's sculpture of David, installed in 1476 at the entrance of the Sala dei Gigli in the Palazzo Vecchio. Zephyr, on the other hand, appears to be based on the so-called Tazza Farnese, an ancient cameo, which was at the time in Lorenzo de' Medici's collection of antique gems (now in the National Archaeological Museum, Naples). All these figures would reappear in later works, as well as Venus and Flora, who recall the type of the early Judith (in reverse) and announce Minerva with their long right arm and counterpoise. It was possibly as part of the creative process that Botticelli executed what is considered today to be one of the most beautiful drawings of Quattrocento Florence: described as an *Allegory of Abundance*, it might have formed part of Giorgio Vasari's *Libro de' Disegni*. The two daughters of Jethro from the Sistine Chapel's *Temptations of Moses* echo with some variations the group of the Graces (with the exclusion of the third figure on the far right), one of them being similarly represented from the back. The many stylistic correspondences and fundamentally new spatial arrangements suggest that the execution of *Primavera* might have been closer in date to the Roman commission than previously thought.

The *Birth of Venus*, on the other hand, is generally dated after Botticelli's return to Florence and belongs, like *Pallas and the Centaur*, to a small group of paintings on canvas rather than on panel, as was more customary in Florence.[27] Botticelli's painting captures the mythological birth of the goddess of love and beauty, who rises from the sea in the form of a fully grown woman. The symbolic meaning of the *Birth of Venus* is another subject of great debate, but above all a Neoplatonist interpretation dominates: Venus 'rising from the sea' ('anadyomene' in Greek) is understood as the embodiment of the celestial Venus, a manifestation of the divine. This interpretation might explain why the pagan goddess shares the same beautiful features as the Virgin in Botticelli's art. Following the conceptual line set forth by Marsilio Ficino, Venus and the Virgin are two beautiful manifestations of the same divine love. This idea must have appealed to the artist, who had already developed a single type of idealized female beauty to transpose and adapt to secular and sacred contexts alike. In addition, Botticelli was at the time already engaged in illustrating Dante's *Divine Comedy*, which, as already seen, follows a similar logic. In 1481 Cristoforo Landino published his commentary of the famous poem with illustrations attributed to Baccio Baldini after Botticelli's designs but of 'inferior style, because the plates were badly engraved', as reports Vasari.[28] Another incentive to Botticelli must have been the testimony that Apelles himself also painted the same subject twice, one painting being damaged and later destroyed during Apelles' lifetime, the other left unfinished.[29]

Compared to *Primavera*, the *Birth of Venus* marks a further step towards a new, simplified set-up while using similar model-types. We encounter Zephyrus from *Primavera* again, this time in an embrace with Chloris. The arrangement reflects the sculptural source of the Tazza Farnese even more closely. One of the Horae (Hours), the female figure who welcomes Venus on the shore, is the mirror image of the Grace near the God Mercury in *Primavera*. Venus herself is based on an ancient marble statue called the Venus of Cnidos. Attributed to the great ancient sculptor Praxiteles, the statue was destroyed during antiquity but is known through a series of Roman copies, the most famous perhaps being the so-called Medici Venus (now in the Uffizi). This was probably not Botticelli's direct model, as the work appears in later inventories, but her modest pose, described as 'Venus pudica' as she hides her pubis and breasts, was well known. The sculptor Giovanni Pisano (*c.* 1250–after 1314), for instance, repeated her stance in a statue of Temperance, or Chastity, in the pulpit of the Cathedral on Pisa (still in situ).[30] The *Birth of Venus* confirms Botticelli's new artistic vision, which favoured nearly life-sized figures brought into the foreground, a trait that would dominate his production of paintings of the 1480s.[31]

Pallas and the Centaur and the enigmatic spalliera traditionally identified as *Mars and Venus* belong to this category of works (see illus. 49 and 65). Both derive from a Roman stone sarcophagus showing *Bacchus Discovering Ariadne at Naxos* and other bacchanalian scenes in low relief, which Botticelli probably copied in Rome before returning to Florence.[32] *Mars and Venus* is particularly interesting as it sheds light on another type of production, typically Florentine, which might have also

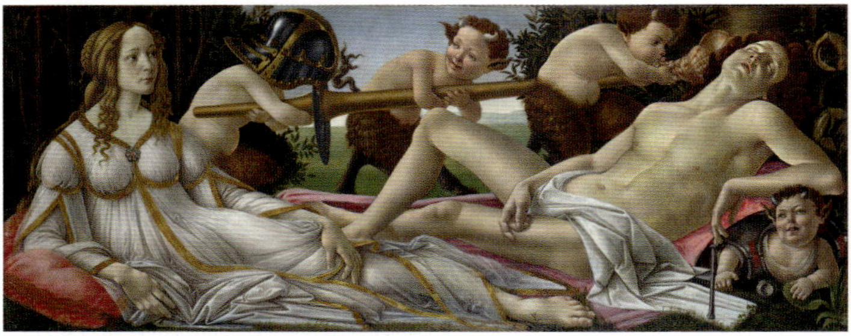

inspired Botticelli. Wedding chests (*cassoni* or *forzieri*) were often decorated with painted scenes, including the inside lid. In this hidden spot, almost life-sized figures of recumbent naked men and women were represented, their elbows leaning on cushions, a detail reproduced in Botticelli's painting. These were propitious images, meant for the eyes of newlyweds only as they were traditionally thought to stimulate sexual activity and hence guarantee the dynastic line. The great beauty of these figures was equally believed to help conceive beautiful children by means of a reciprocity enacted by the act of viewing.[33] Generally dated 1483–4, Botticelli's spalliera was itself most likely a wedding gift (perhaps for a member of the Vespucci family) meant to be set in the bedchamber of the spouses.[34] Botticelli's remarkable invention may therefore represent a subtle elevation of the genre, combining together antique sources such as the Roman vestiges with vernacular imagery.

There are today three surviving partial replicas of the *Birth of Venus* (illus. 66, 67 and 68). It is probably within that decade that Botticelli extracted the figure of Venus from the celebrated mythological composition and reproduced it standing on a ledge against a plain dark background. The simplified

65 Botticelli, *Mars and Venus*, c. 1483–4, tempera and oil on poplar.

setting of these replicas likely meant that they could reach a wider public. These paintings can probably be identified as the 'many female nudes' (*femmine ignude assai*) that Vasari described and possibly saw in the patrician houses of Florence. We do not know anything about their commission, or how they were displayed in the home, but it is possible that they were visible only to a limited audience of relatives. The versions now in Berlin and Turin were certainly transferred from the same cartoon by the master himself using the method of *calco*. The third replica, however, differs significantly from the other two; it appears to be a much later version, copied freehand by a less gifted follower. Anecdotally, further variations of approximately the same dimensions were executed by fellow artists. Lorenzo di Credi painted a similar *Venus*, which clearly derived from Botticelli's design (illus. 69), while another version was made in 1512 by Lorenzo Costa (1460–1535), a painter active in Ferrara. These two paintings attest to the success of Botticelli's innovative design and the breath of his influence beyond his native city of Florence.

The dark, plain background, which characterizes Botticelli's series of Venus, also coincides with a stylistic shift in his portraiture, starting with two male portraits from the mid-1480s.[35] Patrizia Zambrano relates this new phase to a passage in Leon Battista Alberti's *On Painting*, which praises 'those faces which seem to stand out from the picture as if they were sculpted'.[36] In accordance with these precepts, Botticelli developed his interest in the sculptural rendering of painted portraits further, with an enigmatic work (illus. 70) probably executed in the same period as the multiple Venus.[37] Long interpreted as an idealized portrait of Giuliano de' Medici's

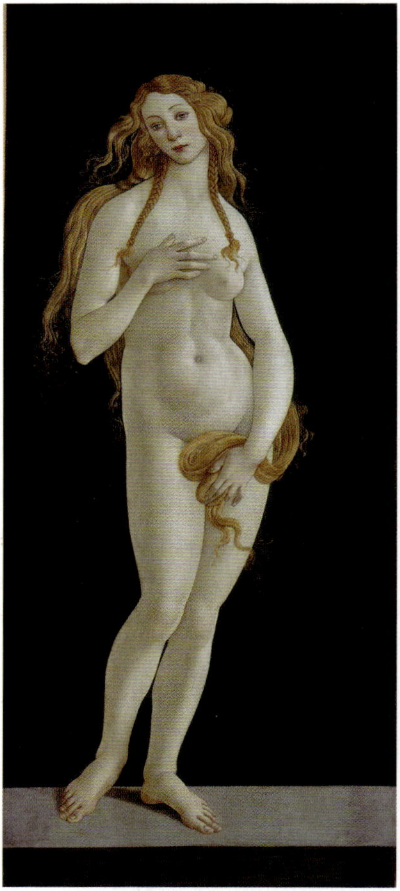

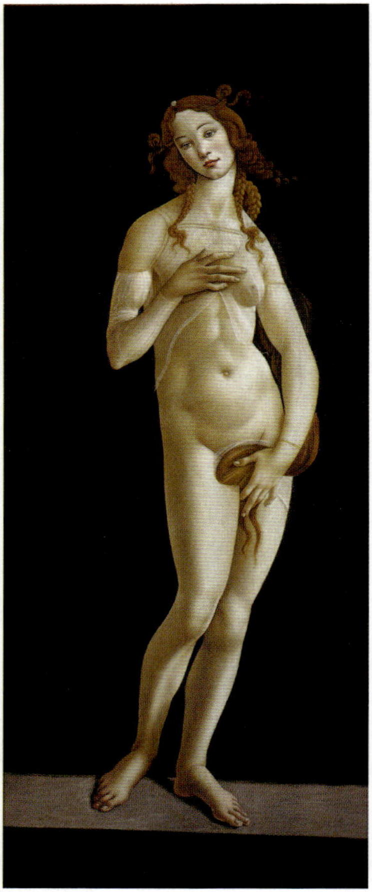

beloved, Simonetta Vespucci, who died prematurely in 1476, this painting can be likened to a veritable cameo as it echoes the colour scheme and plasticity of the famous gem represented on the figure's chest. This gem reproduces, in reverse, the famous carnelian *Sigillo di Nerone* ('Nero's seal') attributed to the ancient Greek sculptor Dioskourides and acquired by

66 Botticelli, *Venere pudica*, *c.* 1490, tempera on wood.
67 Botticelli and workshop, *Venere pudica*, *c.* 1490, tempera on wood.

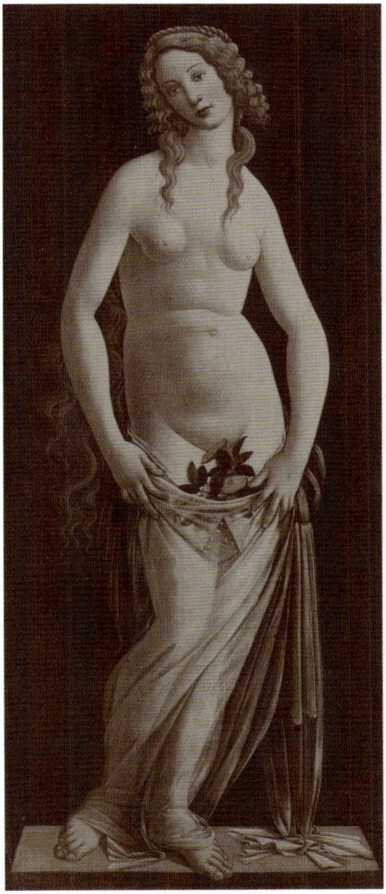

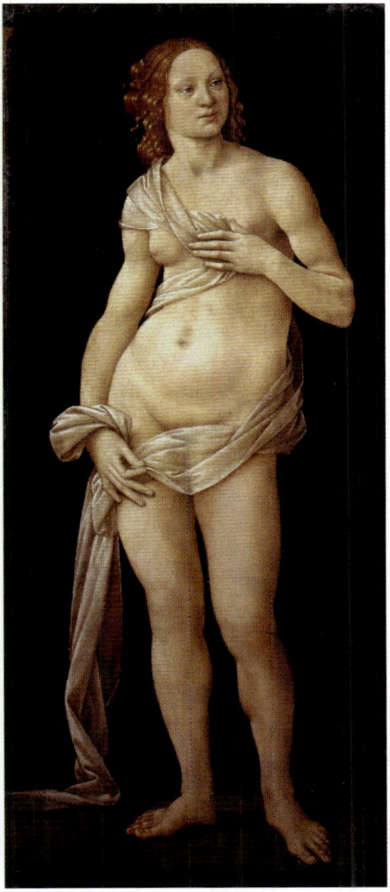

Lorenzo de' Medici in Venice in 1487. The gem was already known in Florence through several replicas, one of which was possibly made by Lorenzo Ghiberti in the first half of the fifteenth century.[38] With this painting, which appears on a much larger scale than contemporary portrayals, Botticelli blurs the boundaries between a real portrait (Simonetta

68 Botticelli's workshop, *Venere pudica*, *c.* 1490, tempera on wood.
69 Lorenzo di Credi, *Venere pudica*, *c.* 1490–94, oil on canvas.

Vespucci?) and an idealized, beautiful head deriving from the Petrarchian tradition, two genres much in vogue in Renaissance Florence.[39] Like the series of Venus, Botticelli's 'portrait' can be construed as a celebration of Florentine beauty transformed into a vernacular and truly 'Botticellian' type, through the imitation and revival of an ancient model. Through his creative process, Botticelli managed to develop a highly personal style, immediately recognizable and yet always new.

Over the course of the 1480s and '90s Botticelli also received commissions for a number of large altarpieces representing Holy Conversation, for which he explored new compositional solutions. These form the fourth group of our study. The aforementioned Bardi and San Barnaba altarpieces, for example, the latter commissioned by the Arte dei Medici e Speziali in the late 1480s, inaugurate a new era of highly refined architectural space enlivened by sophisticated features in a slightly darker palette. Botticelli also paid particular attention, as always, to the effect of perspective, carefully calculated so as to allow for the painting to be seen at a certain height and great distance and stand out among the other paintings present in the church.[40] The San Barnaba altarpiece borrows figures from the artist's own repertoire but also from his former pupil Filippino Lippi. Sandro probably looked attentively at Filippino's altarpiece for the Palazzo della Signoria completed after 1487. The two paintings share a similar, highly sophisticated, ornamental setting, suggesting a continuous dialogue between the two artists. Botticelli reproduced in the upper background of the San Barnaba altarpiece the two tondi depicting the Annunciation that Filippino had executed in 1483–4 for the city hall (Palazzo Pubblico) of San Gimignano,

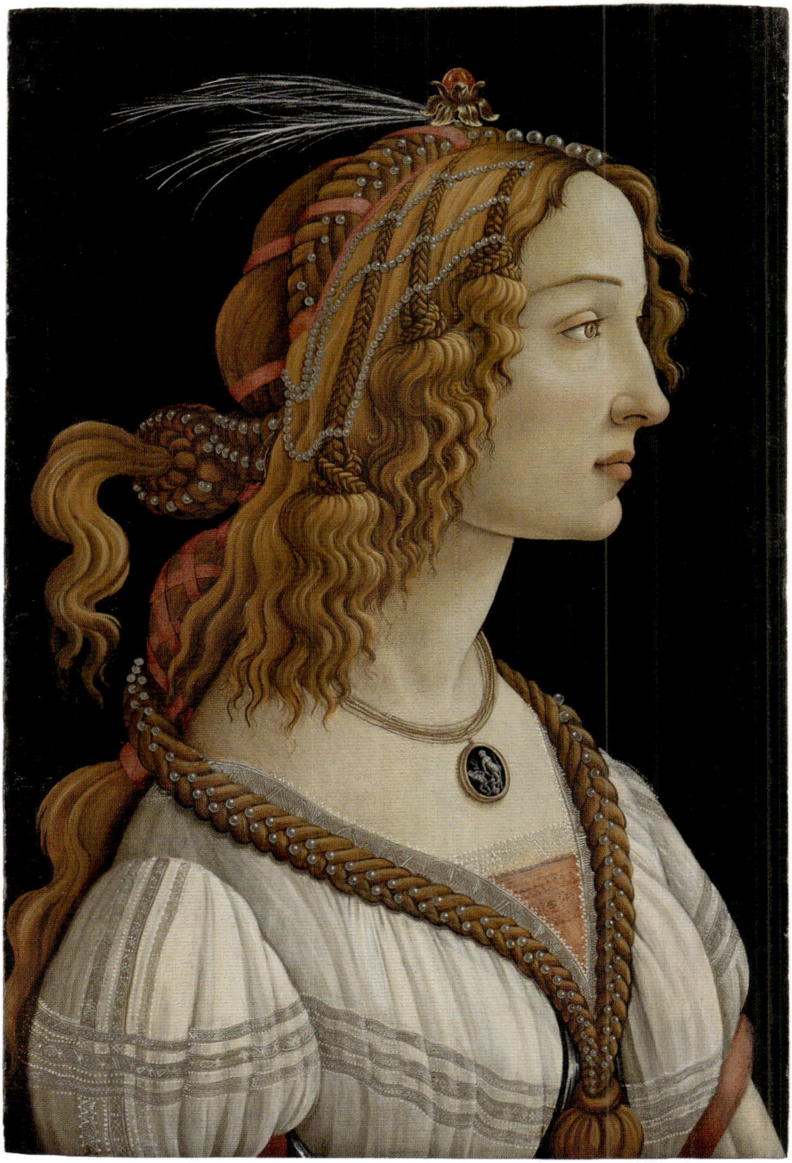

70 Botticelli, *Idealized Portrait of a Woman (La Bella Simonetta)*, *c.* 1480–85, tempera on wood.

themselves reminiscent of Botticelli's own design.[41] This renewed artistic dialogue after Filippino left Botticelli's workshop and became an independent master would continue in the following years.

Botticelli's adherence to Savonarola's ideas remains an open question. While his art of the 1490s may suggest an apparent approval for this severe reformative movement, the few surviving documents argue for the opposite. We know that Botticelli's brother, Simone, was a convinced 'piagnone' (as Savonarola's followers were called at the time) but he never mentions Sandro in his *Cronaca*, a detailed account of these turbulent events and their aftermaths covering the period 1489–1509. Botticelli did not sign either of the two petitions in defence of the friar against the pope's condemnation and, on the contrary, had welcomed in his workshop the leader of Savonarola's opponents, Doffo Spini. It was customary at the time to find gatherings of artists working in different media in Florentine workshops, mingling to discuss a variety of subjects as Vasari describes in the life of the sculptor Baccio d'Agnolo. Botticelli probably needed time to reflect in company of others, as many Florentine scholars – who formerly embodied the humanist *renovatio* that had inspired, among others, his great mythological pictures – had become fervent followers of the friar; it was also at the request of Lorenzo de' Medici himself that Savonarola returned to Florence.[42]

The large altarpiece in the church of San Marco (see illus. 51), commissioned from Botticelli by the Arte della Seta or Por Santa Maria specifically for the chapel of Sant'Alò (or Eligio), patron saint of goldsmiths, marked a new turning point in Botticelli's artistic development. It demonstrates his attempt to respond to the changing taste of the time or, according to some, even anticipating it. Completed by 1492, this painting marks a return to traditional features, such as the gold background, and a new stylistic development. Cited by some as one of the first examples of altarpieces divided into two distinct spheres, Botticelli's invention offers a neat demarcation between the Queen of Heaven in the upper register and the saints set in the lower half, as they are traditionally considered to mediate between the human world and the divine sphere.[43] Furthermore, Botticelli articulates the space without the help of any architectural device, but relies entirely on the placement and scale of the figures to structure the composition. This was an important innovation. Among the four saints of imposing stature in the lower register, the figure of St John the Evangelist, modelled on the elderly Moses in the Sistine Chapel fresco, stands out. St John is holding a book, alluding to his writings on the Apocalypse, upon which Savonarola based his inaugural sermons, preached in the adjacent convent of San Marco as early as August 1489.[44] Although Botticelli's rivals, such as Piero del Pollaiolo and Domenico Ghirlandaio, had developed similar compositions,[45] Botticelli's formula stands out with its the prolific use of gold applied with a highly refined technique, which enhances the divine character of the scene set in the upper register. This bold move at a time when such a feature was seen as considerably out of fashion, as well as the designs of the Virgin and God the Father, were probably inspired by Sandro's memory of Filippo Lippi's own version of the subject in the apse of Spoleto cathedral. There Lippi had painted one of the most ravishing coronation scenes, set against a rich gold background and enlivened by a retinue of angels.

Such extensive use of gold also possibly alluded to the main material used by the goldsmiths, commissioners of the altarpiece. Indeed, the two versions of the same composition executed later for the Badia of San Giusto in Volterra and the church of San Francesco in Montevarchi do not contain any gold and show a greater intervention of the workshop (see illus. 52, 53).[46] The altarpiece originally made for the Badia in Volterra was in fact long held to be a collaboration with Domenico Ghirlandaio, who would have executed the lower register while Botticelli concentrated on the upper half. Such division of labour is unlikely since characteristic hands from Botticelli's workshop are recognizable in this work, as well as in the Montevarchi version. The latter even shows the participation of the master in the lower register given the pictorial quality of certain figures, in particular St Lawrence of Toulouse on the left, strongly reminiscent of Donatello's gilded bronze sculpture of St Lawrence (1423–5), while the upper register might have been left entirely to the workshop.[47] The inversion of roles between the master and his assistants was not uncommon in Botticelli's workshop. As a matter of fact, Botticelli would increasingly favour smaller formats, possibly owing to a lack of large commissions but also probably because of a project that would preoccupy him for several years: the drawings for Dante's *Divine Comedy*. According to a sixteenth-century source, the Anonimo Magliabechiano, this large cycle of drawings was commissioned by Lorenzo di Pierfrancesco de' Medici.[48] Vasari reports that this daunting task, which he left unfinished, led Botticelli to waste a lot of time and brought him much disorder in his affairs.[49] Yet the surviving documents prove the opposite. Despite a drop in his finances in the mid-1490s,

Botticelli managed to stay afloat for the whole decade.[50] The aforementioned paintings are perhaps the largest surviving works executed by Botticelli in this period, including the altarpiece for the church of the Convertite, today in poor condition (currently in the Courtauld Gallery, London). Botticelli was therefore executing a number of works in those years, alternating between large and smaller devotional panels, while working at the same time on his series for Dante's poem.

Paradoxically, very few drawings survived from Botticelli's workshop, but this set of 92 surviving drawings on parchment are among the largest cycle drawn in the Quattrocento. The task possibly started with the supply of designs for Cristoforo Landino's publication in 1481. The drawings, now divided between the Apostolic Library in the Vatican (7) and the Kupferstichkabinett in Berlin (85), testify to Botticelli's extraordinary power of invention as a designer while offering real insight into his stylistic development. The critical literature on this set is vast as the nature and function of these drawings are still subject to debate. Their fairly large oblong format also raises questions about the appearance of the finished project had it been brought to completion. Their main characteristic is the lack of an architectural framework, hence constraining Botticelli to use the figures as structural devices. This compositional strategy was further complicated by the repetition on the same page of the two protagonists, the Latin poet Virgil and Dante, as their journey progresses through the three realms of the afterlife: Hell, Purgatory and Paradise (these three sections of the poem, called 'cantiche' in Italian, are themselves subdivided into 34 canti for *Hell* and 33 for the last two).

A unique oeuvre in Renaissance art, this cycle expressed Botticelli's highly personal style developed from the early 1480s stretching well into the 1490s. By dedicating only a single sheet to each canto, Botticelli had to fit multiple episodes into one pictorial space and renew the multi-scenic approach that he had previously developed in the Esther panels and the Sistine Chapel frescoes. Following his habitual practice, Botticelli fused old conventions and new inventions so as to visually translate this highly philosophical vision and ascetic experience. Hence, many of the *Divine Comedy* drawings are structured without the use of linear perspective, a skill that Botticelli unquestionably mastered. Each sheet displays a complex chronological order that not only reflects the structure of each canto but that of the poem as a whole, blurring the boundary between space and time. Each canto contains a series of events that Botticelli deploys in a unified space, and reflects, in this intermingling of events and individuals, what the *Divine Comedy* really is about: the sense of the transience of life and its aftermath presented as theatre. Two poets, Virgil and Dante, are leading the way in this spiritual journey, even though their encounter would have been impossible in any other situation as Virgil lived in the first century BC and Dante in the late thirteenth century AD.

Hell comprises a series of highly elaborate images, most of them occupying the whole surface of the picture plane, and fewer unfinished sketches than in the following two *cantiche*. The first *cantica* abounds in 'wandering motifs' such as the head of Medusa, already represented on the shield of Minerva in the aforementioned tapestry (see illus. 48), which appears in reverse in the page for *Hell*, XI, while the centaurs in the following canto are modelled on her companion in the mythological painting *Minerva and the Centaur* (illus. 49). Some of the giants' heads in the drawing corresponding to *Hell*, XXXI, recall the features of St John the Baptist in the Bardi and San Barnaba altarpieces. All these correspondences may be used as clues to date the execution of the drawings and inform us about Botticelli's creative process. For example, the illustration of *Purgatory*, XXVIII, which comes much later in the narrative, evokes the earlier *Primavera*, suggesting that Botticelli did not always follow the narrative order of the poem but instead worked through the illustrations at his own will and pace.[51] While the description of the punishment of the souls in *Hell* is highly metaphorical, the following two *cantiche* are much less so. This is demonstrated by the different treatments of the scenes: large spaces are left blank in the latter two *cantiche* while the figures themselves often appear to float in an empty space. This characteristic may be owing to the fact that most of the drawings were left unfinished, but it may also denote a certain struggle in Botticelli's creative process, due to the increasingly ethereal vision of the poet.

The first drawing for *Paradise* shows Dante and his beloved Beatrice rising up from the Garden of Eden. Beatrice has taken over from Virgil and will be Dante's guide for the rest of the poem. For the first time in the series, Botticelli introduces a sudden change of scale as she appears much larger than Dante himself. Such an archaic trait, underscoring Beatrice's blissful condition, appears perhaps for the first time in the *Madonna del Padiglione*.[52] At the same time, Botticelli tends to elongate forms, an inclination particularly visible in the figure of Truth in the *Calumny of Apelles* and in the *Paradise* drawings, marking at the turn of the 1490s a new stylistic approach. Such disproportions were often related to the influence of Savonarola, who advocated for less naturalistic and more austere images that should not visually ravish the viewers (one of the main criticisms directed at art under the rule of the Medici) but function as an aid and memento within the limits of religious obligations. This is why many ornaments, games, cosmetics and paintings construed as distracting, frivolous and immoral were burnt during the bonfire of the vanities organized in place of Carnival in February 1497 and 1498.

The retinues of angels that pervade some of the scenes of *Paradise* recall the graceful flying angels of the large San Marco altarpiece, re-worked in the small *Mystic Nativity* (illus. 71), held to be Botticelli's most sophisticated response to Savonarola's influence.[53] Dated 1500 and signed in the inscription in Greek atop the composition, the painting was probably made for a follower of the friar, whose influence lasted well after his death. Yet Botticelli offers an image of serene reconciliation, contrasting with the inscribed threatening message and the recent religious and political upheavals that concluded with the execution of the monk on the Piazza della Signoria on 23 May 1498.[54] This painting, together with similar pious images such as the small *St Augustine in His Study*, executed during this period for a public predominantly devoted to Savonarola's cause, derived conversely from the predella of the San Marco altarpiece. Together with the *Last Communion of St Jerome* (illus. 72) – executed in collaboration with Bartolomeo di Giovanni (for the lunette) and of which several replicas exist – and the small *Agony in the Garden*, these paintings are all pervaded by an intense sense of religiosity immediately

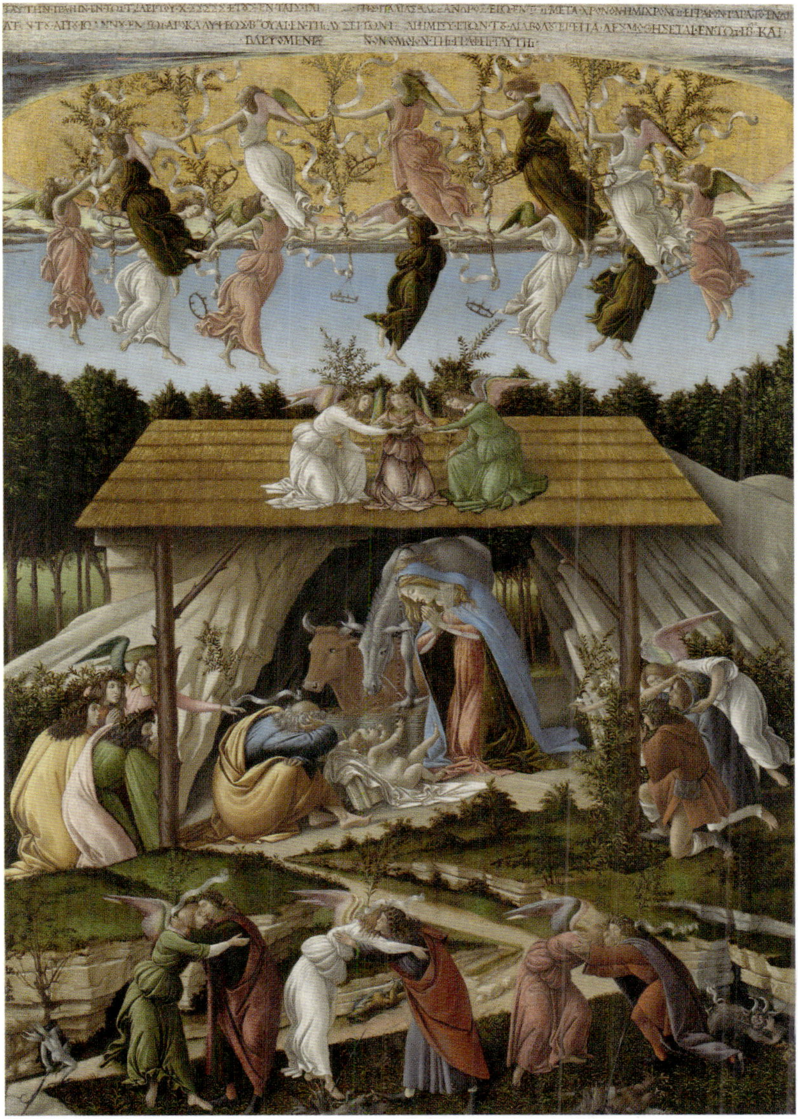

71 Botticelli, *Mystic Nativity*, 1500, oil on canvas.

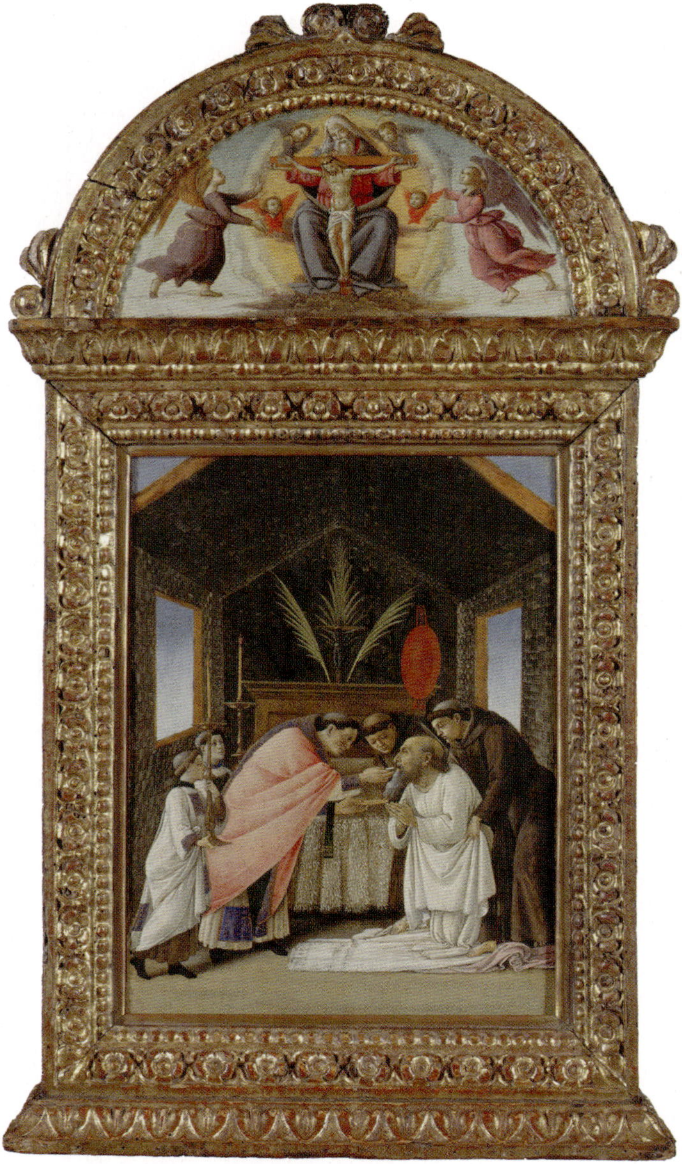

72 Botticelli, *Last Communion of St Jerome*, 1490s, tempera and gold on wood.

transmuted into a calm and meditative scene.[55] Such an approach finds its full expression in a recently rediscovered painted crucifix (illus. 73). This object, which would have been used in the ritual processions of some confraternities or religious communities, synthesizes Botticelli's multifaceted production in this period. The figure of Christ shows an elongated and harmonious body and limbs, typical of that period, while its delicate modelling on both sides of the cross recalls such early examples as Cimabue's and Giotto's, adding a hint of archaism to a vision of timeless beauty. At the same time, this figure of Christ constitutes another 'wandering motif' since it closely relates to the Convertite altarpiece and the *Mystic Crucifixion* (currently in the Fogg Museum, Harvard University). This crucifix must have encountered some success, as at least two replicas survived: one in reduced format and another of the same scale, executed by a still functioning workshop.[56]

The viability of Botticelli's workshop after 1500 was long doubted until the discovery of a contract for a large altarpiece commissioned in 1505 by the Compagnia dello Spirito Santo in Montelupo, only five years before Botticelli's death.[57] This new evidence confirms that Botticelli remained somewhat active until at least 1505, but the extent of his activity remains an open question. The altarpiece has been identified as the large – albeit trimmed – Pentecost scene today in the Birmingham Museum and Art Gallery. While it is undeniably Botticelli's design, its painterly execution shares many characteristics with a group of works issued by collaborators working from his designs. Such works include fairly large compositions such as the *Flight into Egypt* (currently in

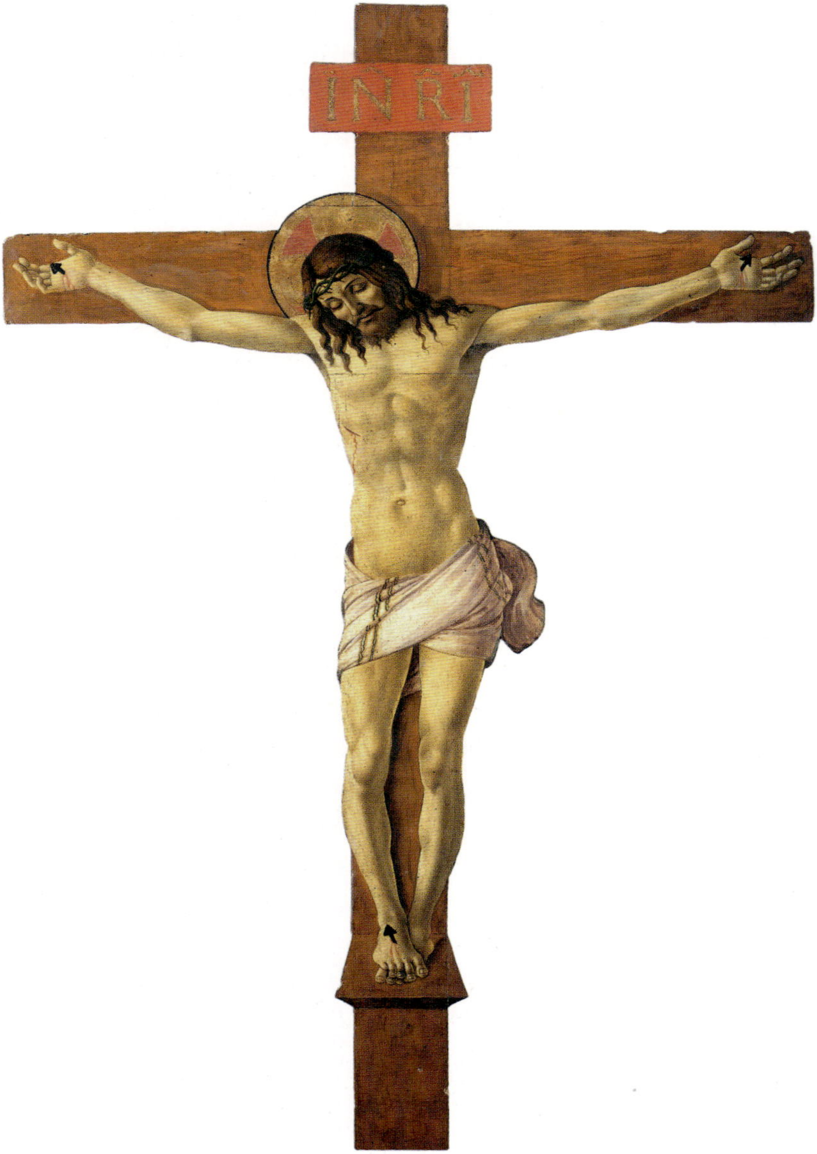

73 Botticelli, *Crucifix*, 1490s, tempera on silhouetted panel.

the Musée Jacquemart-André in Paris) and to some extent the two mirroring compositions of the *Virgin and Child with St John the Baptist* and their replicas, derived from the same cartoon (illus. 74). These works further develop a stylistic approach that Botticelli experimented with in the 1490s. In particular, two large scenes depicting the *Lamentation of Christ* (one being a new version of the former in an upright format) present a group of figures covering almost the entire surface of the picture plane.[58] This dramatic arrangement, strongly reminiscent of Donatello's own sculpted versions of the subject, still allows for a sense of construction in space, nearly completely lost in these later works.[59] This compositional strategy focuses on the physical presence of the figures and their gestures, which express a wide range of emotions, while the background is reduced to a minimum, echoing the staging of Donatello's ensemble and bringing the scene forwards in closer proximity to the viewer. Similarly covering almost the entire surface of the substrate, some later works appear extremely 'Botticelli-esque' without displaying the subtlety of his authentic designs. It is therefore possible that the stock of drawings and cartoons in the workshop was used to inform a new production with little input from the master, or even none.

Botticelli's finances must have plummeted in his very last years, since his nephews and brother Simone refused his inheritance after he died in May 1510.[60] Consequently, no inventory was drawn; his collaborators might have recovered some of the contents of the *bottega* that were used in later compositions, still reminiscent of Botticelli's 'brand' but much inferior in composition and style.[61] What 'Botticelli after Botticelli' might have looked like is exemplified in a series of four scenes of

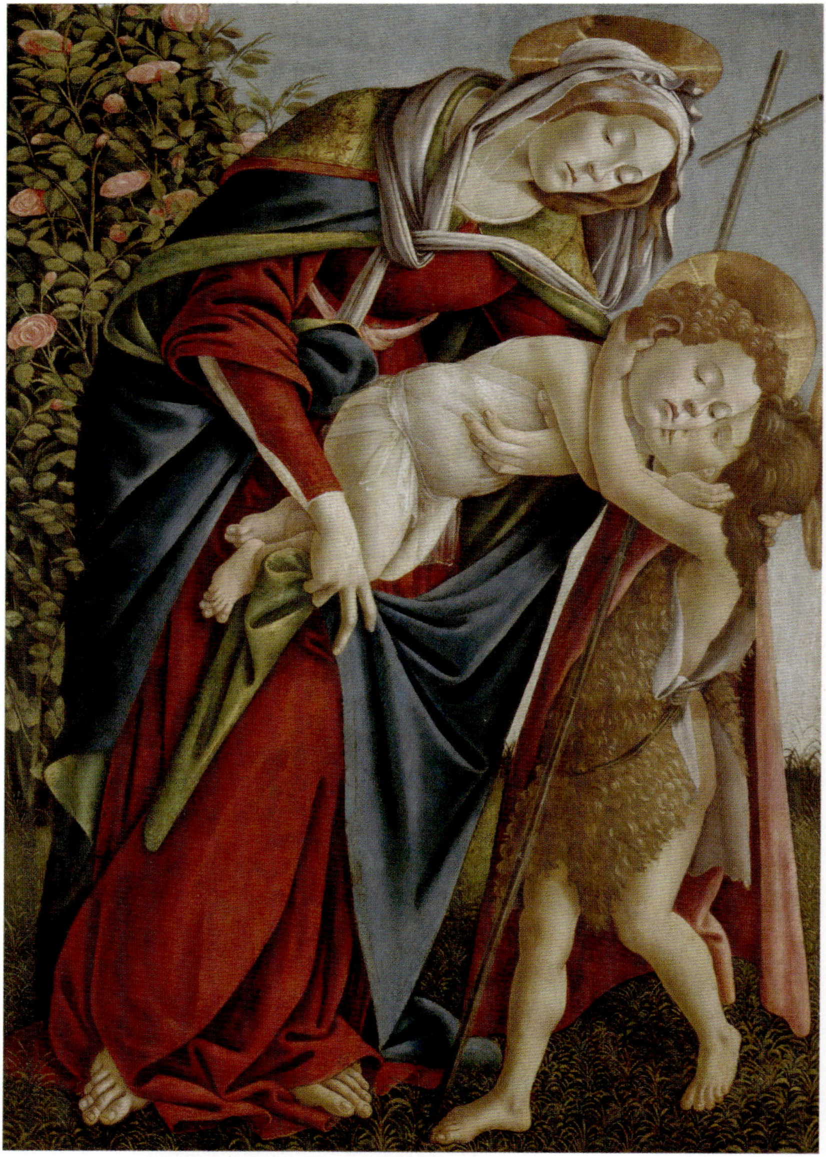

74 Botticelli, *Virgin and Child with St John the Baptist*, 1500s, tempera on wood.

similar dimensions depicting scenes from the *Passion of Christ*, whose function needs to be further investigated, as well as four *Allegories of Seasons* (untraced) derived from Flora in *Primavera* and the woman holding a basket on her head in the foreground of the *Temptations of Moses* in the Sistine Chapel. Another *Allegory of Autumn* reproduced that same figure, probably from the celebrated drawing representing an *Allegory of Abundance* rather than the Roman fresco, giving way to several other copies and derivations.[62]

Botticelli's skills as a designer lie in this important legacy, forgotten for nearly three hundred years and resurfacing only in the course of the nineteenth century. Today, Botticelli's art is almost universally acclaimed. His designs have not lost their ability to adapt to different formats and contexts, including modern ones. In this way they follow the normal evolution of a practice that Botticelli had himself elevated to its full potential.

CHRONOLOGY

1445 Alessandro di Mariano Filipepi is born in Florence to Mariano di Vanni Filipepi, and 'monna Smeralda', residents in the Quarter of Santa Maria Novella

1458 Botticelli appears in his father's tax return ('portata al castato') as of ill health and possibly in training with a goldsmith ('sta allegere ed è malsano')

1459 Benozzo Gozzoli (1421–1497) begins the fresco *Journey of the Magi* in the chapel of the Medici palace on via Larga (today via Cavour). Filippo Lippi (1406–1469) depicts the *Adoration* today in Berlin. Marsilio Ficino (1433–1499) undertakes the translation of Plato's oeuvre in Latin. This year, or the following, Botticelli joins the workshop of Filippo Lippi, already engaged with the fresco decoration of the cathedral of Prato

1464 Mariano Filipepi buys a house on via Nuova d'Ognissanti, called today via del Porcellana, into which his extended family, including Botticelli moves. On 1 August Cosimo de' Medici the elder dies, followed by the goldsmith Maso Finiguerra on 24 August

1465–70 Botticelli paints a series of Madonna and Child indebted to Filippo Lippi's models

1466 The sculptor Donatello dies on 13 December

1467 Filippo Lippi leaves for Spoleto to work on his last commission in the apse of the city cathedral. Botticelli presumably returns to Florence

1469 On 7 February the joust of Lorenzo the Magnificent is organized in Florence. Andrea del Verrocchio depicts his banner. On 4 June Lorenzo de' Medici marries Clarice Orsini (1450–1488). Filippo Lippi dies in Spoleto on 10 October; his son, Filippino, stays for some time with his father's lifelong collaborator and assistant Fra Diamante, then returns to Florence. Lorenzo de' Medici's father, Piero il Gottoso, dies on 2 December. Lorenzo succeeds him as the ruler of Florence

1469–70 Botticelli probably executes his first known altarpiece, Sant'Ambrogio, for a Medici or a close member of the family, as well as the two small panels representing the *Discovery of the Murder of Holofernes* and *Judith Returning to Bethulia*. He has recently set up his own workshop on the ground floor of his father's house

1470 Benedetto Dei mentions Botticelli as an independent master in his description of the city of Florence. Filippino Lippi possibly joins Botticelli's studio. Botticelli receives his first known commission on 18 June for the depiction of two of the seven virtues for the merchants' court (Mercanzia), originally commissioned to Piero del Pollaiolo; he completes only one, *Fortitude*, for which he receives payment on 18 August

1472 Botticelli features on the register of the Company of St Luke, with Filippino as a member of his workshop. Leon Battista Alberti dies on 25 April

1474 Botticelli delivers a painting of St Sebastian probably installed in Santa Maria Maggiore on 20 January. Over the summer Botticelli collaborates with the woodcarvers and architects Giuliano da Maiano, Il Francione and Baccio Pontelli for a series of inlaid works in Pisa Cathedral where he starts a fresco depicting the *Assumption of the Virgin*, left unfinished and presumably destroyed in 1583

1474–6 Botticelli supplies designs of Minerva and Apollo for the marqueted doors of the room called Sala degli Angeli, and the designs for some of the virtues in the *studiolo* in the Palazzo Ducale, Urbino

1475 Botticelli creates the banner for the joust of Giuliano de' Medici, held on 28 January. Michelangelo Buonarroti is born on 6 March in Caprese, near Florence

1475–8 Poliziano writes the *Stanze per la giostra* of Giuliano de' Medici

1476 Cristoforo Landino translates Pliny the Elder's *Natural History* into Italian. Simonetta Vespucci, née Cattaneo (1453), beloved of Giuliano de' Medici, dies on 26 April

1477 Botticelli receives payment for a tondo commissioned by Cardinal Francesco Gonzaga

1478 The Conspiracy of the Pazzi results in the assassination of Giuliano de' Medici on 26 April. Botticelli receives payment from the Otto di Guardia e di Balia to portray the persons responsible on the facade of the Palazzo Vecchio (Jacopo, Francesco and Renato dei Pazzi, Francesco Salviati, archbishop of Pisa, Jacopo et Bernardo Bandini Baroncelli and Napoleone Francezi). These 'images of infamy' are painted in 1494 after the elder branch of the Medici are banned from the city. Botticelli produces a series of posthumous portraits of Giuliano, of which at least three (and possibly four) versions survive

1478–80 Botticelli paints the *Primavera*, possibly for Lorenzo di Pierfrancesco, cousin and ward of Lorenzo the Magnificent

1480–81 Botticelli paints the fresco *St Augustine in His Study* for a member of the Vespucci family in the church of Ognissanti and a large *Annunciation* in the hospital of San Martino alla Scala. He supplies the design of the figures of Dante and Petrarch for the marqueted doors of the Sala dei Gigli in the Palazzo Vecchio. Filippino starts to work on the frescoes in the Brancacci chapel in the church of Santa Maria del Carmine. Ugolino Verino praises Botticelli and Filippino in his *Epigrammata*: *Tuscus Alexander . . . successor Apellis – haec mira Etruscus depinxerat ante Philippinus*

1481 Lorenzo de' Medici sends Botticelli to Rome in July to execute the frescoes of the Sistine Chapel in the Vatican Palace, alongside a group of painters including Pietro Perugino (1448–1523) Domenico Ghirlandaio (1448/9–1494) and Cosimo Rosselli (1439–1507)

	Cristoforo Landino publishes his *Comento sopra la Comedia di Dante*, with illustrations engraved after Botticelli's designs
1482	Lorenzo de' Medici sends Leonardo da Vinci to Milan. Mariano Filipepi, Botticelli's father, dies on 20 February. The Sistine Chapel frescoes are completed in April/May. Botticelli returns to Florence. Botticelli paints *Minerva and the Centaur*, possibly for the marriage between Lorenzo di Pierfrancesco and Semiramide Appiani on 19 July
1483	Botticelli and his collaborators produce four spalliere illustrating the story of *Nastagio degli Onesti* for the marriage of Gianozzo di Antonio di Puccio Pucci (1460–1497) and Lucrezia di Piero di Giovanni di Jacopo Bini (1467–1494?). Girolamo Savonarola (1452–1498) arrives at the convent of San Marco in Florence in April
1485	Botticelli receives payment on 3 August for an altarpiece in the Bardi Chapel in Santo Spirito
1487	Savonarola leaves Florence
1489	Botticelli receives payment on 19 March for the *Annunciation* in the church of Cestello, today Santa Maria Maddalena dei Pazzi, and again, between 31 January and 11 April, for a tondo commissioned by Luigi d'Ugolino Martelli
1490	Girolamo Savonarola returns to Florence in May/June
1492	Lorenzo de' Medici dies on 8 April. Botticelli receives payment on 8 November for an altarpiece for the goldsmiths' chapel in the church of San Marco
1494	Piero il Fatuo, Lorenzo's son, is banned from Florence on 9 November; Charles VIII's troops enter the city on 17 November
1495–9	Botticelli executes an altarpiece in the Villa del Trebbio for Lorenzo di Pierfrancesco de' Medici
1497	Bonfires of the vanities organized in February on Carnival day by Savonarola
1498	Savonarola is arrested and put to trial; he is hanged and burned on the Piazza of the Signoria on 23 May
1499	Marsilio Ficino dies on 1 October. Botticelli features on the register of the Arte dei Medici e Speziali (15 November)

1500–1501	Botticelli paints the *Mystic Nativity*
1502	Botticelli is described as an excellent master in a letter to Isabella d'Este, dated 25 September
1503	Piero il Fatuo dies
1504	Filippino Lippi dies in Florence on 18 April
1505	Botticelli and his assistants depict the altarpiece of the Pentecost for the Compagnis dello Spirito Santo in Montelupo
1510	Botticelli dies in Florence and is buried in the family tomb in the church of Ognissanti on 17 May

REFERENCES

The abbreviation ASF is used to refer to sources from the Archivio di Stato di Firenze.

1 Becoming Botticelli

1 Lorenzo de' Medici, 'Simposio ovvero i Beoni', poem number XIV in *Opere*, ed. A. Simioni, vol. II (Bari, 1914), ch. I, 160, vv. 46–51: 'Tutti n'andiam verso il Ponte a Rifredi, / ché Giannesse ha spillato un botticello / di vin che presti facci i lenti piedi. / Tutti n'andiamo in fretta a ber con quello: / quel ci fa sol sí presti in sulla strada, / e veloce ciascun piú che un uccello.'

2 Alessandro Cecchi, *Botticelli* (Milan, 2005), pp. 12–27.

3 Jacques Mesnil proposed to identify their house as the current no. 28 (see J. Mesnil, 'Quelques documents sur Botticelli', *Miscellanea d'arte* (1903), pp. 87–97, esp. 87); Jacques Mesnil, *Botticelli* (Paris, 1938), p. 1; but no further evidence can sustain such identification.

4 Cecchi, *Botticelli*, p. 20. This happened in September 1490.

5 Vasari reports that Botticelli died in misery and with many debts in Giorgio Vasari, *Le vite de' più eccellenti pittori, scultori ed architettori*, ed. R. Bettarini and P. Barocchi (Florence, 1966–87), vol. III, p. 519; see also Alessandro Cecchi, 'Nuovi documenti sulla casa e sulla bottega del Botticelli', *Paragone*, anno LXVII, III Ser., 128 (July 2016), pp. 45–55.

6 According to Cirri, the last family member of the Filipepi, Cesare di Lorenzo di Mariano, died on 17 May 1640 and was buried in the external graveyard of Ognissanti, no longer extant. See Cecchi, *Botticelli*, note 102, p. 27: BNCF, Sepoltuario Cirri, vol. XI, 5576.

7 On Vasari and Botticelli, see Richard Stappleford, 'Vasari and Botticelli', *Mitteilungen des Kunsthistorischen Institutes in Florenz*, 39 Bd., H. 2/3 (1995), pp. 397–408; A. Cecchi, 'Le Vite del Botticelli e

Filippino della Torrentiniana', in *Giorgio Vasari e il cantiere delle Vite del 1550*, ed. Barbara Agosti, Silvia Ginzburg and Alessandro Nova (Venice, 2013), pp. 231–9.

8 Richard A. Goldthwaite, 'Realtà economica sociale e status culturale dell'artigiano', in *Arti fiorentine: la grande storia dell'artigianato, Il Quattrocento*, ed. Franco Franceschi and Gloria Fossi (Florence, 1999), p. 13.

9 I am employing here the word used by Richard A. Goldthwaite, *The Economy of Renaissance Florence* (Baltimore, MA, 2009).

10 Ibid., pp. 499–500.

11 Vasari, *Le vite de' più eccellenti pittori, scultori ed architettori*, vol. III, pp. 511–12; Vasari, *The Lives of the Painters, Sculptors and Architects*, trans. W. Gaunt (London and New York, 1912), vol. II, p. 84.

12 Ibid., both editions. Original quotation: '*si era volto tutto al disegno, invaghitosi della pittura, si dispose volgersi a quella*'.

13 Giorgio Vasari, *Le vite de' più eccellenti pittori, scultori ed architettori*, ed. R. Bettarini and P. Barocchi (Florence, 1966–87), vol. VI, p. 5: '*Tutto il tempo che poteva mettere di nascoso lo consumava nel disegnare*'.

14 Giorgio Vasari, *Le vite de' più eccellenti pittori, scultori ed architettori*, ed. R. Bettarini and P. Barocchi (Florence, 1966–87), vol. IV, p. 16: '*Non lasciò mai il designare et il fare di rilievo; come cose che gli andavano a fantasia più d'alcun altra*'.

15 Marsilio Ficino, 'Ep. 6, De divino furore', in *Lettere, I. Epistolarum familiarum liber I*, ed. S. Gentile (Florence, 1990), pp. 19–20.

16 Leon Battista Alberti, *De pictura*, III, esp. p. 53; see also Cristoforo Landino, *Comento sopra la comedia di Dante* (Florence, 1481): '*el primo grado tiene Apelle, da tutti reputato etiam ne' futuri secoli insuperabile.*'

17 Lucian, *Dialogues*, LIX.

18 Vasari, *Le vite de' più eccellenti pittori, scultori ed architettori*, vol. III, p. 512; *Lives*, trans. W. Gaunt, vol. II, p. 84.

19 See A. Guidotti, 'Battilori e dipintori a Firenze fra Tre e Quattrocento: Bastiano di Giovani e la sua clientela (dal Catasto del 1427)', in *Scritti di storia dell'arte in onore di Roberto Salvini* (Florence, 1984), pp. 239–49.

20 See for instance Neri di Bicci, *Ricordanze (10 marzo 1453–24 aprile 1475)*, ed. B. Santi (Pisa, 1976), esp. nos. 53, 113, 120, 263, 448 and 738.

21 See A. Mascaro, *L'arte del battiloro. Cenni storici, tecnici, statistici* (Venice, 1928); B. Dini, 'Una manifattura di battiloro nel Quattrocento', in *Tecnica e società nell'Italia dei secoli XII–XVI (Atti del congresso Internazionale di Studi di Storia e di Arte di Pistoia, 28–31 Oct. 1984)* (Pistoia, 1987), pp. 83–111.
22 See ASF Carteggio Mediceo for proof of Antonio receiving payment in 1475 for the casting and the gilding of medals. G. Mandel, *L'opera completa del Botticelli* (Milan, 1978), cat. no. 41, p. 89; U. Baldini, *Sandro Botticelli* (Florence, 1988), p. 48. For a summary of all proposed identifications see Nicoletta Pons in *Botticelli e Filippino: l'inquietudine e la grazia nella pittura fiorentina del Quattrocento*, ed. Daniel Arasse (Florence, 2004), n. 34, pp. 220–23.
23 ASF, Capitani di Parte Guelfa, Numeri rossi, 29, c. 13v., in Cecchi, *Botticelli*, p. 19.
24 See A. Bernacchioni, 'Botteghe di artisti e artigiani nel XV secolo', in *Gli antichi chiassi tra Ponte Vecchio e Santa Trinità. Storia del Rione dei Santi Apostoli, dai primi insediamenti romani alle ricostruzioni postbelliche*, ed. Giampaolo Trotta (Florence, 1992), p. 211.
25 Neri di Bicci, *Ricordanze (10 marzo 1453–24 aprile 1475)*, no. 555.
26 This was the interpretation of Herbert Horne (1908) while Mesnil (1938) proposes to relate the expression to the goldsmith's activity. The majority of the critics follow Horne's interpretation.
27 See Neri di Bicci, *Ricordanze (10 marzo 1453–24 aprile 1475)*, no. 74; *Ricordanze di Bartolomeo Masi calderaio fiorentino dal 1478 al 1526*, ed. G. O. Corazzini (Florence, 1906), p. 89.
28 L. Melli, *Maso Finiguerra* (Florence, 1995), p. 8.
29 ASF Catasto #814 (*portata* di Mariano 1457) : 'Antonio mio figliolo sta all'orafo, aveva di salario fiorini 25 l'anno, quando a da fare sta per lavorante, traghone punt'utile', in Cecchi, *Botticelli* (Milan, 2005), pp. 18–19; Melli, *Maso Finiguerra*, p. 8.
30 L. Melli, 'Antonio del Pollaiolo, orafo e la sua bottega "magnifica ed onorata in Mercato Nuovo"', *Prospettiva*, 109 (January 2003), pp. 65–75, esp. p. 65.
31 Andrea del Verrocchio, *Baptism of Christ*, 1470–75, tempera and oil on panel, Uffizi, Florence, Inv. 1890 no. 8358.
32 Apart from the pioneering work of Martin Wackernagel, see for instance the more recent exhibition and accompanying catalogue

Maestri e botteghe (Florence, Palazzo Strozzi (Milan, 1992)); Anabel Thomas, *The Painter's Practice in Renaissance Tuscany* (Cambridge, 1995); and *Arti fiorentine. La grande storia dell'artigianato,* vol. II: *Il Quattrocento*, ed. Franco Franceschi and Gloria Fossi (Florence, 1999).

33 Ugo Procacci, 'Di Jacopo di Antonio e delle compagnie di pittore del Corso degli Adimari nel secolo XV', *Rivista d'arte*, XXXIV (1960), pp. 3–70. Apollonio, who was without an heir, left his share to Marco's son, who became in turn his father's collaborator.

34 Patrizia Zambrano in Patrizia Zambrano and Jonathan K. Nelson, *Filippino Lippi* (Milan, 2004), p. 18.

35 Jeffrey Ruda, *Fra Filippo Lippi: Life and Work* (London, 1993), p. 25.

36 Cristoforo Landino, *Comento sopra la Comedia*, ed. Paolo Procaccioli (Rome, 2001), p. 8.

37 Michael Baxandall, *Painting and Experience in Fifteenth-century Italy* (London, 1972), pp. 118, 128–39. See also Ruda, *Fra Filippo Lippi*, p. 309.

38 Vasari, *Le vite de' più eccellenti pittori, scultori ed architettori*, vol. III, p. 339.

39 Neri di Bicci, *Ricordanze (10 marzo 1453–24 aprile 1475)*, for instance no. 48.

40 '*Una dimestichezza grandissima, e quasi un continova pratica tra gli orefici ed i pittori*': Vasari, *Le vite de' più eccellenti pittori, scultori ed architettori*, vol. III, p. 512.

41 Ruda, *Fra Filippo Lippi*, p. 23.

42 Statuto del 1315, Rubrica IX in Raffaele Ciasca, *Statuti dell'Arte dei Medici e Speziali* (Florence, 1922), no. 9, pp. 81–2.

43 Neri di Bicci, *Ricordanze (10 marzo 1453–24 aprile 1475)*, para nos. 412, 440, 441, 459, 637, 638, 644, 646.

44 Martin Wackernagel, *The World of the Florentine Renaissance Artist: Projects and Patrons, Workshop and Art Market* [1938], trans. Alison Luchs (Princeton, NJ, 1981), p. 302, n. 4; Vasari, *Le vite de' più eccellenti pittori, scultori ed architettori*, ed. G. Milanesi (Florence, 1906, repr. 1981), vol. II, p. 362, n. 1.

45 Ruda, *Fra Filippo Lippi: Life and Work*, p. 34.

46 Cennino Cennini, *The Craftsman's Handbook (Il libro dell'Arte)*, trans. Daniel V. Thompson Jr (New York, 1954, repr. 2016), p. 2.

47 Ibid., ch. IV.

48 Ibid., p. 8.

49 Alberti, *De pictura*, vol. II, 48.
50 See *Giovanni Rucellai ed il suo Zibaldone*, ed. Alessandro Perosa (London, 1960–81), vol. I, p. 24.
51 Giuseppe Marchini, *Filippo Lippi* (Milan, 1975), p. 100; Ruda, *Fra Filippo Lippi: Life and Work*, p. 259.
52 Ruda, *Fra Filippo Lippi: Life and Work*, p. 259, remarks that these two figures 'would be the best candidates in the cycle for a separate attribution'.
53 Ibid., cat. D4, pp. 495–6; ASF MAP, Florence, f. VI, c. 255.
54 Ruda, *Fra Filippo Lippi: Life and Work*, pp. 197–8, cat. 49, pp. 443–4.
55 Cennini, *The Craftsman's Handbook*, pp. 2–3.
56 Ruda, *Fra Filippo Lippi: Life and Work*, p. 235.
57 Vasari, *Le vite de' più eccellenti pittori, scultori ed architettori*, vol. III, p. 331; Ruda, *Fra Filippo Lippi: Life and Work*, p. 230.

2 Making an Impression: The Painter's Debut in Context

1 See Marco Parenti, *Ricordi storici 1464–67*, ed. Manuela Dori Garfagnini (Rome, 2001), pp. 58, 122–31; Luca Landucci, *Diario fiorentino dal 1450 al 1516*, ed. Jodoco Del Badia (Florence, 1883), p. 9; Nicolai Rubinstein, *The Government of Florence Under the Medici, 1434 to 1494* (Oxford, 1997), pp. 227–34; Paula C. Clarke, *The Soderini and the Medici: Power and Patronage in Fifteenth-century Florence* (Oxford and New York, 1991).
2 Francesco Guicciardini, *Storie fiorentine dal 1378 al 1509*, ed. A. Montevecchi (Milan, 1998), p. 105.
3 The seven Virtues count three theological virtues: Charity, Faith and Hope; and four cardinal virtues: Fortitude, Prudence, Temperance and Justice.
4 Giorgio Vasari, *Le vite de' più eccellenti pittori, scultori e architettori, nelle redazioni del 1550 e 1568*, ed. R. Bettarini and P. Barocchi (Florence, 1966–87), vol. I, p. 483. The drawing is in the Gabinetto Disegni e Stampe degli Uffizi (hereafter GDSU) in Florence, Inv. 208E.
5 See the two deliberations of 18 August and September 1469 in ASF Mercanzia, Deliberazione dell'Ufficiale e dei Sei di Mercanzia. Libro segnato 305, ff. 44 and 84, published in A. Wright, *The*

Pollaiuolo Brothers: The Arts of Florence and Rome (New Haven, CT, and London, 2005), pp. 229–31, and no. 18 on p. 469.

6 ASF Mercanzia, Deliberazione dell'Ufficiale e dei Sei di Mercanzia. Libro segnato 305, f. 84: 'per officium dictorum sex fuit locata ad faciendum picture virtutis caritatis pro illa ponenda in loco ubi est similis picture in sala magna inferiori Piero . . . del Pollaiuolo pictori'; see ibid., p. 240.

7 R. Lightbown, *Botticelli* (London, 1978), vol. I, pp. 31–2; Wright, *The Pollaiuolo Brothers*, pp. 229–31.

8 ASF Mercanzia, Deliberazione dell'Ufficiale e dei Sei di Mercanzia. Libro segnato 305, f. 159v.; published in Wright, *The Pollaiuolo Brothers*, n. 19, p. 469.

9 Antonella Astorri, *La mercanzia a Firenze nella prima metà del Trecento: il potere dei grandi mercanti* (Florence, 1998); Wright, *The Pollaiuolo Brothers*, p. 230.

10 Carlo L. Ragghianti and Gigetta Dalli Regoli, *Firenze, 1470–1480. Disegni dal modello* (Pisa, 1975), p. 79, fig. 35; Roberta Bartoli, *Biagio d'Antonio* (Milan, 1999), p. 31.

11 See for example, E. Gombricht, 'The Early Medici as Patrons of Art' [1960], repr. in *Norm and Form* (London, 1966), pp. 35–57.

12 On the conditions of this important commission see P. Zambrano in J. K. Nelson and P. Zambrano, *Filippino Lippi* (Milan, 2004), pp. 186–91. Filippino depicted there a few members of the Medici circle: Tommaso Soderini himself, but also the young painter Francesco Granacci, Piero Guicciardini, Piero del Pugliese, the poet Luigi and the painter Antonio Pollaiuolo. See G. Vasari, *Le vite de' più eccellenti pittori, scultori e architettori, nelle redazioni del 1550 e 1568*, ed. R. Bettarini and P. Barocchi (Florence, 1966–87), vol. III, p. 561.

13 Cosmé Tura, *A Muse (Calliope?)*, 1455–60, oil with egg on poplar, National Gallery, London, Inv. NG3070.

14 See L. Pulci, 'La giostra', in *Opere minori*, ed. P. Orvieto (Milan, 1986), pp. 61–120; *Ricordo d'una giostra fatta a dì 7 febbraio 1468, sulla piazza di Santa Croce* (Magl. VIII, 1503, BNF), in P. Fanfani, *Il Borghini. Giornale di filologia e lettere italiana*, Anno 2 (Florence, 1864), pp. 474–83.

15 Wright, *The Pollaiuolo Brothers*, p. 29.

16 See for instance Marsilio Ficino, *De amore*, IV, 3: 'Nunc autem puros colores, lumina, vocem unam, fulgurem auri et argenti candorem, scientiam, animam, que omnia simplificia pulchra delectant'; (author's translation: 'What delights us are beautiful pure colours, lights, a sound, flaring gold, shiny silver, knowledge, spirit, which are all simple beautiful things.'). See A. Debenedetti, 'Dans l'antre des nymphes: études sur la pensée magique de Marsile Ficin à Florence au XVe siècle', unpublished PhD thesis, École Pratique des Hautes Études, Paris, 2015, pp. 62ff.

17 For instance, Cristina Acidini Luchinat draws attention to Philostratus' *Life of Apollonius of Thyana*, which was illuminated by Cosimo Rosselli with a 'frame that imitates the geometric tracery of an enamelled and gem-set necklace' in C. Acidini Luchinat ed., *Renaissance Florence. The Age of Lorenzo de' Medici 1449–1492*, exh. cat., London, Accademia italiana delle Arti e delle Arti Applicate (Florence, 1993), p. 120.

18 Gino Corti, 'Two Early Seventeenth-century Inventories involving Giambologna', *Burlington Magazine*, CXVIII (1976), pp. 629–34, esp. p. 633: 'Dua forze di Ercole, di Antonio Pollaiolo, miniate, cosa singularissima, con adornamento, a uso di libro che si serra'; see also Cecchi, *Botticelli* (Milan, 2005), p. 102.

19 Nicole Dacos, Antonio Giuliano and Ulrico Pannuti, eds, *Il tesoro di Lorenzo il Magnifico* (Florence, 1973).

20 Domenico Veneziano, *Carnasecchi Tabernacle* (main section), *c.* 1440, fresco transferred to tile, National Gallery, London, Inv. NG1215.

21 These differences were observed in 1998 during a campaign of restoration on *Fortitude*, *Charity*, *Faith* and *Temperance*; see A. Cecchi, *Botticelli* (Milan, 2005), p. 100, and n. 13, p. 176.

22 The large frame enclosing the whole group together (now lost) was delivered on 23 March 1472 and provides a likely date for the completion of this cycle. See Wright, *The Pollaiuolo Brothers*, p. 231.

23 This was first suggested by Jacques Mesnil, 'Les figures de vertus de la Mercanzia, Piero del Pollaiolo et Botticelli', *Miscellanea d'arte*, I/3 (1903), pp. 43–6; Jacques Mesnil, *Botticelli* (Paris, 1938), p. 22.

24 Botticelli, *Madonna of the Rosegarden*, *c.* 1470, tempera on wood, Uffizi, Florence, Inv. 1890 no. 1601; Lightbown, *Botticelli*, vol. II,

B2, pp. 18–19; Cecchi, *Botticelli*, p. 54, and n. 52, p. 57, with previous bibliography.

25 The eight-pointed star atop its frame which may correspond to several guilds, for example, the Giudici and Notai, the Proconsolo, or the Fornai e Albergatori.

26 Botticelli, *Virgin in Glory of Seraphim*, 1469–70, tempera on panel, Uffizi, Florence, Inv. 1890 no. 504.

27 Botticelli, *Virgin of the Humility*, c. 1470, tempera on poplar, Louvre, Paris, Inv. MI 478.

28 *Virgin and Child with St Mary Magdalen, St John the Baptist, St Cosmas, St Damian, St Francis of Assisi and Saint Catherine of Alexandria*, c. 1470, tempera on wood, Uffizi, Florence, Inv. 1890 no. 8657.

29 See Cecchi, *Botticelli*, p. 54.

30 See proposed reconstruction in A. Schumacher, ed., *Florence and Its Painters* (Munich, 2018), p. 359.

31 Fra Filippo Lippi, *Coronation of the Virgin (Maringhi Coronation)*, c. 1439–47, tempera on wood, Uffizi, Florence, Inv. 1890 no. 8352; Jeffrey Ruda, *Fra Filippo Lippi: Life and Work* (London, 1993), pp. 140–41, cat. 36, p. 333.

32 S. Scarpelli, 'La Pala di Sant'Ambrogio di Sandro Botticelli. Relazione sull'intervento di restauro', in *Itinerario laurenziano* (Florence, 1993), pp. 63–71.

33 D. Carl, 'Documenti inediti su Maso Finiguerra e la sua famiglia', *Annali della Scuola Normale di Pisa, Classe di Lettere e Filosofia*, series 3, 13, 2 (1983), pp. 507–54, esp. 518–22; H. Chapman and M. Faietti, eds, *Fra Angelico to Leonardo, Italian Renaissance Drawings*, exh. cat., Florence, Uffizi and London, British Museum (London, 2010), p. 21.

34 Benvenuto Cellini, *Vita*, ed. Ettore Camesasca (Milan, 1985, repr. 2009), pp. 106–7.

35 Catasto 1481 'dipintore e lavora in casa' in Cecchi, *Botticelli* (Milan, 2005), p. 18. See Benedetto Dei, who lists it in his supplement to the *Descrizione della città di Firenze* written in about 1470.

36 BRF, Codice Ricciardiano 1853, c. 45r, see Giuseppina Carla Romby, *Descrizione e rappresentazioni della città di Firenze nel XV secolo con la trascrizione inedita dei manoscritti di Benedetto Dei e un indice ragionato dei manoscritti utili per la storia di Firenze* (Florence, 1976), p. 7; A. Cecchi, *Botticelli* (Milan, 2005), p. 60.

3 Building the Picture: Invention and Delegation

1 See A. Cecchi, *Botticelli* (Milan, 2005), pp. 60–61.

2 Neri di Bicci, *Le ricordanze (10 marzo 1453–24 aprile 1475)*, ed. Bruno Santi (Pisa, 1976), no. 646: 13 March 1469. For the denunciation for sodomy attesting Betto's presence in Botticelli's workshop in Jan 1473: ASF, Ufficiali di Notte e Conservatori dell'Onestà dei Monasteri, 15–17, 16 [13 July 1472–10 July 1473] *deliberazioni dal 1470 al 1473*, cc. 18v, 49v, 78v, 79v. See J. Mesnil, *Botticelli* (Paris, 1938), p. 98, 204, n. 83, R. Lightbown, *Botticelli* (London, 1978), vol. I, pp. 154, 188, ch. 14, n. 11; Cecchi, *Botticelli* (Milan, 2005), pp. 60 and 91, n. 2. ASF, Accademia del Disegno, 2 (debitori, creditori e ricordi), cc. 56v–57r, see Herbert Horne, *Botticelli* (London, 1908), vol. II, p. 47.

3 J. K. Nelson in P. Zambrano and J. K. Nelson, *Filippino Lippi* (Milan, 2004), p. 16, doc. 3, p. 619, c. 56v; Cecchi, *Botticelli* (Milan, 2005), p. 66 and n. 30, p. 91.

4 ASF Catasto 1000, c. 309r and catasto 1035, c324r, identified by Jacques Mesnil, *Botticelli* (Paris, 1938), p. 203, n. 78 without archival reference; see A. Cecchi, *Botticelli* (Milan, 2005), p. 80, and n. 59, p. 92, n. 61, p. 93. See also Bernard Berenson, *Italian Pictures of the Renaissance, Florentine Schools* (Oxford, 1963), vol. I, pp. 207–8.

5 Leonardo reproves Botticelli for his careless approach to landscape, making Botticelli the only fellow artist mentioned in Leonardo's treatise, see *Trattato della Pittura di Leonardo da Vinci condotto sul Cod. Vaticano Urbinate 1270*, ed. G. Milanesi (Rome, 1890), p. 38.

6 See Chris Daly, 'New Identifications in Botticelli's Workshop' (forthcoming September 2021), in A. Debenedetti, ed., *Botticelli. Un laboratoire de la Renaissance*, exh. cat., Paris, Musée Jacquemart André; Gigetta Dalli Regoli, *Lorenzo di Credi* (Milan, 1966), p. 192.

7 Typically, no work was signed at the time, with some exceptions. This would include the use of the *cartellino*, a small label bearing the painter's name and sometimes the date, especially in the Veneto, and another form of signature, and this is especially true for large compositions such as frescoes for introducing the artist's self-portrait, such as Filippino's in the Brancacci chapel, his father in the frescoes in Spoleto, Benozzo Gozzoli's in the *Journey of the*

Magi in the Medici chapel and Lorenzo Ghiberti on the Paradise door and so on.

8 See Jaynie Anderson, *Collecting Connoisseurship and the Art Market in Risorgimento Italy: Giovanni Morelli's Letters to Giovanni Melli and Pietro Zavaritt, 1866–1872* (Venice, 1999).

9 For a reconstruction of Bernard Berenson's reasoning, see Patrizia Zambrano, 'Bernard Berenson e l'Amico di Sandro', in Bernard Berenson, *Amico di Sandro* (Milan, 2005), pp. 9–70, esp. pp. 53 sq. See also Bernard Berenson, 'Amico di Sandro' in *Gazette des Beaux-Arts*, I/XLI (1899) pp. 459–71; Bernard Berenson, *The Study and Criticism of Italian Art* (London, 1901), pp. 46–69; Bernard Berenson, *Italian Paintings of the Renaissance. A List of the Principal Artists and Their Work with an Index of Place* (Oxford, 1932), where Amico di Sandro no longer appears. Not all the works assigned to this 'artist' were given to Filippino, but the great majority were. Herbert Horne had a fundamental role in dismantling Berenson's 'Amico di Sandro'; see Carl Brandon Strehlke, 'Bernard and Mary Berenson, Herbert H. Horne, and John G. Johnson', *Prospettiva*, LVII–LX (1989), pp. 427–38.

10 For the context of this commission see P. Zambrano in Patrizia Zambrano and Jonathan K. Nelson, *Filippino Lippi* (Milan, 2004), pp. 116–23, nn. 4, A–B, pp. 308–9. J. Byam Shaw, *Paintings by Old Masters at Christ Church, Oxford* (London, 1967), pp. 48–50, nn. 35–6. See Jonathan Nelson, 'Filippino nel ruolo di discepolo, collaboratore e concorrente di Botticelli', in *Botticelli e Filippino* (Rome, 2004), p. 91.

11 Marsilio Ficino, *De Christiana religione. Della cristiana religione* (Florence, 1474), chapters XXIV and XXV. See also P. Zambrano in Zambrano and Nelson, *Filippino Lippi*, pp. 116–23 and cat. 4 and 4b, pp. 308–9 with previous bibliography.

12 Museu Nacional d'Art de Catalunya, Barcelona, Inv. nos. 64968 and 64967, tempera and gold leaf on wood, *c.* 1460–70. See also *Dal giglio al David, Arte civica a Firenze fra Medioevo e Rinascimento*, ed. Maria Monica Donato and Daniela Parenti, exh. cat. Galleria dell'Accademia (Florence, 2013), cat. 71 A–B, pp. 264–7 with previous bibliography.

13 Traditionally, the sibyls are creatures inspired by the divine to convey prophetic visions in a poetic and enigmatic vein.

14 Biagio d'Antonio, chest and spalliera with the arms of Vaggia Nerli and Lorenzo Morelli (the Nerli Chest), 1472, tempera on wood, Courtauld Gallery, London, Inv. F.1947.LF.5). See also Roberta Bartoli, *Biagio d'Antonio* (Milan, 1999), pp. 30–31.

15 Now dismantled, these panels are dispersed between Ottawa (Fine Arts Museum), Paris (Louvre), Chantilly (Musée Condé), Florence (Horne Museum) and Rome (Paravicini-Rospigliosi collection). All six panels come from the Torrigiani family. For a full reconstruction, see *Fra Angelico, Botticelli . . . chefs d'oeuvre retrouvés*, exh. cat., Musée Condé, Chantilly (Paris, 2014), cat. 26–7, pp. 110–17.

16 For a reconstruction of the rediscovery of this cycle, see Jonathan K. Nelson, 'Botticelli or Filippino? How to Define Authorship in a Renaissance Workshop', in *Sandro Botticelli and Herbert Horne: New Research*, ed. Rab Hatfield (Florence, 2009), pp. 137–67.

17 For a different analysis which attributes the execution of all panels as well as their invention to Filippino alone, see P. Zambrano in Zambrano and Nelson, *Filippino Lippi*, pp. 141–55.

18 Tomas Markevicius, 'The Invisible Story of Esther: Revealing Botticelli and Filippino Collaboration and Approaches to Underdrawing', in *Virtù d'amore, pittura nuziale nel Quattrocento fiorentino*, ed. Claudio Paolini, Daniela Parenti and Ludovica Sebregondi, exh. cat., Florence, Galleria dell'Accademia and Museo Horne (Florence, 2010), pp. 210–13.

19 Ibid., p. 210.

20 It has been hypothesized that the cassoni might correspond to the wedding of Dianora di Niccolò Tucci and Antonio Torrigiani, celebrated in 1475, on the basis that they were mentioned as being in Palazzo Torrigiani-Del Nero in the nineteenth century. See also Fiammetta Gamba, 'Per una interpretazione critica dei primordi di Filippino Lippi', *Annali della Scuola Normale Superiore di Pisa*, series II, XXII (1954), I–II, pp. 151–65. For another hypothesis see Marianne Haraszti-Takács, 'Fifteenth-century Painted Furniture with Scenes from the Esther Story', *Jewish Art*, XV (1989), pp. 14–25.

21 The text can be found in Alessandro D'Ancona, *Sacre rappresentazioni dei secoli* XIV, XV *e* XVI (Florence, 1872), vol. I, pp. 129–66. On sacred representations in general, see Alessandro D'Ancona, *Origini del teatro in Italia: studi sulle sacre rappresentazioni* (Florence, 1877), vol. I, pp. 505–15.

22 D'Ancona, *Sacre rappresentazioni dei secoli* XIV, XV *e* XVI, p. 137.

23 Ibid., p. 140.

24 Ibid., p. 150: 'O Idio, onde procede tal sentenzia? / O tristo caso, acerbo, aspro e molesto! Oïme, chi fa dar tanta licenzia? /O padre eterno, or tu non vedi questo ? / O dolce Idio, ara' tu pazïenzia ? / Oïme, popol misero e afflitto ! / O giusto Idio, àlo tu derelitto?'

25 Ibid., p. 159: 'La reina si getta in sul letto, e il re va . . . di giù e di su tutto irato.'

26 Ibid., p. 162: 'Signor, morto è Aman, come dicesti, / E in prigion son e' figli e la moglie.'

27 The story illustrated here is variously interpreted. The interpretation of the right-hand side in particular is the author's reading. Most critics refer to the story of Haman visiting Esther in her bedchamber and being sentenced to death, but this reading does not follow the scene here as it is clearly King Assuerus who is depicted and not Haman.

28 See, for instance, Botticelli's own version of the theme (covered in Chapter Two of this volume) and Donatello's famous bronze statue of Judith and Holofernes, originally commissioned by Cosimo de' Medici and installed in his palace on via Larga in 1457. The statue was moved to the piazza della Signoria in 1494 and is today in the Sala dei Gigli in the Palazzo Vecchio.

29 Published by A. Della Torre, 'La prima ambasceria di Bernardo Bembo a Firenze', *Giornale storico della letteratura italiana*, XXXV (1900) pp. 264–8, esp. p. 267: 'eadem sententia nulla est: / Pulchrius est pictis istud imaginibus'; see also Paolo Orvieto, *Poliziano e l'ambiente mediceo* (Rome, 2009), p. 260; see also Paul Holberton, 'Classicism and Invention: Botticelli's Mythologies in Our Time and Their Time', in *Botticelli Past and Present*, ed. Ana Debenedetti and Caroline Elam (London, 2019), pp. 53–72, esp. p. 54. For a debated interpretation of this passage see Jonathan K. Nelson, 'Renaissance Perspectives on Botticelli: Paolo Cortesi, Giovanni

Aurelio Augurelli, Francesco Sansovino, and Leonardo da Vinci', in *Encountering the Renaissance: Celebrating Gary M. Radke and 50 Years of the Syracuse University Graduate Program in Renaissance Art*, ed. Molly Bourne and Victor Coonin (Ramsey, NJ, 2016), pp. 103–12, esp. p. 103, n. 4.

30 Leon Battista Alberti, *On Painting*, trans. Cecyl Grayson (London, 1972), vol. III, §40, pp. 78–9.

31 See Abramo/Abraham, Bishop of Souzdal, *Ragguaglio intorno alla rappresentazione dell'Annunciazione della Vergine allestita nella chiesa dell'Annuziata il 26 marzo 1439*, in Alessandro D'Ancona, *Origini del teatro in Italia: studi sulle sacre rappresentazioni* (Florence, 1877), pp. 246–50. On similar apparatus see also Vasari's life of Filippo Brunelleschi in Vasari, *Lives*, trans. W. Gaunt (London, 1963), vol. I, p. 295: 'It is said that the apparatus of the Paradise in S. Felice in the Piazza of that city was invented by Filippo for the representation or the feast of the Annunciation according to the time-honoured custom of the Florentines. This thing was truly marvellous, and a heaven full of living and moving figures, and a quantity of light which flash in and out.'

32 On the influence of the sacred plays on narrative painting, see for instance Ludovico Zorzi, *Il teatro e la città: saggi sulla scena italiana*, (Turin, 1977), p. 89. See also Vasari, *Lives*, trans. Gaunt, vol. II, p. 89: 'he was one of the first to find a way of making standards and other draperies by joining pieces together, so that the colours do not run, and show on both sides. He also did the baldachino of Orsanmichele, full of Madonnas, all different and beautiful. It is clear that this method of making standards is the most durable, as they do not suffer from acids, which quickly eat them away, although the latter method is most often used because it is less costly.'

33 See Jonathan K. Nelson, 'Le rivoluzionarie composizioni di Botticelli e Filippino Lippi per i dipinti da cassone e da spalliera', in *Virtù d'amore, pittura nuziale del Quattrocento fiorentino*, ed. C. Paolini, D. Parenti and L. Segrebondi (Florence, 2010), pp. 139–47. See also Anne Barriault, *Spalliera Paintings of Renaissance Tuscany. Fables of Poets for Patrician Homes* (University Park, PA, 1994), pp. 58–9.

34 Alberti, *On Painting*, I, I, p. 37.

35 Paola Ventrone, 'La riproposta fiorentina del teatro classico', in *Le tems revient* (Florence, 1992), pp. 221–2; Zorzi, *Il teatro e la città: saggi sulla scena italiana* (Turin, 1977).

36 See the exhibitions dedicated to this pair: Mariacristina Rodeschini and Patrizia Zambrano, ed., *Le Storie di Botticelli tra Boston e Bergamo*, exh. cat., Accademia Carrara (Bergamo, 2018), and Nathaniel Silver, ed., *Botticelli: Heroines and Heroes*, exh. cat., Isabella Stewart Gardner Museum (Boston, MA, 2019).

37 Filippo Lippi, *Adoration of the Magi*, *c*. 1440–60, tempera on poplar panel, National Gallery of Art, Washington, Samuel H. Kress Collection Inv. 1952.2.2.

38 On the relationship between the Magi confraternity and the Medici, see Rab Hatfield, *Botticelli's Uffizi 'Adoration': A Study in Pictorial Content* (Princeton, NJ, 1976), and Rab Hatfield, 'The Compagnia de' Magi', *Journal of the Warburg and Courtauld Institutes*, XXXIII (1970), pp. 107–61.

39 See another two examples: one dated 1478–80 in the National Gallery of Art in Washington (inv. 1937.I.22) and the other dated to the late 1480s in the Uffizi, unfinished with the Virgin heavily repainted (inv. 1890, no. 4346).

40 See specifically Boccaccio, *Decameron*, V, 8.

41 See, for instance, Patricia L. Rubin, *Images and identity in Fifteenth-century Florence* (New Haven, CT, and London, 2007), pp. 229–77.

42 The identification of Botticelli's collaborators is still subject to debate: see Cecchi, *Botticelli* (Milan, 2005), p. 218: Jacopo di Domenico di Pappi and Bartolomeo di Giovanni, the later only for the third panel; N. Pons, *Botticelli* (Milan, 1989), cat. 53 A–D, pp. 68–9; N. Pons, 'Precisazioni su tre Bartolomeo di Giovanni: il cartolaio, il sargiaio e il dipintore', *Paragone*, CDLXXIX–CDLXXXI (1990), pp. 115–28, esp. p. 119. N. Pons, *Bartolomeo di Giovanni, collaboratore di Ghirlandaio e Botticelli* (Florence, 2004), pp. 30–31.

43 See both works reproduced in Mina Gregori, Antonio Paolucci and Cristina Acidini Luchina, eds, *Maestri e botteghe*, exh. cat., Florence, Palazzo Strozzi (Milan, 1992), p. 40, fig. 7 and p. 41, fig. 8.

44 Alberti, *On Painting*, III, 53, pp. 96–7. The original text was translated from Greek into Latin by the humanist Guarino

Guarini of Verona at the beginning of the century. This is probably this version that Alberti followed.

45 Ibid.

46 Stanley Meltzoff, *Botticelli, Signorelli and Savonarola, Theologia Poetica and Painting from Boccaccio to Poliziano* (Florence, 1987), p. 257.

47 For a full description of the reliefs and other ornaments see ibid., pp. 103–204, and Fabbri in *Boccaccio visualizzato: narrare per parole e per immagini fra medioevo e Rinascimento*, ed. V. Branca (Florence, 1999), vol. II, pp. 220–21. Out of a total cf 72 only eight scenes are illegible.

48 For a summary of the different opinions, see Sara Agnoletto, 'Botticelli orifice del dettaglio: uno *status questionis* sui soggetti del fondale della *Calumnia di Apelle*', *Engramma*, 104 (March 2013), www.engramma.it, accessed 28 November 2019.

49 C. S. Singleton, ed., *Canti carnascialeschi del Rinascimento* (Bari, 1936), p. 214; and Rudolph Altrocchi, 'The Calumny of Apelles in the literature of the Quattrocento', *Modern Language Association*, XXXVI/3 (September 1921), pp. 454–91, esp. pp. 476f. For a discussion of the sources that does not include the *canto carnascialesco* see A. Dressen, 'From Dante to Landino: Botticelli's Calumny of Apelles and its Sources', *Mitteilungen des Kunsthistorischen Institutes in Florenz*, 3 (2017), pp. 324–39.

50 Nicoletta Pons, *Botticelli* (Milan, 1989), cat. 119, p. 86.

51 Opinions ranges from a personal affair affecting Botticelli himself (Horne, Gamba, Lightbown) or his friend (Cecchi) to political upheavals under Piero's rule, who succeeded his father in 1492, and Savonarola's violent preaching (Olson and Meltzoff). Segni was also a close friend of Leonardo who gave him a painting depicting Neptune, according to Vasari.

52 Vasari, *Le vite de' più eccellenti pittori, scultori e architettori, nelle redazioni del 1550 e 1568*, ed. R. Bettarini and P. Barocchi (Florence, 1966–87), vol. III, pp. 520–21: 'This little picture warns the rulers of the earth / to shun the tyranny of the judgment false. / Apelles gave its like to Egypt's king / was worthy of the gift, and it of him.' 'Indicio quemquam ne falso laedere tentent / terrarum reges parva tabella monet. /Huic similem Aegypti regi donavit Apelles / rex fuit, & dignus munere : munus eo.'

53 Alberti, *On Painting*, II, 40, pp. 78–9.

54 Luca Pacioli, 'Epistola al Duca di Urbino', in *Summa de Arithmetica geometria proportioni: et proportionalita*, Venice, Paganino de Paganini, 1523 (my translation): 'E in fiorenza Alessandro Botticelli, Phylippino e Domenico Ghirlandaio . . . quali sempre con libella e circino lor opera proportionandi a perfection mirabile e ducano In modo che non humane: ma divine negli ochi nostri sapresentano. E a tutte le loro figure solo el spirit par che manchi.' A former pupil of the important Renaissance painter Piero della Francesca, Fra Luca Bartolomeo de Pacioli (*c.* 1447–1517) is best known for his *Divina proportione*, written in Milan in 1496–8 and published in Venice in 1509 with illustrations provided by Leonardo da Vinci. Both books are based on Piero della Francesca's own mathematical treatises.

4 The Original Multiple and the Wandering Motif

1 See for instance Elizabeth Prettejohn, *Modern Painters, Old Masters: The Art of Imitation from the Pre-Raphaelites to the First World War* (New Haven, CT, and London, 2017).

2 Pietro Perugino, *Assumption of the Virgin*, 1507, oil on panel, church of the Santissima Annunziata, Florence. For questions on the importance of the incident, see Jonathan K. Nelson, 'La disgrazia di Pietro: l'importanza della pala della Santissima Annunziata nelle Vita del Perugino del Vasari', in *Pietro Vannucci: II Perugino*, ed. Laura Teza (Perugia, 2004), p. 70; for a consideration of its meaning, see David Franklin, *Painting in Renaissance Florence, 1500–1550* (New Haven, CT, and London, 2001), chapter 1. On the altarpiece, see Nelson, 'The High Altarpiece of SS. Annunziata in Florence: History, Form and Function', *Burlington Magazine*, 139 (1997), pp. 84–94.

3 Giorgio Vasari, *Le vite degli eccellenti pittori, scultori ed architettori*, ed. Gaetano Milanesi (Florence, 1878–85), vol. III, p. 586: 'Dicesi che quando detta opera si scoperse, fu da tutti i nuovi artifici assai biasimata; e particolarmente perché si era Piero servito di quelle figure che altre volte era usato mettere in opera: dove tentandolo gli amici suoi dicevano, che affatticato non s'era, e che aveva tralasciato il buon modo dell'operare o per avarizia o per non perder tempo.'

4 Leon Battista Alberti, *De pictura*, II, 45 and 49.
5 E. H. Gombrich, 'Ideal and Type in Italian Renaissance Painting', in *New Light on Old Masters: Studies in the Art of the Renaissance*, IV (Oxford, 1986), pp. 89–124.
6 See for instance the so-called *Madonna della Loggia* and *Corsini Madonna*: Lightbown, *Botticelli* (London, 1978), vol. II, cats. A9 and A10, p. 15.
7 See Botticelli, *Madonna and Child with Angels*, 1465–70, tempera on wood, 99.7 × 71.1 cm, Metropolitan Museum, New York, Inv. 29.100.17; and Botticelli, *Madonna and Child with an Angel*, 1465–70, tempera on wood, 87 × 60 cm, MUDI – Museo degli Innocenti, Florence.
8 See Chapter Three in this volume on the importance of the gaze's interplay in the Sant'Ambrogio altarpiece.
9 Scholars agreed that these three paintings, most likely executed before 1470, were entirely autograph.
10 See, for instance, Andrea del Verrocchio, *Head of a Woman*, c. 1475, charcoal heightened with lead white, pen and brown ink on paper, British Museum, London, Inv. 1895,0195.785; Leonardo da Vinci, *Head of a Woman Looking Down*, c. 1475, black chalk or leadpoint, brown and grey wash, heightened with lead white on paper, GDSU, Florence, Inv. 428E.
11 See, for instance, Stéphane Toussaint, '"My Friend Ficino": Art History and Neoplatonism: From Intellectual to Material Beauty', *Mitteilungen des Kunsthistorischen Institutes in Florenz*, LIX (2017), pp. 146–73.
12 On the dating of Ficino's *De amore*, see S. Gentile; 'Per la storia del testo del *Commentarium in Convivium* di Marsilio Ficino', *Rinascimento*, second series, 21 (1981), pp. 3–27.
13 See Ficino, *De amore*, esp. II, 1–6.
14 See Michelangelo, *Rime*, for instance, sonnet 164. See also Girolamo Benivieni, *Canzone de amore* in *Canzoni e sonetti dell' amore e della bellezza divina, con commento* (Florence, 1500).
15 Gemäldegalerie, Berlin 1474, tempera on wood, inv. 1128. See Jacques Mesnil, *Botticelli* (Paris, 1938), pp. 195–6, n. 27; R. Lightbown, *Botticelli* (London, 1978), vol. I, pp. 36–7, vol. II, cat. B14, pp. 27–8; A. Cecchi, *Botticelli* (Milan, 2005), pp. 118–19.

16 Antonio and Piero del Pollaiolo, *The Martyrdom of St Sebastian*, 1475, oil on wood, National Gallery, London, Inv. NG 292.

17 See Botticelli, *Head of an Angel*, early 1480s, silverpoint, heightened with white, on light grey prepared paper, Musée des Beaux-Arts, Rennes, Inv. 794.1.2504; and *Head of a Youth*, 1470s, pen and brown ink, heightened with white on pink prepared paper, British Museum, London, Inv. 1895,0915.450.

18 See for instance, heads of the angels in the so-called Raczinski tondo and the head of Mercury in the *Primavera*.

19 On this iconography, which seems to start with Bicci di Lorenzo's *Nativity* in 1435, see Jeffrey Ruda, *Fra Filippo Lippi: Life and Work* (London, 1993), pp. 221 sqq.

20 Prince Chigi was the last prestigious owner before the painting entered the collection of Isabella Stewart Gardner Museum in Boston after a few peripeties. On this acquisition, see Pat Rubin '"Pictures with a Past": Botticelli in Boston', in *Botticelli: Heroines and Heroes*, ed. N. Silver, exh. cat., Isabella Stewart Gardner Museum, Boston (London, 2019), pp. 10–31.

21 R. Lightbown, *Botticelli* (London, 1978), vol. II, cat. B26, p. 40.

22 According to Ruda, 'a real landmark in altarpiece design'; see Ruda, *Fra Filippo Lippi: Life and Work*, p. 163 sq.

23 Conservation report in press; see www.uffizi.it/magazine/%2Frestauro-dipinto-giovanile-Botticelli-Uffizi, accessed 23 November 2020.

24 These might have been somewhat similar to the exceptionally large number of workshop drawings left by Filippino Lippi, his pupil, which record, among other motifs, many Virgins and Childs in different poses and postures.

25 These include Cosimo Rosselli and Francesco Botticini, see A. Blume, 'Giovanni de' Bardi and Sandro Botticelli in Santo Spirito', *Jahrbuch der Berliner Museen*, 37 Bd (1995), pp. 169–83, esp. pp. 175–6.

26 Botticelli received payment on 3 August 1485 for the altarpiece while the woodcarver and architect Giuliano da San Gallo provided the carved frame, no longer extant. The name of Giuliano da San Gallo is inscribed on the reverse of a painting attributed to Botticelli's workshop in the National Gallery

(NG 275), which may suggest it belonged to the architect and woodcarver unless he was only responsible for its very fine carved frame, still extant.

27 See A. Blume, 'Giovanni de' Bardi and Sandro Botticelli in Santo Spirito', *Jahrbuch der Berliner Museen*, 37 Bd (1995), pp. 169–83.

28 On the various meanings, see A. Blume, 'Giovanni de' Bardi and Sandro Botticelli in Santo Spirito' *Jahrbuch der Berliner Museen*, 37 Bd (1995), pp. 169–183, esp. 175; and Lightbown, *Botticelli*, vol. I, pp. 100–103.

29 '*Con diligenza lavorata e a buon fine condotta; dove sono alcune olive e palme lavorate con sommo amore*': Vasari, *Lives*, trans. W. Gaunt (modified by the author) (London, 1963), vol. II, pp. 84–5.

30 A. Blume, 'Botticelli and the Cost and Value of Altarpieces in Late Fifteenth-century Florence', in *The Art Market in Italy*, ed. Marcello Fantoni, Louisa C. Matthew and Sara F. Matthews-Grieco (Modena, 2003), pp. 151–61.

31 These replicas include the version in the Fogg Art Museum, Cambridge, MA, oil on wood, Inv. 1943.105; another in the Galleria Sabauda, Turin, attributed to a Flemish follower; another is in the Yale University Art Gallery, New Haven, CT, Inv. 1871.50; a painting formerly in the Metropolitan Museum, last seen in Gallery Moretti, London (74.3 × 40.6 cm); and another formerly in the collection of Lord Battersea, whereabouts unknown.

32 These replicas include the three paintings illustrated above as well as another much reduced version (63 cm) formerly in the Mount collection and now in a private collection, as well as a further one formerly in the Hahn collection.

33 R. M. Olson, *The Florentine Tondo* (Oxford, 2000), p. 67. A. Cecchi identifies the carver of the frame as Giuliano da Sangallo and records that the carved French lilies against a cerulean background indicates a public destination: see Cecchi, *Botticelli*, p. 242.

34 These include Cardinal Francesco Gonzaga in 1477–8, whose tondo is identified as the painting now in the Museo Civico of Piacenza and another to Luigi D'Ugolino Martelli in 1489. See Olson, *The Florentine Tondo*, p. 67; Dario Covi, 'A Documented *Tondo* by Botticelli' in *Scritti di storia dell'arte in onore di Ugo Procacci*, ed. Maria

Grazia Ciardi Dupré dal Poggetto and Paolo dal Poggetto (Milan, 1977), pp. 270–72. Another tondo, identified as the *Madonna del Padiglione* in the Pinacoteca Ambrosiana, Milan, is recorded by Vasari in the cell of Guido di Lorenzo di Antonio, prior of the Calmadolese convent of Santa Maria degli Angeli in Florence between 1486 and 1498.

35 Giorgio Vasari, *Le vite de' più eccellenti pittori, scultori ed architettori*, ed. R. Bettarini and P. Barocchi (Florence, 1966–87), vol. III, pp. 517–18.

36 Ibid., p. 518.

37 See for instance at the beginning of the century no less than the great Filippo Brunelleschi, to whom Alberti dedicated his treatise *On Painting*, who also played a rather cruel joke on a 'fat carpenter' (*grasso legnaiolo*) which concluded with the carpenter running away from Florence, never to return. The story was later published by Brunelleschi's first biographer Antonio Manetti.

38 See A. Blume, 'Botticelli and the Cost and Value of Altarpieces in Late Fifteenth Century Florence', in Marcello Fantoni Fantoni, Louisa Chevalier Matthew and Sara F. Matthews-Grieco, eds, *The Art Market in Italy, 15th–17th centuries* (Modena, 2003), pp. 151–61; Michelle O'Malley, 'Quality Choices in the Production of Renaissance Art: Botticelli and Demand', *Renaissance Studies*, XXVIII/1 (2013), pp. 4–32, esp. n. 16, p. 9.

39 GDSU, Florence, inv. 201E, black chalk, pen and brown ink, highlighted with white, on pink prepared paper.

40 Vasari, *Lives*, trans. Gaunt (modified by the author), vol. II, p. 89.

41 Besançon, Musée des Beaux-Arts, Inv. D3112, before 1480, pen and brown ink over black chalk, highlighted with white on prepared pink paper. See A. Cecchi, 'Giuliano e Benedettoda Maiano ai servigi della Signoria fiorentina', in *Giuliano e la bottega dei da Maiano*, ed. D. Lamberini, M. Lotti and R. Lunardi (Florence, 1994), pp. 148–57, who attributes the design of the door to Filippino, followed by P. Zambrano, *Filippino Lippi* (Milan, 2004), p. 21, fig. 5.

42 For an alternative identification of the subject matter, see B. Demling, 'Who Tames the Centaur? The Identification of

Botticelli's Heroine', in *Sandro Botticelli and Herbert Horne. New Research*, ed. Rab Hatfield (Florence, 2009), pp. 63–103.

43 Oxford, Ashmolean, Inv. BB581, 1480s, pen and ink over black chalk, brown wash, highlighted with white, on a prepared pink paper.

44 Louvre, Paris, Inv. 2686, recto, 1480s–90s, pen and brown ink on silk, 296 × 230 mm; Cennino Cennini, *Il libro dell'arte*, ed. Fabio Frezzato (Vicenza, 2003), ch. CLXIV, p. 184.

45 See Gabinetto Disegni e Stampe degli Uffizi (GDSU) in Florence, Inv. 1149E.

46 Botticelli, *Annunciation*, *c.* 1485–92, tempera and gold on wood, Metropolitan Museum of Arts, New York, Robert Lehman Collection, 1975.1.74; Botticelli, *Annunciation*, *c.* 1490, tempera on wood, Kelvingrove Art Gallery and Museum, Glasgow, Inv. 174.

47 See A. Cecchi, *Botticelli* (Milan, 2005), pp. 272–7. According to the scholar, Botticelli is not responsible for the central motif of the Trinity, which is weaker in style and thus could be ascribed to an anonymous hand.

48 Florentine manufacture after Botticelli, *Hood of a Cope with the Crowning of the Virgin*, *c.* 1485–90, silk and gold wrapped threads, Poldi-Pezzoli Museum, Milan, Inv. 444.

49 Louvre, Paris, Inv. 2686: pen and brown ink on silk. On the specific embroidery technique, see Marialuisa Rizzini in Andrea di Lorenzo, ed., *Botticelli nelle collezioni lombarde*, exh. cat., Milan, Poldi Pezzoli Museum (Milan, 2010), cat. 5, pp. 70–73. Further examples of designs for embroidery includes a drawing in Darmstadt, identified as the design for the lower missing section of a large altarpiece representing the Pentecost in Birmingham, which on the contrary displays a structure close to an embroidery showing the *Presentation in the Temple* now in the Opera del Duomo Museum, Orvieto, datable to about 1495. See Annarosa Garzelli, *Il ricamo nell'attività di Pollaiolo, Botticelli e Bartolomeo di Giovanni* (Florence, 1973), pp. 25–34; N. Pons in *Maestri e botteghe*, ed. M. Gregori, A. Paolucci and C. Acidini Luchinat, exh. cat., Florence, Palazzo Strozzi (Milan, 1992), cat. 10.12, p. 268; Cecchi, *Botticelli*, p. 306.

50 Milan, Civiche Raccolte d'Arte del Castello Sforzesco.

51 Francesco Guicciardini, *Storie fiorentine*, ed. A. Montevecchi (Milan, 1998), pp. 129–48.

52 Ibid., pp. 123–7.

53 *Il Codice Magliabechiano*, cl. XVII, 17, ed. Karl Frey (Berlin, 1892), §6, p. 105.

54 Leonardo da Vinci, sketch of Bernardo Baroncelli, 1479, pen and brown ink on paper, Bayonne, Musée Bonnat-Helleu, Inv. 659. Another drawing attributed to Filippino Lippi, Paris, Louvre, Inv. 10715, *c.* 1479–94, pen and brown ink, grey wash, on paper, pricked; silhouetted and framed (by Vasari?), Lorenza Melli suggests it is in fact a model for a 'hanged Man', an iconography that belongs to the tarot cards (*tarocchi*): see Lorenza Melli in *Botticelli: Likeness, Myth, Devotion*, ed. Andreas Schumacher, exh. cat., Frankfurt, Städel Museum (Frankfurt, 2009), cat. 9, pp. 174–5.

55 A fourth painting in this series, now in a private collection, is considered by some to be a forgery. See Luisa Vertova, 'Botticelli tra falsificazioni e reinvenzioni', *Antichità viva*, XXX/6 (1991), pp. 24–9.

56 Florence, Museo Nazionale del Bargello, Inv. 5956 MED, 1478–9, bronze. For additional representations of Giuliano, in marble and terracotta for instance, see Francesco Caglioti in Patrizia Zambrano and Mariacristina Rodeschini, eds, *Le storie di Botticelli fra Boston e Bergamo*, exh. cat., Bergamo, Accademia Carrara (Milan, 2018), cat. 1.3, pp. 78–83.

57 Sometimes identified as a lost drawing which was recorded in three inventories of the Medici household between 1553 and 1637 before disappearing. See Elizabeth Walmsley and Alexander J. Noelle with Babette Hartwieg, 'The Portraits of Giuliano de' Medici by Sandro Botticelli', *Facture*, IV (2019), pp. 2–33, esp. n. 34, p. 31; and Karla Langedijk, *Portraits of the Medici: 15th–18th Centuries* (Florence, 1982), vol. II, pp. 1063–4.

58 Cennino Cennini, *Il libro dell'arte*, ed. F. Frezzaro (Vicenza, 2014), cap. CXXII, pp. 149–50.

59 See for instance Stefan Weppelmann in Keith Christiansen and Stefan Weppelmann, eds, *The Renaissance Portrait from Donatello to Bellini*, exh. cat., New York, Metropolitan Museum of Art (New Haven, CT, and London, 2011), cat. 50–52, pp. 174–7; and Patrizia

Zambrano in A. Di Lorenzo, ed., *Botticelli nelle collezioni lombarde*, exh. cat., Milan, Poldi-Pezzoli Museum (Milan, 2010), pp. 54–7.

60 J. Shearman, 'The Collection of the Younger Branch of the Medici', *Burlington Magazine*, CXVII/862 (January 1975), pp. 12, 14–27, esp. p. 26; Grand Duke Ferdinando I de' Medici was a descendant of Giovanni di Pierfrancesco de' Medici, Lorenzo's brother. It is therefore possible that the portrait passed through generations as a family heirloom.

61 Although the identification of the prototype for this series has been long debated, recent technical investigation suggests that the three panels may have been made at the same time. See also P. Zambrano, *Botticelli and the Birth of Modern Portraiture in the Fifteenth Century* (forthcoming).

62 The print was made by Tobias Stimmer, *Giuliano de' Medici*, 1575, woodcut, and published in the 1575 edition of Paolo Giovio, *Elogia virorum bellica virtute illustrium* (Basel, 1575), p. 159. The book was first published in Florence in 1551. For more details, see Paolo Sachet in C. Rodeschini and P. Zambrano, eds, *Le storie di Botticelli tra Bergamo and Boston*, exh. cat., Bergamo, Accademia Carrara (Milan, 2018), cat. 1.4, pp. 84–7.

63 Further interpretations in, for example, Herbert Friedmann, 'Two Paintings by Botticelli in the Kress Collection', *Studies in the History of Art Presented to William E. Suida* (London, 1959), pp. 116–23; and Stephen Weppelmann in *The Renaissance Portraits from Donatello to Bellini*, exh. cat., ed. Keith Christiansen and Stephan Weppelmann, Metropolitan Museum of Art (New York, 2011), cat. 50–52, pp. 174–7.

64 London, Victoria and Albert Museum, Inv. CAI.100, 1470–75, tempera on wood. This first position is sometimes challenged by Leonardo da Vinci, *Ginevra de' Benci* (1474–8), one of the first known three-quarter-view portraits in Italian art, also gazing directly at the viewer (Washington, National Gallery of Art, Ailsa Mellon Bruce Fund, Inv. 1967.6.1.a). On Botticelli's portraiture, see P. Zambrano, 'Sandro Botticelli and the Birth of Modern Portraiture', in *Botticelli Past and Present*, ed. Ana Debenedetti and Caroline Elam (London, 2019), pp. 10–35.

5 Changing Style, Adapting to the Market

1 See E. H. Gombrich, 'The Early Medici as Patrons of Art', in *Norm and Form* (London, 1960, repr. 1966), pp. 35–57.
2 Piermatteo d'Amelia, *Design for the 15th-century decoration of the ceiling of the Sistine Chapel*, 1475–83, Gabinetto Disegni e Stampe degli Uffizi (GDSU) in Florence, Inv. 711A.
3 For a detailed interpretation of the iconography, see R. Lightbown, *Botticelli* (London, 1978), vol. I, pp. 64–7.
4 Ulrich Pfisterer, *La Cappella Sistina* (Rome, 2014), pp. 26–7 including previous bibliography.
5 For attributions see A. Cecchi, *Botticelli* (Milan, 2005), p. 186.
6 Pfisterer, *La Cappella Sistina*, p. 25, attributes ten figures to Botticelli; Cecchi, *Botticelli*, p. 186, nine figures; and Lightbown, *Botticelli*, vol. II, p. 45, eleven figures.
7 See Cecchi, *Botticelli*, p. 184. Anecdotally, this fresco provides further insight into Botticelli's playful temperament: on the book behind the clock, a line appears that stands out in the context of Euclid's problems: 'Dove fra martino e scappato e dove e andato e fuori della porta al prato' ('Where is Fra Martino? He ran away. Where did he go? He is out of the Porta a Prato').
8 Annunciation, Florence, Uffizi, 1481, detached fresco, Inventory Deposito no. 201; see Chapter One in this volume. Vasari, *Vite*, ed. R. Bettarini and P. Barocchi (Florence, 1966–87), vol. III, pp. 512–13.
9 Vasari, *On Technique*, trans. Louisa S. Maclehose (New York, 1960), p. 221.
10 N. Pons, *Botticelli* (Milan, 1989), cat. 47b, p. 64: Botticelli would be the man in profile at the far left, and Filippino is the figure wearing a red hat.
11 Statue of a girl with a dove, 1st century AD, marble, Roman, Musei Capitolini, Rome, Inv. Scu 738.
12 The narrative on the opposite wall runs from the left-hand side of the altar as follows: *Moses in Egypt* by Perugino, *Temptations of Moses* by Botticelli, *Crossing of the Red Sea* by Biagio d'Antonio, *Conturbation of Moses* by Botticelli, *Death of Moses* by Signorelli and Bartolomeo della Gatta.

13 Botticelli illustrates here the origins of architecture which Vitruvius based on the imitation of nature. Botticelli most likely did not have access to Vitruvius' Latin text of *De architectura* (1st century BC) but was doubtless acquainted with its main ideas discussed in humanist circles, in particular by Leon Battista Alberti, whose own treatise of architecture (*De re aedificatoria*) was prefaced and published in 1485 by Poliziano, Botticelli's neighbour and close acquaintance.
14 Vasari, *Vite*, ed. Bettarini and Barocchi, vol. III, p. 492.
15 These include Pomponio Leto or Giorgio Costa or il Chierigati, Alessandro Farnese, Pope Paul II or Raffaello Riario: see Pons, *Botticelli*, cat. 47c, p. 65 including previous bibliography.
16 They completed the *Death of Moses* after a design by Perugino. See Cecchi, *Botticelli*, p. 186, and n. 17, p. 278.
17 See Lightbown, *Botticelli*, vol. I, p. 66.
18 Paola Ventrone, 'Feste e spettacoli nella Firenze di Lorenzo il Magnifico', in *Le Tems Revient, 'l tempo si rinuova'. Feste e spettacoli nella Firenze di Lorenzo il Magnifico*, ed. Paola Ventrone, exh. cat., Palazzo Medici Riccardi, Florence (Milan, 1992), pp. 21–53, esp. p. 33.
19 *Primavera*, tempera on wood, Uffizi, Florence, Inv. 1890 no. 836.
20 Lorenzo and his brother Giovanni (1467–1498) became wards of Lorenzo the Magnificent upon the premature death of their father Pierfrancesco in 1476, who was Lorenzo the Magnificent's cousin.
21 For a detailed analysis of the iconography including previous bibliography, see Lightbown, *Botticelli*, vol. I, pp. 72–81; and Cecchi, *Botticelli*, pp. 148–51.
22 The identification of the figures is based on the generally agreed interpretation but remains the subject of intense debate. There are no documents on this commission and the earliest record lists the panel in the Medici palace on via Larga, hung above a *lettuccio*, a type of daybed commonly found in Florentine patristic houses. It was later moved to the Villa at Castello, another Medici property just outside Florence, where Giorgio Vasari saw it together with the *Birth of Venus* in 1550.
23 Alberti, *De pictura* (On Painting) [1435], trans. Cecyl Grayson (London, 1972), pp. 35–40.

24 P. Francastel, *La fête mythologique au Quattrocento: expression littéraire et visualisation plastique* (Paris, 1952).

25 N. Carew-Reid, *Les fêtes florentines au temps de Lorenzo il Magnifico* (Florence, 1995).

26 Vasari described the painting as follows: 'un'altra Venere che le Grazie la fioriscono, dinotando la Primavera', in Vasari, *Vite*, ed. Bettarini and Barocchi, vol. III, p. 513.

27 Florence, Uffizi, *c.* 1482–84, tempera on canvas, Inv. 1890 no. 878. Long believed to have been commissioned by the same patron as *Primavera*, and thought to form its pendant, the painting was in fact possibly made for somebody else and later passed into the hands of the Medici in the Villa at Castello where Vasari saw it together with *Primavera* in 1550.

28 Cristoforo Landino, *Comento sopra la Comedia di Dante* (Florence, 1481); Vasari, *Lives*, trans. W. Gaunt (London, 1963), vol. II, p. 87.

29 Pliny the Elder, *Natural History* (XXXV). This Latin text was translated by Cristoforo Landino in 1474, published in 1476 and often reprinted in the following years. See Eliana Carrara, 'Plinio e l'arte degli antichi e dei moderni. Ricenzione e fortuna dei libri XXXIV–XXXVI della *Naturalis Historia* nella Firenze del XVI secolo (dall'Anonimo Magliabechiano al Vasari)', *Archives Internationales d'Histoire des Sciences*, LXI/166–7 (June–December 2011), pp. 367–81, esp. p. 368.

30 Kenneth Clark, *The Nude: A Study of Ideal Art* (London, 1956, repr. 1976), pp. 89–90.

31 On the relationship between *Primavera* and the *Birth of Venus* see also Aby Warburg, *The Renewal of Pagan Antiquity: Contributions to the Cultural History of the European Renaissance*, trans. David Britt (Los Angeles, CA, 1999), pp. 89–164.

32 The tilted pose of the centaur at the extreme left of the sarcophagus inspired the stance of Botticelli's centaur in *Pallas and the Centaur* while Mars and Venus derived from a bacchanalian scene on the top right corner: Musei Vaticani, Inv. 173. See Erica Tietze-Conrat, 'Botticelli and the Antique', *Burlington Magazine for Connoisseurs*, XLVII/270 (September 1925), pp. 124–5, 129.

33 A. Debenedetti, 'Entre art et magie: imagination et participation à Florence au XVe siècle', *Art Italy*, 19 (Summer 2013), pp. 57–64.

Two significant examples of this traditional use of concealing life-size nudes in the inner lids of cassoni are the pair of chests attributed to Lo Scheggia, Masaccio's brother: *c.* 1460, tempera on wood, National Museum of Art, Copenhagen.

34 This spalliera was possibly commissioned by a member of the Vespucci family if we accept that the wasps at top right are an allusion to the heraldry of the family (wasps in Italian is *vespe*, for 'Vespucci'), but it may also be no more than an allusion to the stings of love.

35 See Botticelli, *Portrait of a Young Man*, *c.* 1485, tempera and oil on panel, National Gallery, London, Inv. NG626; and *Portrait of a Youth*, *c.* 1485, tempera on poplar, National Gallery of Art, Washington, Inv. 1937.1.19.

36 Alberti, *On Painting*, trans. Grayson, vol. II, 46, p. 89. See also P. Zambrano, 'Sandro Botticelli and the Birth of Modern Portraiture', in *Botticelli Past and Present*, ed. A. Debenedetti and C. Elam (London, 2019), pp. 10–35, esp. pp. 28–9.

37 Botticelli, *Young Woman (Simonetta Vespucci) in Mythological Guise*, *c.* 1485, tempera on panel, Städelsches Kunstinstitut, Frankfurt am Main, Inv. 936. Botticelli's preparatory drawing for the figure is conserved in the Ashmolean Museum, Oxford, Inv. WA1863.613.

38 Dioskourides, *Apollo and Marsyas* (*Sigillo di Nerone*), 1st century BC–2nd century AD, carnelian, Museo Archeologico Nazionale, Naples, Inv. 26051; Lorenzo Ghiberti and workshop (?), *Apollo and Marsyas*, *c.* 1425–5, bronze, Museo Nazionale del Bargello, Florence, Inv. 225B. See also Botticelli's preparatory drawings for the figures of Marsyas and Apollo: Florence, GDSU, Inv. 112E and 119F.

39 Simonetta is the dedicatee of Giuliano's tournament (*giostra*) in 1475 and the central figure of Angelo Poliziano's related poem, *Stanze per la Giostra*. A true poetic cult grew around her figure in the Medici circle as she gathered all the ingredients of the genre: youth, beauty and tragic fate. See also Charles Dempsey, *The Portrayal of Love: Botticelli's Primavera and Humanist Culture at the time of Lorenzo the Magnificent* (Princeton, NJ, 1992), pp. 114–39.

40 Mesnil, *Botticelli* (Paris, 1938), p. 113; Lightbrown, *Botticelli*, vol. I, p. 104.

41 Filippino Lippi, *Annunciation*, 1482, tempera on wood, Pinacoteca Civica, San Gimignano, Inv. no. 278. See A. Cecchi, 'Pro honore comunitatis', in *Filippino Lippi, L'Annunciazione*, ed. A. Cecchi, exh. cat., Milan, Palazzo Marino (Milan, 2019), pp. 63–8.
42 Lorenzo welcomed Savonarola back under Pico della Mirandola's pressure: see D. Weinstein, *Savonarola: The Rise and Fall of a Renaissance Prophet* (New Haven, CT, and London, 2011), pp. 69–70.
43 C. Caneva, 'L'incoronazione ritrovata', in *L'Incoronazione della Vergine del Botticelli*, ed. M. Ciatti (Florence, 1990), pp. 33–50.
44 R. Ridolfi, *Vita di Girolamo Savonarola* (Florence, 1974), pp. 48–53.
45 Piero Pollaiolo, *Coronation of the Virgin*, San Gimignano, Collegiata; Domenico Ghirlandaio, *Coronation of the Virgin*, Narni, Palazzo Comunale.
46 These works are now respectively in the Bass Museum in Miami and Villa La Quiete near Florence.
47 Donatello's *St Lawrence of Toulouse* is today in the Museo di Santa Croce in Florence. For a different interpretation, see Michelle O'Malley, 'Responding to Changing Taste and Demand: Botticelli after 1490', in *Sandro Botticelli (1445–1510): Artist and Entrepreneur in Renaissance Florence*, ed. G. J. Van der Sman and I. Mariani (Florence, 2015), pp. 101–20, esp. p. 112.
48 *Anonimo Magliabechiano*, cl. XVII, 17, ed. C. Frey (Berlin, 1892), p. 105.
49 Vasari, *Vite*, ed. Bettarini and Barocchi, vol. III, p. 516.
50 A. Blume, 'Botticelli's Family and Finances in the 1490s: Santa Maria Nuova and the San Marco Altarpiece', *Mitteilungen des Kunsthistorischen Institites in Florenz*, 38 Bd., H.1 (1994), pp. 154–64.
51 On this cycle, see, among others: S. Gentile, ed., *Botticelli, Pittore della Divina Commedia*, exh. cat., Rome, Scuderie del Quirinale, 2 vols (Milan, 2000); and H. Th. Schulze Altcappenberg, ed., *Sandro Botticelli: The Drawings for Dante's Divine Comedy*, exh. cat., Royal Academy of Arts, London (London, 2000).
52 Botticelli, *Madonna del Padiglione*, *c.* 1490, tempera on panel, Pinacoteca Ambrosiana, Milan.
53 See, among others, R. Hatfield, 'Botticelli's Mystic Nativity, Savonarola and the Millennium', *Journal of the Warburg and Courtauld Institutes*, LVIII (1995), pp. 88–114; C. Plazzota in *Sandro Botticelli*,

exh. cat., London, National Gallery (London, 2000), pp. 164–7; Cecchi, *Botticelli*, p. 348–50; F. Zöllner, *Sandro Botticelli* (Munich and New York, 2005), cat. 85, pp. 266–7.

54 Guicciardini, *Storie fiorentine*, ed. A. Montevecchi (Milan, 1998), pp. 276–9.

55 Botticelli, *St Augustine in His Studio*, 1490s, tempera on wood, Uffizi, Florence, Inv. 1890 no. 1444/45-M.1510.

56 Portland Art Museum, Inv. 61.54; Fondazione Santa Maria, Florence, Inv. 1979 no. 31.

57 Louis A. Waldman, 'Botticelli and his Patrons', in *Sandro Botticelli and Herbert Horne: New Research*, ed. R. Hatfield (Florence, 2009), pp. 105–35.

58 The *Lamentation* today in Munich, Alte Pinakothek, Inv. 1075, was identified as being for the high altar of the nearby church of San Paolino in Florence (see J. Mesnil, 'Le Pietà botticelliane', *Rassegna d'Arte* (1914), pp. 207–11); the other, in Milan, Poldi-Pezzoli Museum, Inv. 1558, was probably originally in the Florentine church of Santa Maria Maggiore where Vasari saw it in 1568, see Vasari, *Vite*, ed. Bettarini and Barocchi, vol. III, p. 513. See also A. Cecchi and R. Naldi, *Sandro Botticelli: Compianto sul Cristo morto*, exh. cat., Naples, Palazzo della Banca Intesa (Padua, 2019).

59 See for instance Donatello, *Lamentation*, bronze, Victoria and Albert Museum, London, Inv. 8552–1863.

60 Cecchi, *Botticelli*, p. 360.

61 See F. Zeri, 'Questioni di bottega del Botticelli', *Paragone*, CDXIX–CDXXIII/36 (1985), pp. 135–9.

62 Botticelli workshop, *Allegory of Autumn*, *c.* 1505, tempera on canvas, Musée Condé, Chantilly, Inv. PE 16; Botticelli, *Allegory of Abundance*, *c.* 1480–85, black and red chalk, pen and brown ink, heightened with white on paper, British Museum, London, Inv. 1895,0915.447.

SELECT BIBLIOGRAPHY

Primary Sources

Alberti, Leon Battista, *De pictura* (On Painting) [1435], trans. Cecyl Grayson (London, 1972)

Anonimo Magliabechiano, cl. XVII, 17, ed. C. Frey (Berlin, 1892)

Cennini, Cennino, *Il libro dell'Arte* (The Craftsman's Handbook), trans. Daniel V. Thompson Jr (New York, 1954, repr. 2016)

Ciasca, Raffaele, *Statuti dell'Arte dei Medici e Speziali* (Florence, 1922)

Ficino, Marsilio, *Opera omnia* (Basel, 1576)

Guicciardini, Francesco, *Storie fiorentine dal 1378 al 1509*, ed. A. Montevecchi (Milan, 1998)

Landino, Cristoforo, *Comento sopra la comedia di Dante* (Florence, 1481)

Landucci, Luca, *Diario fiorentino dal 1450 al 1516*, ed. Jodoco Del Badia (Florence, 1883)

Neri di Bicci, *Ricordanze (10 marzo 1453–24 aprile 1475)*, ed. B. Santi (Pisa, 1976)

Perosa, Alessandro, ed., *Giovanni Rucellai ed il suo Zibaldone* (London, 1960–81)

Pliny the Elder, *Natural History* (XXXV) [This Latin text was translated by Cristoforo Landino in 1474 and published in 1477]

Poliziano, Angelo, *Stanze, Orfeo, Rime*, ed. D. Puccini (Milan, 1992, repr. 2000)

Pulci, Luigi, *Opere minori*, ed. P. Orvieto (Milan, 1986)

Vasari, Giorgio, *Le vite de' più eccellenti pittori, scultori e architettori, nelle redazioni del 1550 e 1568*, ed. R. Bettarini and P. Barocchi (Florence, 1966–87)

Secondary Sources

Bartoli, Roberta, *Biagio d'Antonio* (Milan, 1999)

Baxandall, Michael, *Painting and Experience in Fifteenth-century Italy* (London, 1972)

Caneva, Caterina, *Botticelli* (Florence, 1990)

Carew-Reid, Nicole, *Les fêtes florentines au temps de Lorenzo il Magnifico* (Florence, 1995)

Cecchi, Alessandro, *Botticelli* (Milan, 2005)

Ciasca, Raffaele, *Statuti dell'Arte dei Medici e Speziali* (Florence, 1922)

Ciatti, Marco, ed., *L'Incoronazione della Vergine del Botticelli* (Florence, 1990)

Debenedetti, Ana, 'Entre art et magie: imagination et participation à Florence au XVe siècle', *Art Italy*, 19 (Summer 2013), pp. 57–64.

—, and Caroline Elam, eds, *Botticelli Past and Present* (London, 2019)

Dempsey, Charles, *The Portrayal of Love: Botticelli's Primavera and Humanist Culture at the time of Lorenzo the Magnificent* (Princeton, NJ, 1992)

Francastel, Pierre, *La fête mythologique au Quattrocento: expression littéraire et visualisation plastique* (Paris, 1952)

Franceschi, Franco, and Gloria Fossi, eds, *Arti fiorentine: la grande storia dell'artigianato, il Quattrocento* (Florence, 1999)

Garzelli, Annarosa, *Il ricamo nell'attività di Pollaiolo, Botticelli e Bartolomeo di Giovanni* (Florence, 1973)

Goldthwaite, Richard A., *The Economy of Renaissance Florence*, (Baltimore, MA, 2009)

Hatfield, Rab, ed., *Sandro Botticelli and Herbert Horne: New Research* (Florence, 2009)

Horne, Herbert Percy, *Alessandro Filipepi Commonly Called Sandro Botticelli: Painter of Florence* (London, 1908)

Lightbown, Ronald, *Botticelli*, 2 vols (London, 1978)

Melli, Lorenza, *Maso Finiguerra* (Florence, 1995)

Meltzoff, Stanley, *Botticelli, Signorelli and Savonarola: Theologia Poetica and Painting from Boccaccio to Poliziano* (Florence, 1987)

Mesnil, Jacques, *Botticelli* (Paris, 1938)

Nelson, Jonathan K., and Patrizia Zambrano, *Filippino Lippi* (Milan, 2004)

O'Malley, Michelle, *The Business of Art: Contracts and the Commissioning Process in Renaissance Italy* (New Haven, CT, and London, 2005)

Pons, Nicoletta, *Botticelli* (Milan, 1989)

—, *Bartolomeo di Giovanni, collaboratore di Ghirlandaio e Botticelli* (Florence, 2004)

Procacci, Ugo, 'Di Jacopo di Antonio e delle compagnie di pittore del Corso degli Adimari nel secolo XV', *Rivista d'arte*, XXXIV (1960), pp. 3–70

Ridolfi, Roberto, *Vita di Girolamo Savonarola* (Florence, 1974)

Rubinstein, Rudolph, *The Government of Florence under the Medici, 1434 to 1494* (Oxford, 1966)

Ruda, Jeffrey, *Fra Filippo Lippi: Life and Work* (London, 1993)

Thomas, Anabel, *The Painter's Practice in Renaissance Tuscany* (Cambridge, 1995)

Tietze-Conrat, Erica, 'Botticelli and the Antique', *Burlington Magazine for Connoisseurs*, XLVII/270 (September 1925), pp. 124–5, 129

Wackernagel, Martin, *The World of the Florentine Renaissance Artist: Projects and Patrons, Workshop and Art Market* [1938], trans. Alison Luchs (Princeton, NJ, 1981)

Warburg, Aby, *The Renewal of Pagan Antiquity: Contributions to the Cultural History of the European Renaissance*, trans. David Britt (Los Angeles, CA, 1999)

Weinstein, Donald, *Savonarola: The Rise and Fall of a Renaissance Prophet* (New Haven, CT, and London, 2011)

Wright, Alison, *The Pollaiuolo Brothers: The Arts of Florence and Rome* (New Haven, CT, and London, 2005)

Zorzi, Ludovico, *Il teatro e la città: saggi sulla scena italiana* (Turin, 1977)

Exhibition Catalogues

Gentile, Sebastiano, ed., *Botticelli, Pittore della Divina Commedia*, exh. cat., Rome, Scuderie del Quirinale, 2 vols (Milan, 2000)

Gregori, Mina, Antonio Paolucci and Cristina Acidini Luchinat, ed., *Maestri e botteghe*, exh. cat., Florence, Palazzo Strozzi (Milan, 1992)

Lorenzo, Andrea Di, ed., *Botticelli nelle collezioni lombarde*, exh. cat., Poldi-Pezzoli Museum (Milan, 2010)

Paolini, Claudio, Daniela Parenti and Ludovica Sebregondi, eds, *Virtù d'amore, pittura nuziale nel Quattrocento fiorentino*, exh. cat., Florence, Galleria dell'Accademia and Museo Horne (Florence, 2010)

Rubin, Patricia L., and Alison Wright, *Renaissance Florence. The Art of the 1470s*, exh. cat., London, National Gallery (London, 1999)

Schulze Altcappenberg, Hein-Th., ed., *Sandro Botticelli, The Drawings for Dante's Divine Comedy*, exh. cat., London, Royal Academy of Arts (London, 2000)

Ventrone, Paola, ed., *Le Tems Revient, 'l tempo si rinuova. Feste e spettacoli nella Firenze di Lorenzo il Magnifico*, exh. cat., Florence, Palazzo Medici Riccardi (Milan, 1992)

ACKNOWLEDGEMENTS

I am indebted to the work of Botticelli specialists, in particular Ronald Lightbown and more recently Alessandro Cecchi, whom I wish to thank for the fruitful exchanges and his friendship. I wish to thank Patrizia Zambrano and Jonathan K. Nelson for generously sharing their knowledge as well as many colleagues and friends who accompanied me on this journey, especially Kira D'Alburquerque. My thanks to François Quiviger and Michael Leaman for their trust, and to Amy Salter, Alex Ciobanu and the extended team of Reaktion Books for their assistance in the preparation of this book. This book is dedicated to my husband, Matteo Andreoletti.

PHOTO ACKNOWLEDGEMENTS

The author and publishers wish to express their thanks to the below sources of illustrative material and/or permission to reproduce it. Some locations of artworks are also given below, in the interest of brevity:

Accademia di belle arti G. Carrara, Bergamo: 23, 55; akg-images/Mondadori Portfolio/Remo Bardazzi: 18; Alte Pinakothek, Munich: 34; The Bass Museum of Art, Miami Beach, FL: 52; Biblioteca Apostolica Vaticana, Vatican City (MSS Reg.lat.1896.pt.A, fol. 98v): 4; British Museum, London: 1; Chiesa di San Salvatore di Ognissanti, Florence: 58; Chiesa di Santa Maria del Carmine, Cappella dei Brancacci, Florence: 5; Christ Church Picture Gallery, Oxford/photos reproduced by permission of the Governing Body of Christ Church, Oxford: 13, 14; Galleria dell'Accademia, Florence: 45; Galleria Nazionale delle Marche, Palazzo Ducale di Urbino: 47; Galleria Palatina, Palazzo Pitti, Florence: 22, 74; Galleria Sabauda, Turin: 67; Gallerie degli Uffizi, Florence: 2, 7, 8, 9, 10, 11, 12, 25, 30, 31, 41, 44, 49, 51, 63, 64, 69; Gallerie degli Uffizi, Gabinetto dei Disegni e delle Stampe, Florence: 6; Gemäldegalerie, Staatliche Museen zu Berlin: 43, 54, 66; Hamburger Kunsthalle, Kupferstichkabinett: 3; Isabella Stewart Gardner Museum, Boston, MA: 24, 39; The Metropolitan Museum of Art, New York: 72; Musée des beaux-arts du Canada, Ottawa: 15, 19; Musée des beaux-arts de Rennes: 38; Musée Condé, Chantilly: 17; Musée du Louvre, Paris: 20, 21, 33; Musée du Petit Palais, Avignon (on long-term loan from Musée du Louvre, Paris): 37; Musei Vaticani, Vatican City: 59, 60, 61, 62; Museo Horne, Florence: 16; Museo di Palazzo Pretorio, Prato: 73; Museo Poldi Pezzoli, Milan: 40, 50; Museo del Prado, Madrid: 26, 27, 28; Museo e Real Bosco di Capodimonte, Naples: 35; The National Gallery, London:

36, 65, 71; National Gallery of Art, Washington, DC: 32, 56; Pieve di San Giovanni Evangelista, Montelupo Fiorentino: 46; private collection: 29 (Pucci collection, Florence), 42, 48, 68; Städel Museum, Frankfurt am Main (CC BY-SA 4.0): 70; © Victoria and Albert Museum, London: 57; Villa La Quiete, Florence: 53.

INDEX

Illustration numbers are indicated by *italics*